The LAST
LOBSTER

ALSO BY CHRISTOPHER WHITE

*The Melting World: A Journey Across
America's Vanishing Glaciers*

Skipjack: The Story of America's Last Sailing Oystermen

Chesapeake Bay: Nature of the Estuary

*Endangered and Threatened Wildlife
of the Chesapeake Bay Region*

The LAST
LOBSTER

*Boom or Bust for
Maine's Greatest Fishery?*

Christopher White

St. Martin's Press
New York

www.stmartins.com

Grateful acknowledgment is made for permission to reprint lyrics from the following:
"Harbor Lights" copyright © 1998 Frank Gotwals and "An Unfamiliar Sea"
copyright © 1998 Frank Gotwals.

Library of Congress Cataloging-in-Publication Data

Names: White, Christopher P., 1956- author.
Title: The last lobster : boom or bust for Maine's greatest fishery? /
    Christopher White.
Description: First edition. I New York : St. Martin's Press, 2018. I
    Includes bibliographical references.
Identifiers: LCCN 2017059442I ISBN 9781250080851 (hardcover) I
    ISBN 9781466892675 (ebook)
Subjects: LCSH: Lobster fisheries—Maine.
Classification: LCC SH380.2.U6 W45 2018 I DDC 639/.5409741—dc23
LC record available at https://lccn.loc.gov/2017059442

Map designed by Jeffery L. Ward

Our books may be purchased in bulk for promotional, educational, or business use.
Please contact your local bookseller or the Macmillan Corporate and Premium
Sales Department at 1-800-221-7945, extension 5442, or by email at
MacmillanSpecialMarkets@macmillan.com.

First Edition: June 2018

10   9   8   7   6   5   4   3   2   1

In memory of Willard A. Lockwood,
editor, mentor, and friend

Contents

AUTHOR'S NOTE

All the key people and places appearing in this account are real. However, a few minor characters and adventures are composites, respectively, of several people or events. Additionally, some names of secondary characters have been changed, and the chronology has been shifted slightly. These modifications are minor in scope.

The fishing comes and the fishing goes
Nothing stays the same
Way up here on this northern coast
It's just a waiting game

Now when things are slow
It's a comfort just to know
Harbor lights are shining—
To light my way back home
Harbor lights are shining—
In the town I call my own

—FRANK GOTWALS, "HARBOR LIGHTS"

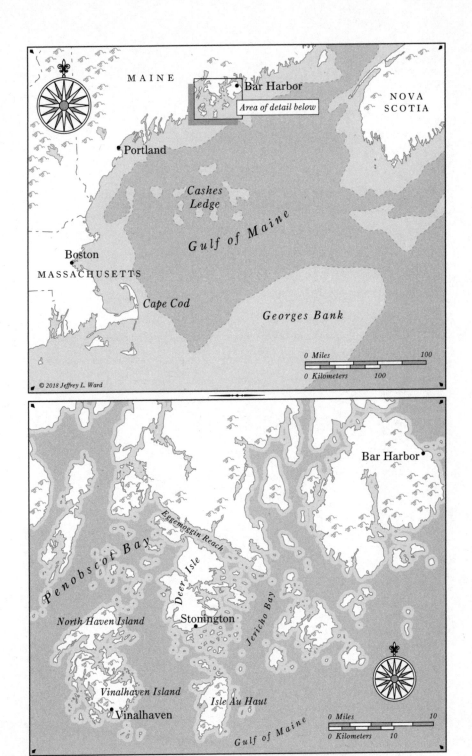

MAINE

Bar Harbor

Area of detail below

NOVA SCOTIA

Portland

Cashes
Ledge

Gulf of Maine

Boston

MASSACHUSETTS

Cape Cod

Georges Bank

0 Miles 100
0 Kilometers 100

© 2018 Jeffrey L. Ward

Bar Harbor

Eggemoggin Reach

Penobscot Bay

Deer Isle

Jericho Bay

North Haven Island

Stonington

Vinalhaven Island

Isle Au Haut

Vinalhaven

Gulf of Maine

0 Miles 10
0 Kilometers 10

The LAST
LOBSTER

Prologue

Thomas Wolfe famously said, "You can't go home again." Wolfe, a New Englander by education if not by birth, visited Maine at least once. Still, he was probably as adamant about the unrepeatable nature of the lobster coast as he was about his home turf in North Carolina. Childhood memories of a revered place, so the logic goes, can never be repeated.

Yet, I discovered recently, this maxim is not always so. There are destinations in Maine where lobstermen still bake blueberry pies derived from wild, low-bush blueberries. Home is where the kitchen is. From my boyhood summering in Maine, I remember this small fruit, tart and sweeter than the larger, cultivated blueberries found in supermarkets. Local cooks are adamant about the tiny berries. Domesticated high-bush varieties would never do, at least not in a Maine kitchen.

Traditional cuisine does not end there. For lunch—while the blueberry pie is cooling—lobster pot pie (with local celery and potatoes) will be created from scratch, all fresh. The succulent lobster itself has been hauled moments ago from the crystal clear Gulf of Maine. Most of a lobsterman's produce comes directly from field or sea. Harvests from each are courtesy of sun and clean water.

My memories return in waves.

Even more than local recipes, I remember the rocky seascapes, still unblemished. I recall cozy harbors with white lobster boats and brightly colored buoys bobbing in the surf. Though fewer, these lobstering coves are still busy, jumping with life. I can smell the mudflats at low tide, rich and rank, an acquired taste that opens up my lungs and even now, from a distance, makes me smile.

Mostly, I remember the people, the faces, the voices, that populate the remote villages where lobstering is a way of life. Rugged crags and rugged faces: The landscape matches the cut of one's jib. The tight-knit communities turn out en masse for a boat launching, a funeral, a fire. Every captain responds to a boat in distress. This way of life persists.

Four years ago, I began my search for the most authentic lobster villages in Maine, places where communities, fishermen, and native cuisine still thrive. A recent glut of lobster and a concomitant drop in prices were putting a squeeze on lobstermen. The Maine lobster culture was threatened. But there was time, I thought, to capture the essence of the lobster coast before it all changed forever.

If any breed could respond and adapt, I figured it would be the seasoned lobstermen in those distant villages. The colorful residents and their fathers and grandfathers had seen booms and busts before. The knowledge of how to survive with versatility had been passed down from generation to generation. To document that legendary resilience was my motivation for crossing half the continent to explore the Maine coast again. I came from the Chesapeake Bay by way of the Rocky Mountains.

Recently, I had spent two years living on Tilghman Island, home of the Chesapeake's famed skipjack fleet, witnessing the crash of another fishery. The Chesapeake watermen were suffering the impacts of overfishing, the scourge of fishermen around the world. But in Maine, the problem was not overharvesting, but, rather, too many lobsters. The challenges were opposite in cause and effect. The biggest mystery was how the glut had come into being. In 2012 and 2013, the market was flooded with lobsters. Prices were at rock bottom. Lobstermen were having trouble selling their catch. However, upon my arrival in 2014, the bottleneck was starting to relax. Catches were still astronomical—six times normal—but the distribution pipeline was unclogged. It was looking like a win-win situation: abundant lobster for everyone. But a boom, the lobstermen reminded me, was a bittersweet gift. Prices could plummet more. Still, after my tenure aboard the last sailing skipjacks, I was ready for some good news, however fleeting it might be.

If I could just solve the puzzle of the boom's origins and impacts, I thought, and perhaps watch the lobstermen bounce back, my odyssey would be complete.

Now back to that lobster pie. More recollections come in with the tide. I recall eating the crust with my fingers. I remember such down-home pleasures from my teenage summers in Maine. Thanks to my table manners, I was considered "from away," or in the parlance of more diplomatic local residents, I was "summer folk." I realize now that I had not fully enjoyed a "pure" Maine experience in the 1970s because I was trespassing. The natives were the lobstermen and I was the interloper. With thousands of onlookers venturing to the Maine coast each summer, the local culture has morphed into a hybrid of sorts: no longer 100 percent authentic. Many lobster villages are now vacation towns, too. Sure, some lobstermen run boardinghouses or boat tours, but the locals are uncomfortable serving two masters—the seafood industry and tourism. This mix comprises a web of modernization. Lobstermen have learned to tolerate, if not accept, the experiment.

Despite some of the coast being overrun, I had heard rumors that a few idyllic villages remained. They are not in any tourist guide. Here, the local residents do not need our business. They are doing fine—for now. Lobstering has come on like a summer downpour. American lobster, which is by far the largest fishery in Maine, had a nationwide harvest value of $460 million in 2013. Out of 149 million pounds caught nationally, more than 127 million pounds (an all-time record), or 85 percent, were landed in Maine. Thirty years ago, the catch was one-sixth that level (only 21 million pounds), and Maine fishermen were suffering. There was talk of overharvesting. Not so today. All talk is about the boom.

The bonanza brought stunning profits to lobstermen and their communities. Older men landed $200,000 or more for the first time in their lives; teenagers made $60,000 in a summer. Young and old fishermen alike bought new trucks and new and bigger boats. They took out larger mortgages and moved into spacious homes. Banks gave away loans like free beer at a picnic. Businesses expanded. Unlike the Midwest's white working class, which has lost touch with the American dream, Maine lobstermen now had money in the bank and were earning their way into the middle class. Locals became dependent on the riches of the sea.

Quickly, lobstering exceeded 80 percent of the catch from all Maine fisheries combined. Yet here's the bittersweet part. The upside: Lobsters became a sure-fire bet in the short term. The downside: Lives became insecure. If the lobster stocks collapsed, there were few other jobs to fall back on. Then and now, the lobstermen became vulnerable to any downturn, any drop in the harvest or price. Rumors of a coming crash began.

Almost immediately, the boom backfired. In 2012 and 2013, thanks to mild winters and warm springs, the lobster season came early—in June, rather than July. Lobsters filled each boat before the summer tourists had arrived. The early surfeit caused a wrench in the distribution chain. Buyers could not move the product. As a result of abundant supply and poor demand, the price plummeted to below two dollars per pound dockside, a 50 percent decrease. No one was prepared for the glut.

The price lifted somewhat each autumn, but the lobstermen had seen into the abyss. They had found a new anxiety. They could lose their security, either from a poor price or a collapse in the fishery.

After the flood of lobsters during those two warm years, lobstermen thought the next season (2014), a cool year, would bring some calm. Not so. The deluge of lobsters continued. So what was going on?

Out of many suspects for stimulating the boom, lobstermen and scientists first pointed to the paucity of predators in the Gulf of Maine. Cod and other groundfish, traditional consumers of young lobsters, had recently been overfished. In their absence, lobsters might be thriving. A second contender was warming waters, new but well known to most fishermen. Carbon loading in the atmosphere was warming the oceans as well as the land, affecting temperature-sensitive lobsters. High summer temperatures might usher in more molting and breeding. But could either of these factors prompt the sextupling of the population? Six times the old harvest seemed a big leap. Perhaps subtler, unseen forces were at work.

To seek answers, I toured the Maine coast until I found the most authentic lobster port to settle upon—a base camp for my investigation. On my journey, I asked scientists, lobstermen, and resource managers, "What caused the boom? What are its challenges? How long can the bonanza last?"

Immediately, I realized what was at stake. Worth $616.5 million ($1.7 billion for its extended sphere), fishing and its spin-offs comprise nearly 5 percent of the economy of Maine. The value to coastal counties is more than five times that percentage. What's more, the culture of the coast is intricately tied to the lobster. Summer tourism depends on the availability of cooked claws and tails. A crash in the lobster fishery would be devastating.

In view of the boom-and-bust history of the fishing industry, I had wondered all the more whether pure Maine could still be found, someplace to match my memories of a simple village life. My tour began four springs ago, when I drove from Portland, Maine, along the coast highway to the Canadian border to find a base camp and to see if any patch of waterfront had escaped gentrification. Gentrification occurs when the authentic character of a place becomes overrun with outsiders. Originality is replaced with quaintness. Former lobster towns become real estate meccas and hubs for vacation rentals. Sailboats line the harbor, rather than lobster boats. SUVs replace pickups. Low-bush blueberries become scarce as gold.

I had a third motivation for touring the coastal villages of Maine. I wanted to locate the fishing ports that adjoin the center, the peak, of the lobster population. I figured my base camp should be near that apex. This center point, where the stocks are most dense, shifts 4.3 miles northeast each year in the open Atlantic. In the face of ocean warming, it has been migrating that much at least since the 1960s. No one knows for sure when the march began. Lobster populations do not migrate in the classic sense, yet each successive year-class of larvae reestablishes itself farther north or northeast.

A research team from Princeton University tracked the movements of 360 marine species during forty years (1968–2008). All these marine animals are temperature-sensitive. Locally, ocean temperatures have climbed over 2° F due to global warming, with the fastest pace during the most recent decade. Surprisingly, during the survey, the American lobster migrated forty-three miles per decade off the northeastern United

States. The center point of the population began at Long Beach Island, New Jersey, in 1968 and ended up off Boston, a 172-mile transposition of the range, forty years later. More recently, the center of the Maine subpopulation moved from Casco Bay (near Portland) in the 1970s to Penobscot Bay (off Camden), just after 2000, a shift of ninety miles in thirty years. They arrived in their present location, northern Penobscot Bay (off Deer Isle), in 2010. This is a similar rate—approximately three miles per year. Marine species have an optimal zone, or thermal niche—for example, cool waters that lobsters seek out along the Maine coast. The cool zone they are seeking is moving north and is getting rather thin.

Not coincidentally, the lobster migrations and gentrification were headed in the same direction, toward the northeast. After the center point crests and declines, the gentry may follow.

I wanted to catch the crustaceans' peak somewhere Down East, the far reaches of the Maine coast. That was my plan: to see how lobstermen in an authentic Maine village handle the deluge, the flood of lobsters, and, by extension, the statewide boom. It would likely be one of the first recorded responses of fishermen, of Americans, to climate change.

The entire rocky coastline of Maine (and New Hampshire and the northern half of Massachusetts) is bordered by the Gulf of Maine, home to lobsters of record size—up to three feet long. The Gulf is a semienclosed basin of the North Atlantic, running from Cape Cod to Cape Sable, at the southern tip of Nova Scotia. As such, it includes the Bay of Fundy, home to the greatest tides in the world. The entire basin is bounded to the east and south by underwater banks. Georges Bank, for example, on its southern side, isolates the Gulf of Maine from the Gulf Stream. Consequently, the basin's waters are cooled by the Labrador Current, coming from the north, making for ideal lobster habitat. Lobsters prefer a chilly 53° F to 64° F. However, the basin's waters are heating up—due to global warming—faster than 99 percent of all the world's seas. Warm air heats the oceans, some more than others, forming hot spots. Already, the Gulf of Maine is too hot for cod, historically its second most important fishery. A portion of the cod population has moved to Newfoundland. Could lobsters be next? They are moving up the coast at a brisk pace.

By my count, there are over eighty-five former or active lobster villages along this stretch of coast. This does not include the fifteen inhabited islands just offshore. In some cases, these isles are pristine. Islands like Matinicus, Swan's, Great Cranberry, and Little Cranberry are completely reliant on lobstering; there is no tourism to speak of. For viable coastal towns and islands, lobster is still king.

You can tell whether you have happened upon a living village by the lobster traps stacked in front yards. The closer these traps are to the water, the more authentic is the town. On the other hand, if traps and buoys are predominantly on lawns two or three blocks removed from the waterfront, then it is likely outsiders are buying up the shoreline. For lobstermen, the biggest threat of gentrification is loss of access to the water. Genevieve McDonald, a lobster-boat captain I came to know, suggested I could gauge a town's purity by how many Maine license tags appear on pickups at the town dock. Too many out-of-state tags and it's a lost cause.

My prospects ranged from genteel Boothbay Harbor to Victorian Camden, from ferry towns like Port Clyde and Bar Harbor to rustic Beals Island and Cutler in the Down East area. I stopped at several—four overnight—to gauge their authenticity.

Every coastal town from Kittery, on the Maine–New Hampshire border, to Boothbay Harbor is close enough to Boston to be a weekend commute. Consequently, they are gentrified, more or less. Still, I found Boothbay Harbor to be beautiful, if tame. Gentrification—particularly the displacement of local residents—is just one of the many impacts of a dwindling catch or climate change. The lobster center point was located off Boothbay Harbor in the 1980s. When lobsters boomed, then faltered late in the decade, the town briefly lost its purpose. Lobstermen were forced to sell. The gentry arrived, and the lobstering community has only partially recovered.

In 1850, the port boasted a population of 2,500—mostly lobstermen, cod fishermen, shipwrights, sailmakers, and riggers. Now, a sleepy town of 6,500 in winter becomes a tourist trap of 35,000 in August, when the cruise ships arrive. Caught between the past and the present, the harbor hosts fewer than thirty lobster boats, moored between puffin tour boats and whale-watching vessels. And yet, Boothbay Harbor is one of the prettiest coves on the rocky Maine coast, scenery that has made the destination famous.

Farther along the Mid-Coast, outside Boston's weekend orbit, Port Clyde was charming but nearly gentrified, too. The lobsters peaked here in the 1990s, though I was getting closer to my goal. The wharves sported lobster traps, although none occupied the backyards. Many locals had moved away. Waterfront taxes and real estate prices were too heavy for those lobstermen. The service industry—for example, puffin tour-boat operators—had eclipsed fishing. Port Clyde's general store, formerly an adventure of mismatched gloves, socks, and one-of-a-kind produce, like dried cod, was now a "country store," catering to vacationers. There was nothing general about it, except the name. An attached restaurant peddled lobster rolls on a bun for seventeen dollars each. Port Clyde was now a summer place, a picture postcard of itself.

Even farther up the coast, the old town of Searsport spoke to the legacy of a seagoing tradition. In the 1800s, ships built here regularly rounded Cape Horn in the perilous China Trade. The local Penobscot Maritime Museum tells the story. Lobstering has also been part of its legacy—cresting around the year 2000—with a dozen lobster boats still harboring here. I discovered that the upward wealth of the town (and taxes) had long eclipsed any downtown lobstermen residences. Today, lobstermen lived outside of town and drove to the harbor to tend their boats. I fear the whole coast could sometime become a museum.

I crossed the Penobscot River at Bucksport, the former home of a paper mill, and relaxed my shoulders. I was now Down East, that northeastern stretch of the Maine coast to the east of Penobscot Bay. The center point of Maine lobsters that year was just south of me now, having peaked a couple of years before. The promise of discovering my base camp very soon spurred me on. I bypassed the towns of Blue Hill and Stonington, pledging to return there to explore the lobsters' hub. I skipped Bar Harbor, as well, another ferry town that caters to tourists. Instead, I took a side road to Beals Island, reachable by bridge, forty-five miles up the Down East coast. Here was an authentic fishing village. Colored traps and buoys adorned every property and pier. Homes were trimmed in red and blue, with paint left over from marking lobster buoys. A single take-out place, called Bayview, was recently awarded the best lobster roll in Maine. Very difficult to find. If you make it, also try the Bayview Burger, which is lobster meat covered with a spicy Thousand Island dressing. Delicious! Too bad only the locals get to enjoy it. There are no novelty shops—their absence is another secret weapon that keeps tourists away. Just a town that knows itself and sticks with it. I did find a cabin to stay in and quizzed the locals about the lobster fishery, which, they say, gets better every year. The mother lode should be at their doorstep in sixteen years.

My fourth overnight stop was Cutler, ninety minutes east of Acadia National Park. I was nearly in Canada on this leg of the trip. Here was another refreshing scene. Lobstermen houses lined the waterfront, looking prosperous. In nearly every front yard were stacks of traps; the white boats were tethered to orange moorings just offshore. The Cutler General Store sold oilskins, fishing knives, pemmican, venison jerky, and, of course, salt cod. In the harbor, children played with "lobstahs" in their dinghies. I had arrived. At last, I was in old-time Maine.

Kittery, Boothbay Harbor, Port Clyde, Searsport, Beals Island, and Cutler represent the breadth of the Maine coast. The modernization, the gentrification, spreads northeast along the waterfront like a rash. All the towns were once authentic—as the lobstermen say, "all wool and a yard wide." Southern Port Clyde resembled northern Cutler one hundred years ago. Now to the south, we find 7-Elevens; to the north, general stores. This homogenization of the landscape pleases some. In the south, shopping is easier. Favorite brands are easy to find. What's missing is originality and local flavor. We travel northward to experience true Maine, then criticize all the inconveniences. We lament the experience not being more like that in Massachusetts. Well, some lament. Others travel deeper into the country.

The single greatest threat to Cutler and other lobster towns is not vacationers, however. As long as a visitor doesn't buy up any waterfront, his impact is mild. But once waterfront homes switch hands, once harbor access is denied, the lobstermen are left high and dry. In the same vein, the biggest peril to the community is a possible crash in the lobster industry, whether a price war or a plummet in the population. If and when that comes, locals may be forced to sell their properties. We have seen a lobster fishery crash before, most recently in Long Island Sound. The case holds poignancy for Maine.

Connecticut and northern Long Island, which together frame Long Island Sound, once hosted an abundant supply of lobster. Then the ocean heated up. At first, the warming ocean stimulated growth of larval lobsters, similar to what we are now seeing in Maine. As late as 1998, over 550 lobstermen caught 3.7 million pounds of lobster, bringing in fifteen million dollars, ranking the region third after Maine and Massachusetts. Then something went drastically wrong. As temperatures continued to climb, the harvest crashed, retreating to 120,000 pounds in 2013, a mere 3 percent of its heyday. Not wanting to acknowledge climate change, the lobstermen pointed to pesticide runoff and parasites as the two preferred candidates for the disaster. New York State sprayed malathion in 2000 to curtail the spread of the West Nile virus by mosquitoes. Some of this nasty pesticide may have found its way into Long Island Sound, killing lobsters, though scientists found nothing detectable in the water column. The connection was never proven. Parasites also proved to be inconclusive. The third suspect was given short shrift by most fishermen: Global warming, or, more correctly, ocean warming, was a possible factor dismissed outright by lobstermen.

Yet three factors favor this theory. First, lobsters are at the extreme southern limit of their inshore range in Long Island Sound. So they are already near the limit of their upper temperature tolerance. Second, temperatures have been climbing in Long Island Sound and now regularly exceed 65° F—sometimes by a large measure. (Some August water temperatures have exceeded 74° F in certain locations around Long Island Sound.) Third, this temperature horizon is near the threshold where lobster metabolism begins to falter. Anything above 68° F is stressful to lobsters. Stressed lobsters either flee to deeper (or more northern) waters or die. Connecticut officials estimate that eleven million lobsters died in Long Island Sound in 2013, nearly 90 percent of the population. Most Augusts, lobsters turn limp and perish. The stress can also bring on other ailments, such as a susceptibility to parasites or shell disease, a wasting illness that makes lobsters unsalable.

Today, the lobstering workforce in Long Island Sound is just 154 men and women, about 28 percent of what it was in 1999. Lobstermen are switching professions or moonlighting as truck drivers, telephone repairmen, and tollbooth attendants. Fishermen are flexible, but it's a far cry from the water.

This past September, lobsterman Dick Sawyer, seventy-six, of Groton, Connecticut, pulled all his lobster traps, nearly seven hundred wire cages, out of the water—maybe for good. He quit midseason to comply with an official three-month closure of the fishery. The state of Connecticut hopes the moratorium will reduce exploitation of the already depressed lobster population by 10 percent. But such a closure implies that overharvesting was playing a decisive role in causing the stocks to fail. Yet overfishing is unproven. While agreeing with his fellow fishermen that overharvesting is not at work, Dick Sawyer breaks stride with the pack by claiming the culprit is not simply pesticides nor parasites.

"Don't forget about the effects of climate change," he says. "The warming water has just killed the Sound. What we now harvest in a week I used to catch in a day."

Sawyer, a third-generation lobsterman, believes reducing the lobster harvest will not fix the problem. "The closure hasn't done anything but stop us from fishing."

In Groton, when the season has been open, the Sawyer family sells their catch to Garbo Lobster Company, a buyer and processor right in town. But Garbo cannot fill its orders by just tapping Long Island Sound anymore. Too few lobsters. To reach better hunting grounds, Garbo's eighteen-wheel trucks head north to Maine, which is crawling with lobsters. Maine is on the "uptick" of the graph. While Long Island Sound is going bust, Maine is celebrating a stampede. One of their last stops is Stonington, Maine, which is now the largest port in the Down East region, thanks to the arrival of the lobster center point. I saw this authentic lobster town on my trip back from Cutler and was intrigued by the place.

So, after my drive along the Maine coast and my visit to Connecticut, my partner, Donna, and I return to the Down East area and settle in

Stonington, halfway between Port Clyde and Cutler. If Down East is the last bastion of authenticity and a sustainable fishery, then Stonington is the hub. The lobster center point hovers right offshore, so winnings are big. The UK-based Marine Stewardship Council just declared the Maine lobster "sustainable." I am curious why it received the badge of honor when the fishery seemed so precarious. Gulf of Maine summer temperatures still hovered below 55° F (on average), but that is only thirteen degrees below the lobster's threshold for stress. I want to know how the warming ocean (or other causes of the boom) could affect sustainability. Certainly, Connecticut no longer has a sustainable fishery. Can Maine fall off the pedestal, as well? What will happen to the lobster villages and, by extension, to the culture and economy of Maine? Will the last authentic stretch of the Maine coast survive?

Rick Wahle, professor of marine biology at the University of Maine, spoke recently about the domino effect a collapse of Maine's lobster fishery would have on the state. "It puts the fear of God in lobstermen to imagine what happened in Long Island Sound happening here," he said. "The magnitude of the fishery is so much greater here and the coast is so perilously dependent on a single fishery."

Stonington is a bustling port with over 350 licensed lobster captains and six dockside buyers who ship across the country and around the world. It ranks first among Maine's ports, with $49 million in commercial fish landings (in 2014). Though it is accessible to big seafood trucks like Garbo's, you have to fight to get there. Stonington sits squarely on the southern tip of Deer Isle, reachable by a high, narrow suspension bridge. The view from the top resembles a ski jump. After another six miles of winding road, the town harbor appears, adorned with boats. Hundreds of white vessels bob with the huge tides. Nothing on the French Riviera can beat the view. The town harbor looks out to Isle au Haut, one of the gems of Maine's fifteen inhabited islands, reliant on the town ferry. There's no other escape, unless you have a lobster boat. Stonington is land's end.

Downtown Stonington comprises a single thoroughfare—Main Street—with two inns and three restaurants frequented by locals. Harbor Café, a lobstermen's hangout, is famous for its haddock sandwich. Yet, rest assured, you can order lobster there and everywhere—even for breakfast, if you want. The homes and storefronts are Victorian, right up to the gables and widow's walks. Salt cod is available at the Harborview General Store. While lobster traps do not sit in front lawns on Main Street, they congregate at the edges of town—leading in and leading out. There's simply no room for lawns or frontage or traps in the narrow commercial district. Still, the rule of thumb applies: Where there are traps, the lobstermen own their own homes, all within a stroll of the harbor.

Stores offer groceries, clothing, fishing gear, engine parts, and books. There are two bookstores and a lending library for a population of eleven hundred. Winters are long, and unless you have a comic for a sternman, your lobster helper, there's no entertainment at all. But come summertime, the Stonington Opera House opens, featuring plays and movies and concerts. *Romeo and Juliet & Zombies* was a big hit last year.

At the edge of town, I strike up conversations with men and women standing in their yards among rows of traps. While I was warned that Maine fishermen are standoffish to anyone "from away," I find the town welcoming. Lobstermen invite me aboard their wooden craft. The residents tell me warm temperatures have brought an oversupply of lobsters. That sounds benign enough until my immersion into the life of the fleet.

Within a day or two, I find myself motoring out of the harbor aboard a lobster boat for a day of setting and hauling traps. The sternman tells me that the flood of lobsters has brought poor prices. The catch may have doubled, but the value has been cut in half. I am curious whether any one of the captains may have the key to reversing the trend. It will take a season to find the answers. I rent a cottage within sight of the harbor to make it easy to go lobstering each season—summer, autumn, winter, and spring.

While I'm unpacking, two cats—Albert Einstein and Charlie Chaplin—make my acquaintance, one cerebral, one comic. In Maine, personalities of boats, pets, and fishermen follow their names. Even the town Stonington, I discover, is eponymous—named for a granite quarry nearby.

Just up Pink Street, behind our cottage, is the weekly Farmers' Market. I take a break from suitcases and hangers to hunt for an organic lunch. That's easy. One vendor offers me a lobster roll—all claw meat.

Divine. Then I inspect the homemade pies. Yes, the blueberries are wild, low-bush—as petite as river pearls. The cook offers me a sweet bite—just tart enough to tickle my mouth into a grin.

I have only one thought: After all my explorations, I've come home again. Thomas Wolfe is wrong.

This is where my story begins.

It is the story of a search for remedies to the predicament of the lobsterman's world. He lives in a boom-and-bust cycle that makes life insecure. Can he adapt to climate change and other challenges on the waterfront? He will have to work fast. There is little promise that the current boom will last long. The world of the lobster is heating up.

1

Summer, Jericho Bay

In the half-light before dawn, Frank Gotwals, sixty, rows a yellow skiff across the gray-blue water of Stonington Harbor, Maine. While other lobster captains employ a motor for commuting, Frank works with his hands, his back, his arms. His progress from the dinghy dock to his mooring is steady, but from my vantage on a floating pier at harbor's edge, he appears to hesitate at each successive curtain of fog. The shreds of mist glance off his shoulders and split into gray curlicues as he makes headway. Pushing through each curtain is like stepping through a waterfall. Thin sheets of fog open and close without memory. They absorb and absolve. Finally, there are only one or two layers of fog left. He's nearly in the clear.

A breath of wind crosses the harbor, kissing my face. The surface of the water undulates slightly in long curves but is more or less "flat ca'm," as they say. It will get choppy later. We are expecting a southwest breeze on the open water today, enough to break up the fog. Yet right now from my pier, from his boat deck, we're in low-lying clouds, like pillows nestled on a hardwood floor.

Frank flicks his right wrist twice so his oar will avoid a rock, barely exposed now at high tide. The tide doesn't simply go in and out here, flood and ebb, as it does in the waters below Cape Cod. Here, in the Gulf of Maine, it much more obviously goes up and down. It is vertical in expression. The tidal range is eight to thirteen feet, depending on the phase of the moon. A boulder on the seafloor can become a navigation hazard in six short hours. Not surprisingly, passage to the open Atlantic is shipwreck-strewn. A captain takes his chances. The Gulf of Maine is a game of all or none.

Earlier this July morning, Frank told me, that with knowledge of the tide, he could row blindfolded to his lobster boat. In the weeks ahead, I would witness the larger truth: Frank knows the bottom and edges, the channels and islands, of the Gulf of Maine just as well as his mooring. He had baited and set 750 lobster traps in these waters over the past few days and he knows where every one is—no chart or inventory needed. We would check one-third of them today. That would require two workers: Frank and his "sternman," Alyssa LaPointe, twenty-six, the woman who now joins me on the float. She seems out of place: young, blond, wearing fingernail polish, but dressed for commercial fishing—yellow oilskins from shoulder to foot. I'm here to observe both captain and crew—for Alyssa, a college of one.

There are over 3,800 active lobstermen in Maine, most limited to working eight hundred traps or fewer. That's over three million pots on the ocean floor, a concentration of effort unparalleled in the history of shellfish harvesting. The Gulf of Maine—and its inshore bays—claims more lobsters, more densely, than anywhere in the world. Estimates place the stock at 248 million individuals. In addition to the lobstermen, another ten thousand people—pickers, cooks, drivers, etc.—provide support to the Maine lobster industry, which is valued at over $1.7 billion annually. I was curious about that level of intensity. What kept the lobster villages going in the face of such pressure and recent volatility—the catch doubling, sextupling, then possibly subsiding again, the price dropping through the floor. How did lobstermen stay in business? Could they endure much longer?

Captain Gotwals is quick to give me some more telling statistics.

Last week, when Frank hauled all 750 of his traps, he caught over three thousand pounds of lobster, or four pounds per trap. That's about half his record of eight pounds per trap (nearly six thousand pounds) set last year. Both harvests were at the height of the first shed, or molt. These are record times for the whole state of Maine, where 127.8 million pounds of lobster were landed in 2013, six times the average harvest of the late 1980s. That's a lobster on the plate of one out of every three Americans. However, the bonanza has come at a cost. The law of supply and demand has forced the overabundant lobsters into a low price range. The market paid Frank only $2.50 per pound (plus a bonus at the end of the year). He is accustomed to getting close to four dollars per pound. It may not be worth it for him to continue, regardless of how many lobsters he lands. The day's expenses will be upwards of five hundred dollars. On top of that, he must pay Alyssa 20 percent of the catch. Profit margins are slim; expenses are fat.

The lobsterman is sometimes called Maine's patron saint of lost causes. But Frank is not a quitter. He is spearheading a statewide campaign to rally demand for Maine lobster. Last year's new prospect was South Korea. This year, there's a redoubled effort toward China. Exports of Maine lobster to Asia are picking up. Captain Frank may have to learn a little Mandarin before it's all over. Yet today he speaks only the language of his great-grandfather, who fished these waters in the 1890s and later. The dialect hasn't changed.

"We'll try to catch some lobstah—that's my idear anyways," he calls from the rowboat.

Frank slips easily in and out of the voice of a "Mainah." While his mother's family is native to Stonington (and surrounding islands), he grew up in Northampton, Massachusetts. His father was a music professor, his mother a choral director, both at Smith College. That lineage gave him a love of music and the water, the two passions of his life. Frank occasionally polishes off words that end in *er* with *ah,* hence "ye-ah" for *year.* He also turns an *a* ending into an *r,* such as in "idear." This is standard Mainahspeak. Yet Frank can sometimes sound cosmopolitan, while Alyssa always "marks her lobstahs with a rubbah band."

Frank shrugs off the last wisp of fog and touches the port side of his white boat, the thirty-eight-foot *Seasong.* Immediately, he ties the rowboat to the mooring and hoists a blue-and-white lunch cooler up to and over the gunwale and rests it on deck. Then he muscles his way into the lobster boat. Even at sixty, he moves like a lanky teenager.

Although it ranges on the continental shelf from Virginia to the Canadian Maritimes, the American lobster is most plentiful in Penobscot and Jericho Bays, our hunting grounds today. It's the third Monday in July and the "shedders" (or newly molted adult lobsters) are running. They've been running for three weeks, since the summer season began. "Nothing's sweeter than a shedder," Alyssa says to me. "We should really think about boiling some aboard." At 5:00 A.M., Frank is anxious to get under way. He releases *Seasong* from her mooring and motors in a wide arc to pick us up.

"Time to haul some traps," Captain Frank says, with the motor in idle while we climb aboard.

"Yeah, it's time," says Alyssa over her shoulder. "I brought the melted butter anyway, mistah, just in case there's a lull."

"Doubtful."

"Exactly."

"Keeping busy used to be a good thing," says the captain.

"Now we're too busy," says Alyssa. "Lobsters coming out of our ears. The price has dropped and I can't pay the rent."

Frank pays her no mind. He hits the throttle. *Seasong*'s stern digs in, as if for traction. The bow lifts up out of the water. My view from the cockpit is obscured for a minute until the boat levels off. Now in full witness, the view through the windshield captures half the foredeck, the water, the sky. Frank steers east, away from Penobscot Bay and into the waters of Jericho Bay. The town of Stonington, pointing like a dial southward at the tip of Deer Isle, divides the two bays: Penobscot to the west, Jericho to the east. The primary feature of the latter is an archipelago of small islands—some covered with spruce trees, some bald. Most are the size of a soccer field; some appear no bigger than the goal. The smell of spruce sap drifts over the water, mixes with the salt air, and delivers a unique combination of odors: sweet and sharp. Green Island, Russ Island, and Camp Island—what I will call the "harborside islands"— are among the first tree-covered isles to materialize out of the fading fog. They are close enough that we can make out the individual trees. But the blue-green water obscures their footprints, including the underwater rock ledges leading up to the islands themselves.

Farther ahead of us is a broad smile of water.

Frank tells me that the number-one hazard in working the shallow waters of Jericho Bay is the hidden granite—the submerged rocks and subtidal igneous aprons at the edges of the islands. More than one hundred rock islands populate Jericho Bay, along with dozens of shipwrecks from previous centuries. Frank knows the contours of each island in three dimensions. He knows where to land at low tide and where to fend off when the water is high. He also knows their names.

Not just a few modern fishermen have punched holes in their boats on the jettylike ledges surrounding these islands. Frank gives wide berth to the islands and their footings. Just now, he swerves wide to avoid a rock point. He is protective of *Seasong,* the second boat he has built with his own hands. In an age of fiberglass and steel, Frank is an anachronism: He constructed his boat of wood. The pine and oak construction makes her "comfortable" in the water. She has a traditional lobster hull, with bunks and a galley below. Frank talks of the "feel" of her being just right. Of her many advantages, the slow-turning diesel engine gives her fuel efficiency—better than his previous boat, *Seahawk,* which is two feet shorter (and now owned by his stepson). Above all, Frank has the pride of authorship. Other lobstermen read her lines and smile. He knows he got this one right.

While submerged rocks are treacherous, fog adds another layer of unpredictability to navigation. Frank slows down through a dense patch yet keeps his nerve. Fishermen are raised on uncertainty; they are taught to expect the unexpected. "Thar're simply too many variables in fishing—wind, weather, tides, stock cycles, the mood of the boat—to forecast accurately the catch outside the current week," he says. "Even that is complicated. It's best to only base the afternoon on the morning, and leave it at that."

Thinking how chancy it appears, I ask Frank if fishing isn't akin to gambling. As he comes out of the fog, he pivots on the heel of his boot and sets me straight.

"It's like playing blackjack with six decks in the shoe," he says. "The odds are always in favor of the house."

By "house," he means nature. She holds all the cards, he says. Nature has her whims. "If she deals you a good hand one day, be thankful," he says, "but don't expect your luck to surface again soon. In fishing, circumstances change fast. You have to take the little victories whenever you can."

Out of all fishermen, lobstermen are least like gamblers, however. Gamblers bet on probabilities; they count on the odds working in their favor a certain amount of the time. Meanwhile, lobstermen accept the unpredictable and unrepeatable nature of their work. There are no odds, no averages, no certain payoff. Frank doesn't believe in probabilities. On a good day, with the tide high and the wind blowing southeast, he may catch some lobsters. If it's one of those perfect days, he accepts his fair share of the ocean's bounty. If the day is a wash, he surrenders to the gods. The most important thing, he says, is to be on the water when that fine day appears.

"The first rule of lobstering," says Frank, "is to not sleep in late."

I'm standing next to Frank at the helm. Alyssa is aft, filling nylon bait bags with herring. The four-inch fish resemble oversized sardines. The air is rank with the rotting fish. We are threading our way through a slalom course of little islands, mostly bald—solid rock, no trees. Suddenly, out of the fog comes a rolling wave—a rogue, it seems, but perhaps another boat's wake—that rocks *Seasong* heavily and knocks me off my feet. My right shoulder slams into a cabin bulkhead before I can lift my hand to protect it. No damage done: a bruise maybe, but that's all. I look over at the captain. He's braced securely, his shoulder lined up over planted feet.

I make the promise to myself not to be surprised again. Little do I know that lobstering is all about surprises. The forecast is that there will be a new forecast. And soon.

Alyssa comes forward, showing no signs of wear or first aid. "That's lobstering," she says. "Hours of calm followed by five minutes of sheer terror."

Gulls appear, flying over our wake. They scavenge bits of herring that Alyssa throws overboard. Five herring gulls in all. And a black-backed gull lands on the bow and manages to maintain its stance with the boat under way. These gulls make a living following the lobster boats and their discarded bait from sunrise to sunset.

When the sun appears, the fog dissipates. The last tendrils dance against the purple curtain of the sunrise like shadow puppets on a velvet stage. Up ahead, an oval patch of sky takes on the same color as the sea—a deep maroon—as if the ceiling were holding a mirror to the sea.

In dawn's soft light, Frank's and Alyssa's faces come into full view. Alyssa has French good looks, with a sharp nose, high forehead, and thin lips. Her long, sun-streaked blond hair hangs loosely. No hat. Frank, on the other hand, looks German, his paternal heritage. He's blond, too, but sandy, not golden. While Alyssa seems born to the water, Frank does not. He resembles a rock star—picture Bon Jovi—in looks. When he plays guitar (Frank is a Maine songwriter and celebrity, with four albums to his credit) and sings at concerts and nightclubs, he appears comfortable. He's a natural showman. When he's onstage, it's hard to imagine him in a lobster boat, and yet here he is, considered a "highliner," one of the best of the best.

Seasong races along at a gallop, the captain burning diesel to recapture the minutes lost to his commute. He turns to port in a broad arc to the south side of Camp Island, the third of those harborside islands we saw. The green trees and blue water of neighboring islands have given them the name Arcadia. Here, I inhale the scent of spruce and seawater and think, This heaven will do.

I still stand next to the captain at the helm, so as not to miss a trick. I discover that there is more to lobstering than meets the eye.

Twenty minutes out of the harbor, Frank reins in the throttle. Breaking his canter, Frank now trots forward toward the gathering ahead, a galaxy of buoys. All are brightly painted, bobbing in the dark sea as if a kaleidoscope of stars had dropped from the night sky. There are shimmering green and white buoys, bright sky blue and yellow ones, even mustard orange and black ones. Most striking are the neon yellows and electric pinks. Frank scans each, searching for his mark. His quest is akin to identifying one rainbow from hundreds. Alyssa spots his trademark red-white-and-blue buoy on the far side of the congregation, and whistles. Her call is shrill and seems to melt the last shred of fog. When I look around next, the sky and water are clear. Frank steers the boat toward the marker, his first buoy of 750 dotting Jericho Bay today.

The red-white-and-blue plug bobs off our port bow. Frank nearly swamps it to get close enough. He comes alongside and reaches over the gunwale with a boat hook. With his other hand, he cuts the engine. With a twist of the wrist, he gaffs the buoy line and pulls it to him. The line is dripping wet. Yellow Grundén oilskins, blue rubber gloves, and black boots keep him dry. He sets the buoy on deck. With his dominant right hand, the captain now wraps the line over a snatch block and around the trap hauler, which is a hydraulic winch that pinches and pulls the line and its treasure to the surface. In the process, the trap hauler deposits a large coil of wet line on deck. Positioned among the wheel, the winch, and the coil, the captain is in a precarious spot. The coil itself is lethal, a noose that can carry a man out to sea. Frank seems as calm as if he were brushing his teeth. When the first of two traps surfaces, Frank stops the winch and lifts the forty-pound trap onto the rail, a work area above the gunwale at the side of the boat. Frank puts the next segment of line into the winch and reels in the second trap. Once both are on the rail, Alyssa tends the first one and Frank the second. The traps are rectangular wire mesh, coated in yellow plastic. Each has two compartments, with doorways giving access, all in plain view. We can see the verdict before they open the gates. One adult flexes its "tail," more accurately called an abdomen, in Alyssa's trap, while two small, immature lobsters— about half the size of the adult—dance around the second compartment of Frank's two-room pot. The catch is just short of empty.

"I better freshen up the bait some," says Alyssa, meaning replace the old with something more rank.

"It's not the bait," says the captain. "We're just in the wrong spot. Maybe it's too shallow. Last week, we caught ten beauties here. Their brothers and sisters must have gotten restless. The trouble is, this bay is just big enough for a lobster to change its mind."

We are fishing the shallows around the islands today because it is the season of shedders, molting lobsters. Immature lobsters crawl out of the depths in summer to shed their shells under the protective cover of rock ledges and stones (and the fissures between). Lobsters must molt periodically in order to grow. A naked lobster is vulnerable to predators, and it takes six weeks to grow a new shell. The shedders gain up to 40 percent in size once they've grown a new, larger covering. At this point, the legal-size lobsters remain in their new clothes until further growth necessitates changing outfits eleven or twelve months down the road. For the first six to eight weeks, the lobster is considered a shedder, recognizable by its softer, shiny shell. Like most everything in the ocean, temperature is the cue for molting. Traditionally, summer temperatures induce larvae and juveniles to molt. Thus the popular summer time for feasts, Frank's best season. Shedders are prized by lobstermen. From all accounts, they taste better—sweeter—and garner a good price.

Alyssa places the keeper on the counting table and tosses the two smalls back into the sea. She tilts the male into the sharp sunlight to show off his colors—green and brown, with a hint of red. Only the red will survive steaming in Alyssa's cooker. Next, she hooks a bait bag of rotting herring into the first compartment of each trap. I am curious why the bait bag goes into the first room and the lobsters end up in the second. I ask her about the bait room first.

"Oh, that's the kitchen," she says. "The lobsters enter the trap at that spot, hungry for bait. But then they try to escape into the second compartment—the parlor—and we have them. I think of it as a two-room cat house made of mesh."

Some sternmen refer to the parlor as the "bedroom," but Alyssa assures me her lobsters are not that promiscuous. "They just eat dinner and try to get free," she says, "like most of the men in this town."

As the morning warms up, Alyssa peels off her oilskin jacket. Underneath, she sports a T-shirt that proclaims:

FISH NAKED
Show off your rod.

There are no pretenses aboard *Seasong*. Everyone and everything is unadorned. What you see is what you cannot forget.

Alyssa picks up a female, notes her small swimmerets, or soft, feathery appendages, on her abdomen, and places her gently in the water tank. Then she inspects a male and his first pair of swimmerets, which are hard and bony. "Don't get any ideas in that tank," she says, and drops him to mingle with the females.

After adding the bait bags, Alyssa closes the trap's doors, which shield both compartments. She locks the doors. Alyssa tosses the aft trap into the ocean and the line plays out. This is called "setting a trap." Frank slides the second trap overboard (in the same order they had arrived on deck) and watches the coil unwind at his feet. The buoys go over last, marking the place he will return to in three days' time. As they fly overboard, it's natural to wonder what greets the empty traps on the ocean floor. Divers and remote video have uncovered the life of the lobster trap and the behavior of its residents and neighbors underwater. The level of activity depends on the freshness of the bait.

When Frank and Alyssa toss the two traps over the port rail, the pots descend quickly and land about one hundred feet apart on the ocean bottom, the breadth of a short fairway. The expanse is full of shimmering fish. Imagine that nearby is a ghost trap, an abandoned pot, its tether severed from its buoy by prop or mischief. The ghost trap has a biodegradable vent so that stranded lobsters can escape. Still, more lobsters enter the kitchen out of habit, even though the bait bag is long empty. The ocean bottom is littered with cracked shells, carcasses of seals, skeletons of cod: the legacy of hungry lobsters.

The lobsters must burrow in the sand for protection. Like sand traps around a putting green, the bottom is pockmarked with depressions, where single female lobsters brood their eggs. At the scent of Alyssa's traps, burdened with fresh bait, the females stir. They are the bloodhounds of the deep. They are joined by males, all clashing for dominance, to see who can prey on the herring first. The lobsters raise their claws, then strike, resulting in a "claw lock," like two antlered elk. Some males are already clawless, having lost their crushers or pincers in combat. These grow back. The winners gain entrance to the kitchens and a feast of herring or pogies. After feeding, most exit the trap through the same porthole. But a few adults advance to the next room—the parlor—and are destined for Frank's boat. The smaller lobsters—as well as Jonah crabs and hermit crabs—can easily escape from the parlor, as well.

There are more dangers on the seafloor than just traps. Predators that lurk in the trap field include wolffish, sculpins, and striped bass. When the big females release their eggs next summer and those eggs transform to floating larvae, voracious fish, ranging from herring to basking sharks, will prey on the newborn. Ninety percent of lobsters die in those first four weeks. Yet, right now, the biggest danger is striped bass, a tiger of the Atlantic, often four feet long. Imagine Alyssa throwing a short off the side. That small lobster, as vulnerable as a baby bird, descends through sixty feet of water—at every turn a waiting striped bass, capable of chomping a grown lobster. "If he can make it to the mud or sand," says Frank, "he's probably safe. Until we catch him."

Frank smiles at Alyssa and me. He is pleased the last sequence, setting two traps, went so well. Alyssa is a seasoned sternman, so he does not have to repeat instructions. A nod or a look will do. "I'm lucky to have a female sternman," he says. "I've had enough young guys swaggering around the deck with too much testosterone in their veins. In a confined space, under stressful conditions, you can't be competing with each other all the time. Alyssa and I tease each other, sure, but we don't compete. We both take our time. When you rush things on a lobster boat is when you get into trouble."

Alyssa does not hear her captain's words above the drone of the diesel engine. But she pitches her voice to ask, "What about this string of traps?"

Frank says, "If we just catch water in the next two traps, instead of lobsters, we'll have to find a new neighborhood for our string."

"Okay, Cap'n."

Things can change fast on the ocean floor. Last week, Frank and Alyssa caught a dozen lobsters in each of these traps—all shedders sequestered in the shallows. Now, with hardening shells, the lobsters are perhaps on the move. They've got hunger on their brains.

In between hauling lobsters, the *Seasong* races from spot to spot, its engine wide open, causing the boat to kick forward like a lurching truck.

On the far side of Camp Island, Frank spies another cluster of buoys. He descends on them, cutting the engine at just the last second, the swells of the wake washing over the buoys, swamping them. They are quick to recover.

Frank's eyes widen, but Alyssa is the first to say, "Aren't those Jason's colors?"

"Yep," says the captain. "That's my boy Jason." His stepson is working the same island, here and there checkered with his white-blue-and-yellow buoys. "He'll be out here today, I imagine. I could use his help aboard this boat. Best sternman I ever had."

Alyssa's jaw sags a little. She bounces back quickly, however. She tells me the second rule of lobstering is to accept that the captain's family comes ahead of everyone else.

"And the first rule?" I ask.

"To remember who told you the second. And the third. And the fourth."

Just now, Frank raises Jason on the marine radio. Jason is out of eyesight, behind an island no doubt. "*Seahawk,* this is *Seasong.* Come back!"

"Got you, Frank."

"You hauling on Camp Island today?"

"Not as fast as you, but I'll get there eventually."

"May not be worth it. Neither lobster this morning. Have a good one."

"You, too."

We haul four more of Frank's shallow-water traps, but Camp Island is a total bust. Alyssa sits these four traps in the stern for placement later in a new neighborhood. The captain calls his stepson again with an interim report. Then Frank retrieves a wild card. In the sixty-foot channel between Camp Island and Coombs Island (the next isle to the southeast), Frank recovers a pair of traps teeming with life. The traps are on the rail, and all manner of thrashing and commotion takes place inside. Upon opening the first door, Alyssa does a little jig. She sings out, "Could be eight or ten legal lobsters, if they gauge out good."

Alyssa holds the metal gauge in her left hand and grabs one of the lobsters in her right. She is gentle with the male, careful not to dislodge a claw. The other nine prospects sit in the counting tray at her waist. She measures the carapace, the defining shell segment over the lobster's thorax, and it's under three and a quarter inches, the limits of legality. Alyssa tosses the lobster overboard. The next lobster is a female with a distinctive V-shaped notch cut out of the right tail flippers. This means another lobsterman caught the same female when she was carrying eggs. That captain cut the notch, as prescribed by law, and let her go. She will be forever protected from the human food chain in this way. Nearly all lobstermen respect the minimum size and V-notch rules. There's also a maximum size of five inches, since larger lobsters are more fecund. These conservation practices may have helped augment the boom. All these measures carry heavy fines for violators. The first mismeasurement prompts a five-hundred-dollar fine, with an additional one hundred for the next five mistakes. It doubles after that. Yet that's not the chief motivator.

The crew have their rules, their morality.

"Fines are the least of our troubles," says Frank, facing the stern and watching Alyssa's handiwork. She is gauging another small lobster. "We want to produce a sustainable crop," he says. "We want to give young lobsters every chance to reproduce before we get to harvest them next year."

Overboard goes the female.

Alyssa backhands the undersize lobster, which sails overboard like a Frisbee. The conservation measure began in the 1890s, when a minimum size was adopted. Very quickly, a positive effect was felt. Suddenly, the population was producing at a higher rate. More lobsters survived to maturity and bred. The annual harvest was around five million pounds. In the 1930s, a maximum harvest size was also implemented to further help the fishery. Then, for sixty years, the stocks stayed at a plateau of from ten to twelve million pounds. But the population has been quirky recently. First, in the 1990s, with the near extirpation of groundfish like cod, which are predators of lobster, the lobster population climbed again. The harvest reached 25 million pounds. The impact of poor predation and good conservation became somewhat normalized. Then, in 2012, landings reached their new level—in excess of 120 million pounds. Some new factor was in play. But what?

"Temperature's my best guess," says Frank. "Most timing in nature— mating, molting, hibernating, et cetera—is prompted by hot or cold. They say the oceans are warming—that's pretty clear. That's why we have all these southern species like black sea bass, summer flounder, and blue crabs entering the Gulf of Maine for the first time in recent memory. Lobsters have probably taken notice of the warmth, too. In 2012 and 2013, the warm spring made them molt sooner than ever before.

"But why the warming would boost the population is anyone's guess. Scientists don't know. Plenty of theories—early molting, expanded nursery grounds, fewer predators—take your pick."

It's nearly a taboo to mention global warming in Maine, which except for the coast is largely Republican, so I'm intrigued by Frank Gotwals's candor. What he leaves unsaid today, however, is the crux of the matter. Were 2012 and 2013 simply abnormally warm springs, part of a cycle perhaps, or is there a trend toward warmer weather overall? In other words, is the temperature in the Gulf of Maine changing permanently—enough to alter the reproductive and molting cycles of the American lobster?

In the summer of 2013, when temperatures were running high and the harvest was six times that of prior seasons, lobstermen reported seeing some shedders molt twice in the summer. They began earlier, too—in June. Rapid molting, say some scientists, brings more of the population to harvest size in a shorter amount of time. The timing of molting in lobsters—like that of crabs and butterflies—is brought on by temperature, nothing more. Turn up the heat and a lobster changes its clothes.

Frank's words inspire me to search for answers. Is there a trend in the Gulf's temperature? How is any pattern in the ocean tied to local weather, if at all? How is lobster affected—not in theory, but actually on the ocean floor?

For me, a single July day has quickly stretched into a plan to wander the waters of Maine for a year or two. More than dipping for any one fact, I will cast a broad net for how Frank and Alyssa and their community view the shifting ocean and how they'll adapt to changing times.

Alyssa is left holding seven keepers. The lobsters squirm and thrash in the counting tray. Alyssa writes the number 7 on the edge of the tray; she'll compare this catch record to those behind us and up ahead. She'll pass the tally along to a captain hungry for data. Next, she employs banding pliers to place blue rubber bands on each of the lobsters' claws—to prevent mischief to humans and other lobsters. The species is cannibalistic. The large crusher claw (adorned with white "molars") and the smaller shredder claw can each do damage to rivals and to human hands. Alyssa is careful. She drops each crustacean gingerly into a holding tank, refreshed with seawater pumped aboard.

Frank motors along the channel to Devil Island, another steep isle crowned with spruce. Devil and Coombs and half a dozen other "mid-channel isles" will be tapped today before we get to the "far islands," about four miles out. Here, in the surrounding waters, he retrieves six traps on three buoys, all in shallow water. They are empty, or nearly so. Alyssa stacks them with the other two on the stern, making eight traps selected for redeployment.

Now Frank guns the motor, making for open water, as if he were trying to forget a bad dream. He crosses the wide stretch between two middle islands, adding more distance from the dawn. The passage is known as Deer Island Thoroughfare, the entrance and exit from the mid-channel islands. At 6:30 A.M., he arrives on the leeside of Eastern Mark Island, a "far" island, just an hour into our voyage. "That's the official name—Eastern Mark, I guess," says Frank, pointing to the isle, "but we all call it 'Dumpling.'"

On the north side of Dumpling, the water depth is sixteen feet, shallow for so close to the channel. Frank and Alyssa had set two traps there, experimenting last Friday. Now they haul the traps. The verdict: two lobsters, one in each trap. These ninth and tenth traps, all low-yield, go in the stern.

Frank now has two priorities for the day: to retrieve lobsters from any deepwater traps he has already set, and, second, to move poorly producing traps to better neighborhoods. First on the agenda is to reset the ten traps on the stern. The captain has a place for them in mind, but he keeps it to himself. His lips are pressed together.

"Deep water," he says finally, his clear hint that we will exit the maze of islands. But he says nothing more. A lobsterman keeps knowledge of his fishing holes close to his chest. Not a hand is shown, lest someone shadow his success. More important, he is guarding his family's lobster territory. All of Jericho Bay—in fact, most of the Maine coast—is partitioned into local territories, defended by kith and kin. These tribes have say over who, among the next generations, can work those waters. The traps within each are marked by the tribe's colorful buoys. (Most lobstermen inherit their buoy colors, like a coat of arms, along with the territory.) A man or woman without a territory is a lobsterman without a country. No lobsters for the taking.

For Frank, it took a few years to build his reputation so that he would be fully accepted into the fluid territory that encompasses the islands and channels we fish today. In the meantime, he had the spindles cut off his buoys more than once, a warning from the tribe that he was not welcome. Over time, this changed. He's a senior tribesman today.

We roar through the narrows that separate two more far islands, Shingle Island and Saddleback, and make for open water. I could see hundred-foot depths on my marine chart, which I consult, to the captain's disdain. He'd rather not have any assistance. Suddenly, Frank pulls up short and circles a red-and-white bell buoy, marked with the letters *SI*. This marker designates where the deeper water from the channel touches the island plateau, or footprint. Depths rise from eighty to forty feet fast. Frank and Alyssa set their string of ten traps, two to a buoy, on this escarpment.

"You like this spot, don't you, Cap'n?" says Alyssa.

"Working the edge, the story of my life," Frank says.

From here, we thread our way back through the mid-channel island gauntlet—Shabby, Sheldrake, Gooseberry, Colby Ledge, and Colby Pup—to retrieve some two hundred other traps that Frank has targeted for the day. The time-honored routine of spotting, hauling, picking, banding, baiting, and setting is followed at each red-white-and-blue buoy. I recall the sequence in my mind's eye as a series of sepia photographs— like those of early railroad workers, tall-ship sailors, or others who built the country—each burnished with the years. Lobstermen are the last photogenic icons in a long line of Maine fishermen.

Frank hopes to land half of the two hundred traps by lunchtime. "We should have three hundred lobsters by then," he says. "That's three pounds per trap."

"Then all we'll need is a little melted Land O Lakes," says the sternman.

Frank gazes at the horizon again and ratchets up the throttle a notch. The Cummins engine whines—all 405 horsepower kicking into gear— so, when he finally speaks, he raises his voice for our benefit.

"Today, the lobster has fooled me. He's a trickster all right. It's never the same month to month, year to year. Each summer something surprises me."

"I'm trying to buy a truck," says Alyssa. "Your brilliant lobster better make my payments—"

"But I've got a secret weapon," says Frank, not paying her any mind. "*Diversity* is the word of the week. You don't want to put all your bait in one basket. So we're spreading the traps around. Shallow, rocky bottom one week; deeper mud the next; hard sand a little later; then back to shoal water on a whim. Still, it's hit-or-miss. You can't second-guess a lobster."

"That's why we go fishing," says Alyssa, "for the humility—to learn that you don't know a damn thing." She tosses another trap into the cold blue sea.

Frank communicates—even engages—minimally with his crew. There is a silent acceptance between them, like two mime players on a stage. One wink or a scowl says volumes. Frank is more gregarious, more loquacious, on land. He is friendly and respected by the community but a bit of a loner. Like most lobstermen, on the water he is solitary, self-reliant, iconoclastic. In figuring out the lobsters' movements, sleuthing their whereabouts, Frank keeps his own counsel. He is Sherlock Holmes without a Watson.

His high level of autonomy can be unnerving. He requires no marine radio, radar, copilot, or charts. Nor another captain's voice. Frank keeps his geography in his head. He is reliant on only one thing: his own ability and experience. That practical knowledge goes back to his twentieth summer, when he first set half a dozen traps from his skiff in Jericho Bay. From the first day, he was hooked, but he tried staying away from the water during a freshman year studying marine affairs at Eckerd College, in Florida. Returning home the next summer, he made 150 wooden traps and tried his luck again. Unlike most young captains, who apprentice under a senior captain's eye, Frank taught himself and owned his own boat at the young age of twenty-one. That was in 1976. He never returned to college. He chose the fishing life because his ancestors had. He found his true north. "I'm not suited to the classroom," he says. "I've always felt at home on the wide-open seas." After a second season of lobstering, he never looked back.

His experience alone on the water, and more recently keeping company with a sternman, has shaped his temperament. Alyssa looks up to him. While just as independent as other lobstermen, Frank is often chosen as their leader. He is open-minded, whereas they are, let's say, "opinionated." He is patient, whereas they are stubborn. He is talkative (on land), whereas they are taciturn.

Frank drives the boat closer to shore, where the water is fifty feet deep. He aims for one of his buoys and snags it with the boat hook. Placing the line in the trap hauler, he reels in the prize—half a dozen adult lobsters ready for banding. The second trap of the pair produces the same. Alyssa scribbles the number 12 on her counting tray.

Swinging around to the leeward side of McGlathery Island, west toward Wreck Island, Frank cuts the depth in half and roams over hard bottom—pebbles, mostly, if the depth sounder is accurate—where shedders like to hide in camouflage. Frank and Alyssa recover five buoys, each a pair, for a total of ten traps. They are empty. Win some, lose some more. Alyssa stacks all ten in the stern.

"They still outfox me," Frank repeats. "Lobstering is like a mystery book. I thought these shallow rock ledges would last awhile longer. Then again, next week is another day."

Frank spins away from McGlathery and races east, down the channel, into the wind. We pass by Ram Island, which is assaulted by our big wake, but Frank pulls up short at Gunning Rock, just at the edge of the main channel. Our direction all morning has been to zigzag across the water from northwest to southeast through various channels into open water. I figure he is going to place the ten traps here, but he has other designs. His eyes are sharper than mine. Frank points to one of his buoys nestled near Gunning Rock, which I finally see in between two chops of the growing sea. The "Rock" is more of a navigational hazard than an actual island. It's shallow water again. He makes a figure-eight turn to bring his port rail alongside the buoy. He hits his mark, making a perfect record for the day. As the trap surfaces, Frank succumbs to a grin at the sight of Alyssa's little dance celebrating the nine lobsters in the parlor.

"Nine keepers," says Alyssa, tossing her brass gauge unused into the counting tray. No need to measure; each specimen is robust. The next trap is a matched set. She writes the number 18 on the tray and bands the lobsters. They go into the holding tanks with a splash.

Alyssa is careful yet confident in banding the harvest. "I don't git bit," she says. "Never on my fingers. That's because I take my time. The men dive right in, say they're not scared. And they git bit either day. I put out a force field and simply say no to those crushing claws. Patience helps, too."

For his part, Frank is relieved that at least one string in shallow water has fared well: the south side of Gunning Rock, twenty-eight feet of water. Frank makes a mental note for next year, as if he could outfox a lobster.

We motor over to No Man's Land, a "far" island just a quarter mile southwest of Gunning Rock. In rapid succession, the team sets the ten reserve traps in forty feet of water, a depth and bottom similar to the other deployments today. Once again, we are just up on a shelf where the channel runs below.

"I see an opportunity here," says the captain. "I'm curious." He'll see if his bet pays off in two or three days.

Resetting thirty traps has been a diversion. Meanwhile, we're doing better landing lobsters than it would seem. Alyssa points into the water tanks for us to see. Frank scans the tanks, which look like the aquarium in the lobby of the Portland Red Lobster. "If we fill these two water boxes today, we're doing good," he says.

"Half-full already," says Alyssa. "Must be time for lunch."

The captain turns the engine off, and we float with the current and enjoy the silence. We assemble on the afterdeck at ten o'clock promptly for the midday meal. We sit on the transom. It is sandwiches all around— each has brought his or her own. Frank has us beat with homemade chicken salad (derived from last night's fried chicken), sprinkled with grape halves and walnuts. I surrender three potato chips for a bite. Frank admits that his wife, Donna, has the corner on lobster-boat cuisine.

For her part, Alyssa keeps threatening us with melted butter, but we see her hands are empty in the galley. Truth be told, she rarely boils water on a boat or at home. She sells all her lobsters. She's just a tease.

Over chips, Frank has a story to tell. He explains how, while growing up in Massachusetts, he spent summers as a boy with his mother's family in Stonington. The lineage descends from the founders of Swan's Island, an inhabited lobstermen's island between Deer Isle and Mount Desert Island. His great-grandfather taught him how to fish, how to clam, and how to live by the fisherman's code.

"My favorite piece of advice was about how to navigate in the fog. He taught me how to read the currents, but most of all how to read my compass. 'Even in a whiteout, it'll always take you home,' he said. 'Then you can show up tomorrow and fish another day.'"

Frank's family skipped two generations before getting back to the water. The legacy and the old advice are never far from Frank's mind. After getting his first lobster boat, the next acquisition was buying his great-grandfather's house back from a stranger. "Closing the circle," he calls it. Now, his mother and he are neighbors, just outside of Stonington.

Alyssa, who has been silent through her captain's story, pipes up, "I don't even know who my grandfather is. Or was. The actual man is lost somewhere in my grandmother's past."

"You can choose your own heritage, then," says Frank.

"That's what I'm doing on this boat."

"Hey, look," says Frank, pointing to some floating kelp about twenty feet off the stern. "That's a harbor seal." The female, an aquatic acrobat, flips her tail and disappears. The rolling sea closes in behind her without a trace. "That seal loves crustacean larvae," says the captain.

"At least one of us is having lobster for lunch," quips Alyssa, and sinks a bite into her bologna and cheese. Fair guess, she won't be boiling water anytime soon.

"Wanna cookie?" she says, holding out a bag of chocolate chips ones.

The captain declines with a shrug. I take one to be polite. It would be smart to have Alyssa on my side in a knife fight.

Frank speaks next. "Let's haul another eighty traps and head in early." For the next fifty pots, our late run of random luck continues. If today's 250 traps average out to three pounds per trap, we'd land 750 pounds. Frank's record is over double that, but the modest take will do.

In the kitchen of the next trap, a large female, still chomping on the bait, carries her brown eggs along her abdomen. They look like tiny berries on a bush. They hitch a ride for up to ten months, whereupon they are released at the female's next molt. Frank picks her up and checks the tail fan, which is unmarked. So he does the honors: cutting a V out of the chitin. The notch will alert any other lobsterman who recatches her that she is an egg-laying, or "berried," female. Thus, she is retired from the menu, forever protected by the fleet.

The captain has returned many V-notched females to the sea this summer, promising a good year for offspring. Once hatched, the larvae take seven years and many molts—up to twenty-five—to reach legal size. Just before they do, a fair percentage becomes mature enough to breed, at least in warming seas. These conservation measures assure a significant percentage of the population breeds before harvesting.

"The stocks seem secure," says Frank. "The fishery is sustainable. At least some would say that. Yet I worry about the economics of the lobster industry. That's not secure at all."

Frank briefly explains the law of supply and demand in the lobster world. The greater the demand from the consumer, the higher the price. But when the harvest is high or the demand is low, then prices can plummet. That's what's happened to Frank. "Stocks are huge and demand is modest," he says. "Those two factors add up to a cheap price. Last year, some buyers refused to take lobsters off the boats. The wholesale pipeline shut tight."

"That cut the price nearly in half," says Alyssa.

"The big question is whether fishermen will consider limiting the huge harvest to control supply. Rarely has it happened before, but when lobstermen do get in agreement, major conservation strides have been made." When Frank began lobstering in 1974, there were no trap limits in Maine. In the wake of some poor annual harvests, a debate surfaced around instituting a twelve-hundred-trap limit for each boat. This was eventually reduced to eight hundred traps, which is still enforced today. Yet tighter local controls are possible. Out on Monhegan Island, the lobstermen voluntarily cut their number of traps by 50 percent—from eight hundred to four hundred. That helps boost the price in winter.

"Now with elevated temperatures or reduced predation bringing on a huge surplus of lobsters, we really need to control the harvest," says Frank.

"Nobody'll go for that here," says Alyssa.

"Some might. It just might elevate the price. The trick is to convince the majority." As former president of the Stonington Lobster Co-op, where he will sell his lobsters today, Frank has some clout among local fishermen. If anyone can convince them to curb the supply, it's him. He's been making the rounds informally, testing the waters. Of course, if the boom goes bust, it will not be necessary. Both ends of the seesaw—high and low—require different approaches. "For lobsters," says Frank, "turning around a low demand requires marketing on a grand scale."

The next dozen traps are slim pickings. I imagine their paucity might add a few pennies to today's price. Prices often shift on Mondays, and it will be interesting to see what our harvest brings at the Co-op.

Frank has one more buoy in his sights. It's floating in a narrow trough between Gunning Rock and Saddleback Island—in about sixty feet of water. I check my watch: 1:00 P.M., eight hours into our voyage. The first trap of the pair goes to Alyssa, who does a few exquisite steps of her dance. "I've got eight beauties," she says. The second trap lands next to the captain, who counts six legal lobsters. Fourteen beauties for the run, topping off some six hundred lobsters for the day. That's 720 pounds, or over $2,088 of lobster ($2.90 per pound dockside).

On the way into port, Alyssa lights up a cigarette and lets it dangle on her lips while she sponges and mops the sides and decks of *Seasong*. Frank does his share, washing the mud and splatter from the instrument panel. On sighting the Co-op, however, he stops and maneuvers the boat in a wide circle to avoid the bottleneck. A dozen other lobster boats have returned at this hour. The wharf and weighing scales can handle only two at a time.

"Even on a modest day," says Frank, "we're catching too many."

"Can the Co-op handle that much product?" asks Alyssa.

"They can if they cut the price. You can sell real estate on the moon if you cut the price enough." Frank scans the fleet, then checks over his shoulder at the next wave of lobster boats crossing the harbor. "I'm going to deeper water tomorrow to get away from all these boats."

"I'll bet some big lobsters patrol out there," says Alyssa, tossing her cigarette into the water.

"Maybe; it's a crapshoot," says Frank. "Lobstering reminds me of those kites we use to fly as kids. Occasionally, an updraft comes your way and you're all smiles. And that's pretty sweet. But a downdraft may be just as likely. You just can't count on it either way."

2

Fishermen's Day

My first voyage aboard *Seasong* was in mid-July, sandwiched between Stonington's two major summer social events: the annual lobster bake and the lobster boat races, where reputations are sealed for the summer. While the Chesapeake has its crab feasts and Texas its barbecues, Santa Fe its chile festivals and Cape Cod its clam dinners, Maine serves up lobster in July. This reaches its zenith on the Fourth, with several Stonington lobster bakes at churches, the town pier, and the Masonic Hall. A lobster bake is the slow steaming of lobster—heated by charcoal—under layers of seaweed, potatoes, and corn. The venue is a sandy beach or barbecue grill. Nearly 2,500 lobsters are required to feed the town, since summer folk double the population. Off Stonington, everyone checks their traps on the first of July and for the three days thereafter. Some holiday harvesters inspect their traps twice a day—what one local calls a "double dippah!"

This season—summer 2015—the lobsters are running late. As of July 1, the rush of shedders is still a week or two off. After the early rush of 2012 and 2013, this apparent delay comes as a surprise to some. But not to seasoned fishermen. Lobsters have been gathering in mid-July for centuries. The previous years were simply an anomaly, they say. Meanwhile, scientists say it was the warming trend. In any case, the crustaceans are arriving at the normal time this year. Once again, this mid-July timetable puts a crimp in village plans for Independence Day. Lobsters are not yet plentiful.

Later in the summer, an order for 2,500 lobsters would be no problem. Frank alone could catch that many in a week. But for the town dinners at the start of July, it takes more than thirty captains to deliver the bounty. Typically, their services are donated, or prices reduced. At best, it's a break-even proposition for the lobstermen.

After the veterans' parade and color guard but before the fireworks, I settle down to an early lobster dinner at the Masonic Hall on Sunset Road, known for its occasional "lobster feeds." About eighty local residents have shown up for the first shift; no summer people. All the license plates in the parking lot are from Maine. The men wear unadorned white T-shirts, the women colorful blouses. So my partner, Donna, and I are honored that the locals at our table welcome us with a smile, and loose lips. Talking lobster is a favorite pastime.

Scratch any Stonington family and you come up with a lobsterman. Out of a population of 1,200, the citizenry comprises 350 lobster captains, 450 sternmen, dozens of dealers and dockworkers, and 50 people in the seafood restaurant trade. In other words, nearly three-quarters of the residents actively work in the industry. The remainder are relatives. The town has a singular purpose; it stands for something—getting lobsters from the ocean floor to the family table, sustainably. So it comes as no surprise that the patrons on either side of our picnic table, covered with a red-checkered tablecloth, are local lobstermen.

The old-timer seated across from me, devouring a lobster tail, is eighty-eight-year-old Pete Clancy. He and his wife, Blossom, now engaged in conversation with Donna, live on Main Street, on Stonington Harbor. Pete still works a gang of 800 traps and hauled 150 for today's dinner. Eighty-two years ago, when he was six, Pete was handling similar gear, just less of it; he was hauling a pair of traps from a rowboat.

As we crack claws with fist-size stones—these are hard-shell lobsters—Pete reminisces a bit.

"I grew up on Little Deer Isle, during the Great Depression," he says. "My neighbors were all farmers and fishermen, but which profession to choose?

"My grandfather had a huge vegetable garden that fed the whole family. One year, he gave me two rows to sow and reap on my own. So I got ambitious. I figured I was going to grow some two-foot carrots, so I put the seeds deep—eight inches in the ground. They never sprouted. I think the Chinaman got them, they were so deep. Right then, I decided I would fish and let somebody else plant the garden."

From the time he was six through his teenage years, lobsters ranged in price from fifteen to forty cents a pound. A good haul was one hundred pounds, so he was making up to forty dollars a day. In the current boom, he's lived long enough to see a three-thousand-dollar day.

Pete dips his lobster in vinegar, rather than butter, a local custom. "This lobster is a little tough," he says. "To do better, you'll have to wait for the shedders in a couple of weeks." Although an expert on the fishery, he's taken aback by the lobster boom. "I've seen the population cycle a dozen times," Pete says. "What goes up must come down. But it's anyone's guess when it will happen. The longer I go, the less I know."

Two weeks later, after lobstering with Frank, I am enticed down to the docks for the Stonington Lobster Boat Races. While many lobster ports—Boothbay Harbor, Friendship, Harpswell, Searsport, and Winter Harbor, among them—hold races in the summer, and local boys and men travel far and wide to compete, there's nothing like winning at home. The Stonington races are Maine's equivalent of the Daytona 500.

This year, 109 boats have signed up for thirty-three races that involve high wakes, hefty horsepower, and unmatched egos. Several boats break the once-impenetrable fifty-miles-per-hour mark. At least one of those fishermen has pushed the envelope by installing a 1,000-horsepower engine in a forty-foot boat, far more power than needed to haul lobster traps. That sort of excess is commonplace where reputations count for more than prize cash.

The winningest contender today is Shawn Alley's twenty-eight-foot *Little Girls*, which wins four races, including the "fastest lobstah boat afloat," at 50.3 miles per hour. Jason McDonald, Frank Gotwals's stepson, places third on *Seahawk* for 600-horsepower diesels, blowing smoke across the finish line. Sid Eaton of the *Kimberly Belle* wins a smaller class of 400-horsepower boats, while his wife, Julie, gets a fourth on *Cat Sass* in the 200-horsepower race. Luckily, there's a race for every size head, big or modest.

In the next week, we settle into our cottage on Pink Street, right off Main Street, with a view of the harbor. In Maine's parlance, I'm "smack-dab" in the middle of things. I wake at 4:00 A.M. to the gurgle of diesel engines in the harbor. There's no need for an alarm clock in this town. It's impossible to sleep in.

Our cottage is a small two-room bungalow with a deck surrounded by planters teeming with flowers. Barrett Gray, the innkeeper, waters the flowers daily, except on this Saturday, which is threatening to rain. Barrett's uncle, a lobsterman named J.B., has a trap-and-buoy repair shop next door; he is up before dawn, making a racket. When J.B. is not lobstering, he's either scalloping or netting herring—to sell as bait. From his shop, a path offers a shortcut to the Farmers' Market up the hill.

The clamor on both sides of the cottage—uphill and downhill—is a mere distraction. I'd been planning on an early start to explore the town. Besides, the din from the harbor is a secondary onslaught to the senses. With this morning's sea breeze, the odor of rank bait wins first prize. On certain days in Stonington, it is impossible to get away from the smell. A whiff of week-old salted herring is better than a dose of smelling salts: It will wake you up and curl your hair.

At dawn, I take in the view. As the largest lobster port in Maine, Stonington is one of the few coastal towns with a working waterfront. The once great ports of Camden and Bar Harbor have none. From our deck, I can watch lobster boats with names like *Ahab, Addiction, Aces High, Jackpot, Killing Time, Peggy Lynn,* and *Naughty Girl* sell their catch to Sunshine Seafood. Captain Pete Clancy, aboard *My Uncle's Angel,* sells here, too. The lobster boats take on more boxes of bait in the evening, which are ripe by sunrise. Some of the summer people complained about the smell of bait recently, which seems counterproductive. If you come to Maine for lobster, bait is just the price of doing business. You cannot have one without the other.

Beyond Sunshine Seafood are the harbor islands, green wooded ones in the distance, bold gray ones in the foreground. The first rock outcrop is Powder House Island, on which sits the old stone storage building that housed dynamite for blasting granite from Crotch Island Quarry, outside of town. Before it was Maine's largest fishing port, Stonington was the premier source of granite in the nation.

The bronze *Stone Cutter* statue at the foot of the harbor hints at the legacy. The granite was accessible, the harbor was deep (ready for loading and shipping), and the stone was beautiful, speckled with a lavender-pink hue. It also featured dark feldspar veins—called "horses"—making each block original and radiant. Like Stonington's lobsters, the rich granite was immediately in demand, once discovered. Some say the lobsters are so prime here because they crawl over rich granite.

Originally known as Green's Landing, the small farming and seafaring community was overcome with "granite diggers" in 1860, when the quarry boom commenced. By 1897, the town was renamed Stonington. During the intervening years, the face of the town changed dramatically. After the Civil War, Americans and immigrants—Italians, Swedes, Norwegians, and Scots—came looking for work. Some sought a fortune. Boarding-houses appeared overnight. Hotels and houses were built in a European style, reflecting the taste of immigrants. The Continental style is still on display today. By 1898, over 100,000 tons of granite were being shipped annually from Stonington.

At the turn of the century, not just stonecutters occupied the town. Many settlers were able seamen, recognized for their skill throughout the world. In those days, sailboats like the Friendship sloop were employed to get to and from the lobster grounds and to schools of herring and cod. A sardine cannery stood at the edge of town. Local fishermen, if not their stonecutting neighbors, were proficient at sail handling. When the New York Yacht Club built *Defender* for the 1895 defense of the America's Cup against Great Britain's *Valkyrie III,* over thirty sailors from Deer Isle and Stonington were selected as crew. They won. Four years later, when *Columbia* was launched to defend the cup against Ireland's *Shamrock,* 80 percent of the crew were Stonington boys, bringing home victory again.

Meanwhile, the stonecutters kept blasting and chiseling. From 1869 to 1969, granite was shipped for construction of the U.S. Naval Academy, Annapolis; Boston's Museum of Fine Arts; the New York County Courthouse in Manhattan; Philadelphia's Market Street Bridge; the Smithsonian Institution; and the JFK Memorial at Arlington National Cemetery.

While the famous pink granite is nearly gone, some beautiful white granite remains. It is still harvested from the quarry. The modern quarry workers, who are die-hard Red Sox fans, had to swallow pride recently in delivering eight million pounds of white granite for the new Yankee Stadium's Babe Ruth Plaza. The contract led to a drowning of sorrows in local pubs.

When sailing into Stonington Harbor, anyone can see that the skyline tells the story of wave after wave of European stonecutters who tried their luck in the quarry. Victorian homes, mansard roofs, cupolas, and widow's walks abound. Most of the waterfront sits on stilts, like that of Venice, the pilings driven into the harbor mud. I sit on our deck and listen to the waves lapping their tongues along the footings. Yet the town is largely silent. No explosions at the quarry. No need anymore for an offshore powder house to protect the town. But there it stands, a reminder of changing times.

I see the schooner *Stephen Taber* anchored for the day just behind Powder House Island. Built in 1869, she is the oldest schooner in continuous use in the country. The *Taber* was the kind of ship used for transporting granite up and down the coast. Today, she caters to tourists, but she must anchor well outside the harbor because of the thirteen-foot tide.

For the same reason, the lobster boats moor in deeper water. Each commercial pier has either a float, which keeps pace with the tide, or an elevator, which lifts lobster crates from the boats to the pier, fifteen feet above. As a result, the main harbor is open water, free for seals to frolic amid the kelp.

After a few days in town, I can recognize which pickups go with which fishermen. In a few weeks, I can identify quite a few boats—their names and their captains. Barrett tells me the next test is to recognize the stripes and colors of each man's lobster buoys. "That can take a couple of years," he says with a smile.

Already I have a sense of what the town values, of what it is in danger of losing if the lobsters were to go away: an almost tribal sense of community.

On Sunday, Donna and I dress up in sunglasses and sunscreen for Fishermen's Day, the annual celebration on the Commercial Fish Pier of past and living lobstermen. It's cloudy, overcast, but that is deceptive. If you don't like the weather up here, wait five minutes. The sun could break out at any moment.

The gates to the Fish Pier open at ten o'clock, so there's time to explore the town some more. I begin at Harborview General Store at one extreme end of Main Street. This grocery and all-purpose market opens at 3:00 A.M. to sell coffee and lunches to lobstermen. Among their sundry offerings are smoked mussels, dried cod, and dried pollock, what can best be described as fish jerky, an acquired taste to say the least. Three teenage boys in knee-high black rubber boots are buying Red Bull, the caffeine-laced energy drink. I stand behind them at the counter, carrying a pound of Maine Trader Coffee. Looks like everyone needs their high.

When it's my turn, Adrienne, the thirty-year-old checkout girl, a striking brunette, asks if I'm going to Fishermen's Day. I nod, raising my eyebrows. "I sure would like a doughboy," she says with a smile. She explains the treat comprises deep-fried dough covered in cinnamon and sugar. I smile back and make a mental note.

The next patron in line is from Connecticut; he asks Adrienne for directions. "Does it make any difference which road I take to Bangor?"

She glances at him. "Not to me it don't."

Outside, the teenagers scuff the sidewalk with their rubber boots and climb into three brand-new pickups, the keys left dangling in the ignitions. The boys can earn five thousand dollars per week lobstering, adding up to sixty thousand dollars for the summer. Reason enough to drop out of school or forsake college plans. If the boom continues, they could be millionaires by the age of thirty.

One by one, the three trucks back out of the parking lot, spinning their wheels. They pull around and tear down Main Street, squealing their tires and tattooing the light-colored road with black rubber.

In front of Island Ice Cream Shack, next to the town newspaper office, I witness the other extreme of the lobsterman's life: old age. Two senior gentlemen stand in line for lobster rolls, the ice cream parlor's unexpected and popular menu listing. The men are stooped over and bow-legged, a common anatomical stance of elderly fishermen. Presumably, their days of racing trucks up and down Main Street are over. The two old-timers chomp on the lobster as if it were cotton candy. Despite the challenges of wayward youngsters and the decrepitude of old age, the townspeople have a common purpose. All efforts at the water's edge, from raising children to painting buoys to selling bait, are geared toward bringing the lobster home.

The two seniors part company. "How's ya lobster?" one codger says in farewell.

"Wicked awesome," says the other octogenarian. "See ya later."

"Take care."

A young teenager tips his hat to the two old-timers as they walk off to celebrate Fishermen's Day. I recognize him as Elliott Neville, the fifteen-year-old son of Liz Perez, one of the organizers of Fishermen's Day. His other hand rests on the shoulder of his girlfriend, Emily. Elliott is one of the youngest fishermen and one of the most industrious. He is one of the teenage elite who catch twenty thousand dollars' worth of lobster in a summer month. Aboard *Tail Grabbah,* a fine lobster boat he purchased himself, he works alone three months a year but shares his experiences with the Skippers Program at his high school. The Skippers Program helps budding fishermen learn how to be businessmen and advocates for issues of the day.

Just now, Emily's sister asks Elliott why he wants to give up his whole summer to go lobstering. "It's something I just love to do," he says. "Then there's the money. Some of my friends mow lawns all summer for four hundred dollars. I make that in half a day."

This morning, the tourists are here in droves. Maine has two seasons: August and winter. An exception can be found in Stonington, where the "August traffic" begins in July. Even then, the locals try to keep the influx of summer people to a minimum. (These people are referred to as being "from away.") No pleasure yachts are allowed in the main harbor or on the wharves; docks are reserved for lobstermen. There are only two guesthouses on Main Street, there's no restaurant service on Wednesdays, and there is no cell-phone service. One of the most popular restaurants, the Clamdigger, announces its fare as "warm beer and lousy food." Get the message? Stonington residents do not want your business; they'd just as well sell their lobsters to China, thank you very much.

The crowd moves past the town library toward a narrow stretch of the road, where there's room for only one sidewalk, and two cars (or two trucks) cannot pass by abreast. One car must stop and pull over, permitting the oncoming vehicle to pass through. On workdays, this congestion causes havoc for the eighteen-wheel seafood trucks trying to get to Greenhead Lobster at the far end of town. Yet today the only inconvenience is the overflow of pedestrians into the street, walking toward the festival. By 9:30 A.M., Main Street is nearly shut down to motorized traffic.

I shoulder my way toward the post office, where I want to mail a letter. On the way, I pass up a haircut at Suzy Shepard's Scissor Shack, although I'm intrigued by her sign, which reads THAT SEAGULL DID WHAT IN YOUR HAIR? In the post office foyer, a brilliant orange cat named Dundee jumps up on the counter, then purrs briefly to win me over, only to wander out the front door. On Friday the postmistress seemed to know everyone as well as when they graduated from her high school. Dundee leads me a hundred yards along the street, never once peering over his shoulder, to Dockside Books, his home.

Al Webber, the seventy-year-old proprietor of the bookstore, accepts Dundee's wanderings with a shrug of his shoulders and a stroke of Dundee's chin. Al is the self-appointed arbiter of town gossip.

"Stonington is one of the last holdouts of coastal village life," he says, "but even we are beginning to change. Wealthier people are moving in and property taxes are going up. They expect me to pay ten thousand dollars a year, and I have a modest house. So, now, only five or six fishermen—Pete Clancy, a few others—remain on Main Street. Some houses are for sale, but the only buyers are people from away—summer people. In a few years it may look like a ghost town in winter. The local twentysomethings have plenty of cash but don't want waterfront. They want to build a castle back in the woods. Money to burn. One boy told me he wants a five-car garage just to fill it with sports cars." Al shakes his head. "It makes no sense—you can't drive a Porsche through a Maine winter.

"The generations have split. They're now miles apart. The older guys are thrifty, always saving for a rainy day or a poor season. Meanwhile, the young bucks shoot for the moon. They live for today only, mortgaging houses, boats, and trucks to the hilt. Whatever money can buy, with no thought of the future. The banks hold the paper. Sure, lobsters have been on the make lately, but if that reverses, those same banks will own a lot of property. And those boys will be out on the street. They have nothing to fall back on, not even a high school diploma." With that tirade complete, Al permits Dundee to jump off his lap.

The pressure to lobster at an extreme pace comes, in part, from the demand for the product. From Al Webber's bookstore, I can count seven dealers perched around the harbor, ready to buy whatever the lobstermen can bring ashore. Stonington boasts three piers with buying stations—Co-op II, Sunshine Seafood, Greenhead Lobster—and another wharf that houses Little Bay Lobster. Stonington Co-op I, where Frank sells, and Damon Seafood, which is on a float, round out the six dealerships. Between them, they purchased over twenty million pounds of lobster in 2015, to lead the state.

The street is bustling with hundreds of people when I make my way toward the Stonington Fish Pier gate. Parting the crowd, a familiar blue GMC pickup steers toward me. Frank rolls down the driver's window and smiles. He says he's on the way to church. In fact, he's late and cannot stop off at the Fishermen's Day festivities. Frank is wearing blue jeans and a Hawaiian shirt; a guitar sits next to him on the seat. He does not appear dressed for the Sabbath. His religion is "alternative." Indeed, it would be another month before I would discover how unorthodox his church might be.

Slapping my forehead, I promise to return his fishing boots—now long overdue.

"No worries," he says. "Would you like to stop by for supper Monday night?"

"Absolutely," I say. "What better chance for our two Donnas to meet?"

Fishermen's Day is a waterfront festival put on by the Island Fishermen's Wives Association (IFWA) to honor living and deceased watermen. In its twenty-sixth year, the celebration raises funds for widows of drowned captains, payments to injured lobstermen, purchases of safety and survival gear, and scholarships for teenagers going on to college or into fishing as a profession. The community looks after its own.

The festivities begin with a prayer at the granite memorial to drowned captains, which reads IN MEMORY OF THOSE WHOSE LIVES HAVE BEEN LOST AT SEA. Harry Vickerson, a local minister, offers these words while a couple of hundred people gather round: "Lord, thank you for this wonderful creation, especially for the ocean and the creatures that live here, for letting our community sustain us with this bounty. We ask you to guide today's fishermen and their families. And we bless the fishermen who left us too early. We remember them well."

After a moment of silence, Vickie Hardie, the copresident of the IFWA, grabs the microphone to address the assembly. I notice that most spectators are chatting with their neighbors like long-lost friends. Everyone knows one another. I spot Alyssa LaPointe, Frank's sternman, with her two daughters, Madison and Audrey, and wave. She smiles back. Vickie taps the mike and the clamor dies down.

Eight wives flank Vickie, four on either side of her. These are the founding members of the IFWA—Debbie Robbins, Suzy Shepard, Su Oliver, and Julia Trundy—and the current officers, Liz and Jenni Steele (Jenni is also a founder), Shauna Schmidt, and Genevieve McDonald. Each sports a gray T-shirt with *Island Wives* in pink lettering. They look like young sisters. Most are young mothers. Genevieve is both a fisherman and the wife of a fisherman, so she has double duty.

In August 1989, Debbie Robbins lost her father, Clyde Haskell, at sea. He had been lobstering aboard his boat, *Margaret L.,* off Isle au Haut when he fell overboard. He could not swim. He clung for two hours to a rope but succumbed to hypothermia. He was a very popular man. Six weeks later, a second Stonington captain, Allen Thompson, drowned off the *Melissa Sue.*

"Everyone was devastated," says Debbie during a lull. "We started the Wives Association the following spring. Right off, we established a bereavement fund, but we wanted to do something to prevent these tragedies in the future. So we set up swimming lessons for island kids. Very few fishermen could swim when we got started; now quite a few can."

"We were thinking and breathing the Wives Association," says Suzy Shepard. "We were brainstorming all the time. So we came up with CPR courses, safety training, a Fishermen's Ball, and the award for the dirtiest truck. Well, that was a low point, but our high mark is scholarships—two graduation gifts, one for college and one for future fishermen who may need help with a boat or other gear but don't want more school."

"Last year, from the proceeds of Fishermen's Day," says Genevieve, "we gave first-aid kits to four hundred captains. This year, we're donating emergency blankets, which can fend off hypothermia."

"Rope ladders are coming next," says Debbie. "These fishermen cannot get back into their boats if they fall out. A rope ladder would have saved my father." She searches my eyes for understanding. "You know, we help the lobstermen, but it works both ways. I called one captain the other day to ask for a donation of lobster for today's feed. I said, 'Thank you,' and he cut me off. 'No, thank *you*,' he said. 'I can't imagine the Stonington community without the Island Wives.'"

After another moment, Vickie Hardie blows into the microphone. The speaker hisses with static. "Thank you, everyone," she says. "It's now time for the new inductees into the Fishermen's Hall of Fame, our pantheon of exemplary fishermen."

North and south of the fishermen's memorial, dozens of young lobstermen, mostly in their twenties and thirties, inspect the placards of previous inductees. The surnames on the testimonials read like an island Who's Who: Billings, Boyce, Blackmore, Eaton, Robbins, Greenlaw, McDonald, and other large families are represented. These are the young men's mentors and idols, the great highliners of years past. The newcomers revere the old-timers much as Little Leaguers honor an MVP. Twenty-seven placards, each celebrating three inductees, are arranged in sequence for the years 1990 through 2016. I recognize a few, including Andy Gove (2012), Bob Williams (2013), and Elva Ames (2003), the first woman to be inducted. The Robbins family has the most members honored: James Robbins (1995), his brother Steve Robbins, Sr. (1994), and Steve Robbins, Jr. (2014). The older Steve mastered several fishing types, including trawling, seining, scalloping, and lobstering. In those days, before World War II, fishermen would rotate in and out of fisheries as the seasons progressed. This versatility made fishing a more stable livelihood.

The sources of their income from a variety of species were more flexible. They adapted to new conditions easily, as if they were changing a pair of shoes. Today, fishermen buy only a single pair—for lobstering.

Vickie Hardie now asks the eight other wives on the stage to come forward in sets of three—she's with the first pair—to introduce the new inductees: Junior Bray, Wesley Hutchinson, and Dave Steele, all elderly fishermen. Elderly and still lobstering. The audience has doubled by now to sixteen hundred visitors: Thin male fishermen and plus-size women, mostly smoking cigarettes, are dressed in short-sleeved shirts and shorts. Laughter ensues when the three inductees try to climb into a single life raft, big enough for only two. Just for good measure, a buxom granddaughter flops onto the trio inside.

The laughter and applause break up as people wander off to their favorite booth or food kiosk. The same vendors reappear each year, so spectators anticipate their "darlings," or preferences. Stretching 150 yards to the end of the pier are a variety of jewelers, potters, publishers, and flea markets. Lobster wire sculptures, created from trap wire, seem popular this year. At midmorning, it's already hot—July will go down as the hottest month on record—so the lemonade stand has the longest line. Walking around from vendor to vendor, I quickly see a pattern: Women are the most common proprietors. On a Stonington Sunday, it's a matriarchal society.

In short order, I stop in my tracks. I am mesmerized by photographs of winter and summer lobstering on the table in front of me. There are panoramic shots of the islands, haunting images of lobster boats in the fog, and an unbelievable portrait of a bald eagle swooping over the water. The sign reads JULIE EATON PHOTOGRAPHY. Behind the table sits an attractive redhead. "Auburn," she says, correcting me. I ask her how she made these photographs. "You had to be on a boat, right?"

"That's easy. I'm a lobsterman," she says. "I'm out on the water every day. The tough part is knowing when to haul the trap or lift the camera. Unfortunately for my art, the lobster paycheck usually comes first. But then, I love lobstering. I couldn't possibly give it up."

The patron next to me buys a set of note cards from Julie, featuring a baby harbor seal poking its head just above the water in Stonington Harbor. The man, a local lobsterman named Dickie Bridges, says he was happy to see Julie's husband, Sid, win his event at the Stonington Lobster Boat Races.

"Sid is the Mario Andretti of lobster boat races," she says, beaming. "He wins every year."

Next, an elegant woman with a thick New York accent steps up to the booth. "Oh," she says in a haughty voice, "I like your photograph of the boats in the fog. They look so close; everything's in focus. Tell me, what f-stop did you use on your camera for that one?"

"Well," says Julie, "I'll tell you. You're from away, and I'm a commercial lobsterman. The only f-stop I know is when we're out on the water and the shit hits the fan. Then it's, Oh my, time to f-ing stop, you betcha."

She sells the photograph.

More gawkers brush up against the booth and capture Julie's attention. The New Yorker—now down a peg—and I share a glance of recognition. We don't want to hog the space, so we mosey on. I make a promise to myself to track down Julie Eaton later.

Time to canvass the menus at the lunch kiosks. The offerings range from lobster rolls to fish and chips to fried clams, from crab rolls to scallop rolls to a full lobster dinner, complete with corn on the cob. Once again, the local fishermen have donated the lobster to maximize proceeds for the Island Wives. As such, lobster dinners are going for ten dollars apiece.

I meet Donna at Julia's Grilled Shark Pit at a prearranged time—noon sharp. The line for this island specialty is fifty-deep. We join the queue, which includes Jason McDonald, Frank's stepson. Julia wears a hat with an animated shark on top. She has three barbecue grills going at once, coals glowing red, from which she flips mako shark fillets with a long spatula and gloves, as protection from the heat. When our turn arrives, we get two platters—five bucks each—of the grilled fish. The shark tastes like swordfish, but flakier, sweeter, and more moist. Knowingly, Jason gives us a wink. A highlight of the day.

Four events dominate the afternoon. First, we watch the Wacky Rowboat Races, performed with one oar. Donna watches the Fish Face Contest, where ten-year-olds pucker their lips for the title, while I observe the Cod Fish Relay. This contest, among children, is like a sack race, but kids must dress in yellow oilskins and carry a greased codfish for fifty yards. Natalee Gardiner, all of seven, runs down the course, her tiny hands and fingernails clawing into the fish, which is half her size. The cod slips loose. She drops it, scoops it up (no penalty), the cod's tail at her knees, the mouth puckered next to hers. She rushes forward. The cod slips slightly. Six feet from the finish, little Natalee throws the cod across the line, clinching victory. The checkered flag comes down, and Natalee collapses into a heap, the smile spreading across her face.

Meanwhile, Natalee's older brother Ben, who is all of ten, is aboard Elliott Nevell's skiff in the middle of the harbor. Ben and other ten-year-olds must haul five lobster traps to qualify for a raffle. Elliott is both captain and lifeguard.

The last event of the day is the Survival Demo, where six teenagers—four boys and two girls—don red-and-black dry survival gear and swim to a life raft in the harbor. Tiffany and Kennady Eaton, Julie's grand-nieces, win the day. The survival training is part of the Eastern Maine Skippers Program, which nurtures future fishermen at eight high schools in coastal Maine.

The survival demonstration is monitored by two officers of the U.S. Coast Guard. One has to dive into the water to assist a struggling teen-ager, but generally the training comes off without a hitch. Just to make sure, Genevieve and Cory McDonald hover offshore in Debbie Robbins's husband's outboard. The demo is right next to the Island Wives' booth, so the women are able to see the success of their efforts. I run into Debbie Robbins again. She says survival suits, though expensive, would have saved some of the Hall of Famers, like Ronnie Haskell, who, not know-ing how to swim, drowned in Barstow's Cove in 1993, and Stephen Poi-tras, who drowned when his boat upset on the first day of scallop season in 1981.

"Someday, every boat will have survival suits," she says. "Then we can finally sleep at night."

After the events, the crowd disperses. Julia is clean out of shark. She'll need a great white, rather than a mako, next year. Natalee, the codfish girl, gives an interview to the local newspaper. I buy a doughboy for Adri-enne. And Julie Eaton packs up whatever photography didn't sell and puts it into her truck, careful to make room for traps to go lobstering to-morrow.

The sun comes out. Anyone in long sleeves strips down to a T-shirt or skin. With the growing heat, there's a run on the lemonade stand. Despite the demand and a dwindling supply, the beverage holds its price.

The three miles to Frank's farm, through the Oceanville section of the township, is a trip backward in time. The rural landscape is full of vegetable fields and grazing pasture, punctuated by country houses. The homes were built before World War II. No new structures, just additions. Yet each property is in good repair, the lawns cut and gardens thriving. Stacks of lobster traps and colored buoys accent the driveways.

The Gotwalses' main house is a spacious brown-shingled dwelling, built by Frank's great-great-grandfather in the 1850s. The homestead has not been in family hands all that time. To reestablish the continuity, Frank and his wife, Donna, bought the old family place in 1974, the year Frank began lobstering in earnest. That was the year he reclaimed his heritage on every front.

Just before we reach Frank and Donna's farm, we pass the Oceanville cemetery on the left, decorated with more than two hundred granite headstones. The Gotwalses (and Joyces—on his mother's side) have a deep history here, which the vitality of the present seems to obscure.

Behind the Gotwalses' farmhouse, over three acres are planted in rows and groves. The orchard features apples, plums, and peaches. A maze of fences is orchestrated to keep deer out of the orchard and raccoons out of the corn. While Frank and Donna point out the other vegetables, three dogs—all shelter animals—roam the garden, on the lookout for rabbits. A path through the orchard leads to a beach at the edge of Penobscot Bay. Donna takes the dogs—Buddy (a white shepherd), Dino (a black Lab), and Lulu (an English setter)—to the shore to retrieve driftwood every day.

In the garden proper, Frank points out beefsteak tomatoes, lettuce, carrots, beans, cucumbers, squash, and asparagus. Many are not yet in fruit and the rows are unlabeled, but Frank knows where everything is buried. Same as with his fishing gear. When the carrot shoots rise, it's like a lobster trap coming up to its buoy. Ahoy there, we have a keeper.

The berries and brambles wrap around an old shed, which Frank keeps threatening to tear down and replace with a proper music studio. The blueberries are low-bush, wild and natural. Close by is a raspberry patch. Our enthusiasm for raspberries leads to some picking and an argument between Frank and his wife.

Let's call it a debate.

Frank says, "I can always tell when the shedders are coming on in July—early or late—by when the raspberries are ripe."

Donna frowns. "It's not the raspberries," she says. "You can tell it's shedder time by when the earwigs show up in the yard or, especially, the house." She stoops to pick up a thin black insect about an inch long. "See, here's one. We must be having shedders tonight." She laughs, and Frank puts his arm around her shoulders and squeezes. The earwig theory wins the day.

Like a pioneer, one apple tree stands in front of the vegetable garden, not back in the orchard. My partner, Donna, asks Frank about this singular tree, its trunk gnarled, its limbs drooping like a willow's, weighed down by the most beautiful red fruit, now barely off the ground. He says his great-grandfather planted the apple seedling; Frank's mother, now eighty-eight, used to play in the tree as a little girl.

By now, the two Donnas are walking arm in arm toward the house. Frank and I follow with six live lobsters out of his truck. Four are greenish brown, the normal coloration, but one has a yellowish cast and one has blue highlights. A totally blue shell, with odds of one in two million, would be a candidate for a city aquarium and not dinner for us. The house is an extension of the garden. From the root cellar to the staircase (stacked with produce) to the kitchen (decorated with tomatoes and corn), we find vegetables ripened or cured on every surface and landing.

Frank serves the cooked lobster to us as we sit at the kitchen table. He has broken the lobsters apart, so the platter contains only claws, knuckles, and tails in the shell. We are encouraged to pick our favorite parts—three tails, for example, if we so wish. I start with a large crusher claw. I look around for the mallets and claw crackers; none are in sight.

"You don't need them," Frank says. "These are shedders—new-shell lobsters—you can break them open with your hands."

Sure enough, a little thumb pressure pries open the paper-thin shell, exposing the succulent meat. The white morsels are tender and sweet.

Rather than the chewy hard-shell lobster I experienced with Pete Clancy—and most of my life—this lobster melts in our mouths. I skip the butter, as does everyone at the table.

Donna Gotwals passes her thick-sliced tomatoes, served with a sprig of mint. She also offers the cucumbers and corn, which has alternating yellow-and-white rows. For the second time tonight, I forgo the butter. Sweet corn, yes, but buttery, too.

"We're saving a lot of money on butter with this meal," Donna says.

"Now we can skip the grocery," says Frank. It is true: Everything on the table comes from the Gotwalses' garden or boat, and nothing is wasted.

Frank tells us a little about his music-touring days up and down the East Coast. He played his own music, as he does today, written for the guitar, and traveled solo. He released three albums along the way.

My partner, Donna, asks why he gave it up.

"I loved making music while touring," he says, "but hated everything else—the moneymen and managers and groupies. I loved the music but hated the life." He passes around the lobster platter again, selecting a tail for himself, which he pops open like a soda can.

I ask, "So, do you ever go to the grocery store?"

"I went last week for salt and vinegar," he says. "I like vinegar on my mussels and clams."

I realize, then, not only that their farm is self-sufficient, much like the town itself, but that Frank is self-sustaining. He has lobstering, his garden, and his music, and that's all he needs. He does not want for anything.

Frank Gotwals may be the most content man in America.

"I'm not an ambitious man," he says. He is where he wants to be and recognizes that he's there.

Upon this, everyone reflects for a minute. Donna Gotwals is the first to speak.

"Frank is so perfect," she says. "It's so infuriating. The dogs and I are so flawed. That feels better to me—to be a little human."

Everyone has a good laugh over the words of Frank's wife. She passes tomatoes and corn, second round, to her bug-eyed guests.

"It's a big garden," she says, "but the kids help out." Frank and Donna have two children, Chastity, thirty-nine, and Jason, forty-two, the lobsterman, and four granddaughters. "Neighbors help out, too," she continues. "Frank's mother lives next door."

"Everyone helps each other around here," says Frank.

"Even mortal enemies put aside their feuds to help someone in trouble."

"That's the code."

"We live by it."

Frank puts down his second ear of corn, kernels gone, with the pride of a farmer-lobsterman. "When Clyde Haskell died out near Isle au Haut," he says, "friends recovered his traps; they sold his lobsters and gave the proceeds to his widow. That's the way it works around here. We're all family."

"We're all in this together."

"That's right—whatever happens. Everyone thinks about the inevitable—the crash of fishing—from time to time. Maybe our big catches won't be sustainable after all. There's a saying: In the lobster business, eventually you're gonna get bit. The most important question is, Can we survive a downturn? The key survival measure will be our ability to bounce back. The town has reinvented itself before—first as a granite town, then a shipbuilding center, next a fishing port—once dependent on cod, now dependent on lobster. Just as when switching harvests from season to season, our fishermen are flexible, resilient. The town has always been able to adapt."

Frank Gotwals is betting on Stonington's doing it again. One thing is certain: Frank can feed his family and canines in case of a crisis. The dogs feasted on the lobster legs when we were done.

3

Anatomy of a Boom

At three in the afternoon on Labor Day, the fog has not budged. Men are fishing blind. If the holiday is not going to keep them in port, then a little mist will not tie them up, either. The fog hovers like a bale of cotton suspended in midair, beginning three feet above the green water and reaching to the top of the radio antennae of the lobster boats. Above this white mass is blue sky. From my stance on the town wharf, my outstretched hands are lost in the void, but, to a toddler, my feet would appear clearly below the floor of the mist. Even at the edge of the basin, the fog has opened up at my boots and above my cap. It bunches in the middle.

My eyes strain into the mist, searching, trying to catch up with my ears, which have picked up a clue of boat traffic coming this way.

Out of the white bank emerges a red trawler, its nets stowed in the stern, its bow headed for me on the wharf. A trawler is a motor vessel that hauls weighted nets behind her. Stepping beside me now on the pine boards is Ed James, a lobster captain I met the year before. He used to catch finfish. Groundfish, like cod and pollock, were his domain—now all but gone. But that was years ago. He was a big fish killer, they say, which is a compliment. We shake hands. Ed, a small angular man, points to the red trawler, now coming alongside the wharf. "Here's one of the last of the bottom trawlers," he says. "A century's worth, she's at the end of the line."

I nod at Ed just as the trawler swings her stern toward the wharf. Except for the folded nets, the decks are empty—no cod or other ground-fish for sale. I notice the boat's name on the transom: *Ketch's Catch Can.*

Ed and I handle the lines, already bearing bowlines, and secure the boat to the pilings. Captain Ketch cinches them tight. He is a barrel-chested man, a little top-heavy. He seems to be a cantankerous fellow who is angry at the fog for some reason. Yet witty.

"The fog is so thick, you can't tie your shoe," he says.

"You don't have any laces in your boots," says Ed.

"See what I mean?"

Like any unemployed fisherman, Ketch has a lot on his mind and lays out his latest argument to Ed with intricate design—many strands braided together into a strong line, a pleated rope.

"They shut us down on Thursday," Ketch says.

"I heard," says Ed. "The cod closure is statewide. Only one-fourth of the grounds are open."

"Not where I fish. All my secret spots are west of here—all closed. They've put a hurt on me."

"I hear you."

"The problem isn't overfishing. The state has cut off the cod's food by damming the rivers."

"Ay-yuh."

"If we can't have cod, at least we have haddock. The state has dou-bled the haddock quota to one point three million pounds."

I do some quick arithmetic in my head and realize the haddock boom will not make up for the cod bust. Groundfishermen will have a hard go this year. More will turn to lobstering, putting increased pressure on a single resource. In the Gulf of Maine, the population of cod of reproduc-tive age has hit an all-time low—only 3 to 4 percent of what's required for a sustainable fishery, according to scientists. Cod will likely be a long time coming back.

Ed sits on a low pier piling. That's seniority. "Some—flatlanders mostly—have the idea that cod are wicked predators of lobster," he says. "So, to them, with cod disappearing, lobster is coming back."

"Oh, I know it. In the winter, when cod and lobster are both hunkered down in the deep and it's darker than the inside of yer pocket, all them cod can eat is baby lobster and other shellfish. Ah'm telling you, it's a clambake down there."

"Ay-yuh, but not when the cod don't show up."

"Hard telling, not knowing."

"Besides," says Ed, "I doubt many cod are feasting on lobster anyway. In my thirty years of trawling and skinning cod—thousands of fish—I only found one lobster in the stomach of a cod. Go figure."

"Maybe so. But all the groundfish in the Gulf of Maine—cod, haddock, pollock, redfish, halibut—add up to a lot of predators. They may not eat adult lobsters, but a three- or four-inch juvenile must be appealing. But lobsters aren't hunted by all those groundfish like they use to be. That's brought on the lobster bonanza. Lobster bottom is like a stadium full of Christians and no lions in sight."

"I don't know," says Ed. "I'm more worried about the warming waters than the lack of predators. We've got too many lobsters, and the price suffers for it."

"You're not gonna preach that climate change bullshit, are you, Ed?" Before Ed can answer, Ketch trolls his eyes farther down the wharf. Along comes a young lobsterman named Kevin Joyce, wearing a Red Sox baseball cap. He doesn't wave or hail Ketch or Ed or me. In Stonington, everyone's family, and greetings rarely exceed a perfunctory grunt. Ketch sits down on the gunwale of his red boat, legs dangling over the wharf; Ed stands up to face him, joining the rest of us standing in a huddle—a half circle, with Ketch as the quarterback.

He throws the first pass. "We were just saying," he tells Kevin, "that lobster is coming on strong, with few predators to keep 'em in check."

"Maybe," says Kevin. "Hard supposing. But I expect the size limits have something to do with the rush of lobster. We throw little lobsters back in the ocean. That's gotta give some more time to breed. We spare the big lobsters, too. They the ones with the most juice. They make the most children."

Ed nods his head at Kevin and picks up the ball. "The greatest help to the boom may be saving our egg-bearing females. I always said lobstermen love their mothers."

"Ah-yuh," says Ketch. "But what's new today? Yer talking a century ago. Why have lobsters come on like gangbusters all of a sudden—in five or six years? It can't be size limits, as wise as they are. If it's not more breeding, it's got to be a lack of dying—fewer teeth chasing after 'em."

"Or else the water is changing," Ed chimes in. "To a lobster, it's pretty near a sauna out there. Maybe they're breeding more because of it."

The warming of the Gulf of Maine, I recall, is well documented. I think over the statistics in Ed's defense. Waterproof thermometers dangling off buoys across the Gulf have recorded surface temperatures since 1854. Between 2001 and 2013, the mean annual water temperature at a depth of sixty-six feet climbed from 42.4° F to 48.1° F, an increase of 13.4 percent. On average, the water temperature jumped a degree every two years. Temperature spikes have been even more impressive during the summer months, when the mercury in submerged thermometers hit 54.3° F in August 2012. Since lobster metabolism begins to shut down at 68° F, these record highs are a major concern for scientists, resource managers, and lobstermen.

"Heat's been rising since the Civil War," says Ketch.

"Not as fast as now," says Ed. "In twenty years, we've lost four weeks off winter, two weeks beginning and end."

Point taken. Both men know that seasonal temperatures—especially autumn and spring measurements—control the range of marine species and their migrations. Fishermen have seen the species profile of the Gulf change dramatically in the last decade. Their traps and nets are landing unfamiliar species. Northern shrimp have migrated from Maine into Canadian waters, canceling one fishery and enhancing another. Meanwhile, southern species like black sea bass are moving north of Cape Cod, new territory for them. Maine trawlers, opportunistic as ever, want to start a sea bass fishery. This may become important financially for fishermen in the southern stretch of the state. They have also seen the center point of the Maine lobster range shift from Portland to Down East, leaving southern lobstermen with near-empty traps.

Ed still has the deck. "All I'm saying is lobsters are sensitive to temperature and we're seeing the heat rise in the Gulf by over ten percent. Something's gotta give."

"Global warming is a hoax," says Ketch.

Kevin is unfazed. "I guess Vinalhaven across the water there is better off making electricity with those windmills."

"Ah-yuh," says Ed.

"Ah'm not convinced," says Ketch.

"Just because you don't believe in global warming, Ketch, doesn't mean it isn't happening. The heat is climbing, whether you like it or not."

"Hard telling, not knowing."

Ed and Ketch stare at each other for a moment without speaking, like two bulls in a ring. Ed breaks the silence first. "Haven't you heard of glaciers melting, my friend?"

"Sure. They've been melting ever since the last ice age."

"Not like this. The seas are rising faster and faster from glacier melt-water."

"Well, Ed, you know I'm lucky. I'm always at sea level on my boat. I just rise to the occasion."

Ed tips his hat to his skeptical friend. Five years ago, he might have laughed at Ketch's avoidance of his facts, but every year the price of denial becomes more costly. Ed risks a wry smile.

Meanwhile, impacts of warming appear in every ocean, along every shore. While not at the extreme pace of the Gulf of Maine, every ocean is heating up. The sea level itself is rising not just from addition of glacial meltwater but also from actual expansion of seawater as it heats up. The same principle as a thermometer is at work: Rising temperature causes the mercury (or seawater) to expand and climb. This phenomenon is responsible for perhaps half of the oceans' ascent of eight inches since 1880. Heating up the oceans also affects their resident species. Marine fish and shellfish possess trademark geographic ranges, based on water temperature. For example, blue crabs—those popular for steaming with Old Bay—traditionally range from Mexico to New Jersey. Above Cape Cod has historically been too cold for the species. Likewise, cod have typically ranged from Newfoundland to Cape Cod, with the Labrador Current being too cold for them and Long Island Sound too warm. Blue crabs and cod rarely overlapped. With the current warming of the North Atlantic, all that has changed. Populations are moving north. Blue crabs are swimming around Cape Cod into the Gulf of Maine. It's now warm enough for blue crabs to extend their range by hundreds of miles.

Meanwhile, cod—those that are not staying put and munching on immature blue crabs and lobsters—are swimming farther into Canadian waters—up to Newfoundland and beyond. Cod are joined by other groundfish. The whole species profile of the North Atlantic is changing, and with it, the ecosystem.

Decades of overfishing have reduced the cod to a fraction of its former abundance. Historically, cod was the most important fishery in the Gulf of Maine and the Georges Bank. European empires, enriched by the transatlantic trade in cod, were built on the salted flesh of this prolific species. Since 2010, resource managers have set out to reverse the cod's decline by issuing severe limits on commercial fishing. A 77 percent cut in the harvest quota was imposed at first. Next, in 2015, the Gulf of Maine quota was slashed another 75 percent, or an 84 percent cut overall. Stocks were so low that fishermen could not even catch that quota. Since then, in the absence of significant fishing pressure, the cod have not bounced back in Maine. There is some recovery in Newfoundland, but elsewhere nets are empty. To the south, something is keeping stocks low after overfishing has ceased.

It's looking like ocean warming may be to blame. Andrew Pershing, chief scientist at the Gulf of Maine Research Institute, points to a relationship between warming and increased fish mortality, either from starvation or increased exposure to predators. Apparently, young cod are moving to cooler, deeper water to avoid the heat. In doing so, they inadvertently trespass into territory where predators gather. Due to the higher mortality of larval and immature cod, the species has less reproduction and recruitment, the graduation of fish into the adult population.

Ocean warming is a juggernaut for fisheries managers. How do they plan for it? Cod and lobster are cold-water species; they have their limits. In the face of ocean warming, Andrew Pershing suggests, we need even more stringent catch limits to allow cod to recover. In this way, climate change would constitute another dimension for assessing and implementing fishery models and plans.

One question looms: Does the heat actually kill the fish and shellfish, or does it impact them indirectly? The answer is: both.

At the very base of the marine food web, we find one clue as to why so many fish are migrating north. They follow their food supply, which reacts to warming seas. Marine species are marching north ten times faster, on average, than species on land. When dodging the heat, striped bass are faster than a snowshoe hare. For finfish, the quest is often to catch up with the northbound plankton on which they depend.

Plankton productivity, especially of the zooplankton species favored by larval cod, is linked to water temperature. Warmer seas can reduce abundance. At elevated temperatures, researchers have also discovered a shift in the dominant species of zooplankton. Cod may miss their favorite meals. Cod may starve. The survival of fish larvae is dependent on the availability of certain food. Thus, mortality and reproduction are tied to plankton as well as to predators.

As cool oceans warm up, conditions become more optimal for certain phytoplankton, the plantlike organisms consumed by zooplankton and some larger species, such as northern shrimp. As temperatures rise, it is expected that more phytoplankton will thrive around the poles and less so in the tropics. Meanwhile, locally in the Gulf of Maine, phytoplankton productivity and distribution are already shifting. In 2014, the spring bloom of phytoplankton was so small that it barely registered as one of the typical annual events. For this reason, in part, federal regulators canceled the Gulf of Maine shrimp season for the second year in a row.

Only five years ago, the first international scientific study was released showing the shift in the range of marine species due to ocean warming on a global scale. Like melting glaciers and sea-level rise, this shift northward in our hemisphere furnishes evidence of the far-reaching impacts of global warming. Each species, it was discovered, has a "thermal niche," a temperature zone to which it is best adapted. Warming the water in a part of the fish's range can alter the species distribution. For sardines and hake populations off Nova Scotia, the southern ends of the species' ranges have become vacant as numbers move north. Across the Atlantic, in the North Sea, sardines, anchovies, mackerels, and other pelagic fish are highly vulnerable to changes in ocean temperature. The study found their displacement north toward the Baltic Sea to be an excellent measure of the speed and direction of climate change. Marine species are extending their range poleward at an average speed of five miles per decade.

Dr. Camille Parmesan, a professor in the Marine Institute at Plymouth University (UK), is one of the study's researchers. She has a word of caution. "These results are from a very, very tiny amount of climate change—0.7 degrees centigrade worldwide over, say, the last hundred years," she said in an interview. "You don't have to be a mathematician to think, 'Gee, what are we gonna see with four degrees of warming?'" Four degrees Celsius (centigrade) is one of the estimates for temperature gain in the next eighty years.

Already along U.S. coasts, we have seen at least two major range shifts: Dungeness crab in the Pacific and American lobster in Long Island Sound. In 2015, along the West Coast, the Pacific Ocean was warmer—by 2° to 4° degrees C—than the year before. The warming trend continues. As a result, Dungeness crab, caught commercially in California, Oregon, and Washington, may be slowly moving toward British Columbia. Of special concern is the appearance of a hot spot in the Pacific, which has nurtured the massive blooms of an algae, called *Pseudonitschia,* that produces domoic acid, a potent neurotoxin that accumulates in shellfish. When ingested, the toxin has human health symptoms ranging from headaches, vomiting, and dizziness to death. When the algae bloomed in proximity to Dungeness crabs in the autumn of 2015, the crab season had to be delayed, for fear of human contamination. Since the crab industry exceeds $170 million, fishermen suffered extreme hardship, losing two months of their usual season and income. When the season finally opened in January 2016, the Oregon boat price for crab was $2.95, a 12 percent leap over the previous years. That's the price when fishermen can actually find them. The range of the species may have shifted a few miles north in a decade, depending upon local hot spots and hypoxia (low oxygen), making for a longer boat ride.

Across the continent, the western Atlantic has increased generally about 2° F since 1901, and the Gulf of Maine far more. Consequently, thirty-six major fish species have moved north. Tarpon, the Florida game fish, is now caught routinely six hundred miles north in the Chesapeake Bay.

In southern New England, lobster have suffered from warming waters, as well. In western Long Island Sound, bordered by Connecticut and New York, where a local lobster industry was concentrated, the lobster population has declined by 95 percent in twenty years, prompting a closure of the fishery. A $100 million industry has shut down overnight. Global warming has pushed water temperature into the red zone, placing the animals under extreme stress and making them more prone to shell disease. This plight, marked by discolored and eroded shells, which can make lobster unsalable, has also spread to the eastern Sound. These lobsters have a bad case of the uglies. High temperatures have also forced a retreat from important breeding and nursery grounds. One reason that Long Island Sound lobsters are so vulnerable is that they are already at the southern limit of their range, where water is warmest, even without temperature rise. A little more heat throws the lobsters into physiological distress. The crash of lobsters began with a 1999 die-off, when waters exceeded 68° F, considered the upper limit of their comfort zone. When the lobsters moved to deeper, cooler waters, they probably encountered hypoxia. To escape the heat and the rarefied water, the lucky ones managed to crawl father east and north. The viable southern limit for lobsters is climbing north every few years.

So far, temperatures in the Gulf of Maine have been warm enough to prompt a boom in production but not hot enough to retard reproduction and growth, as in Long Island Sound. Still, the lobster population is steadily shifting northward in search of cool waters. Lobsters will not stand still for climate change. Already, the center point of the lobster's range has migrated ninety miles northward, from Casco Bay, around Portland, to Down East. The northeastern counties have doubled their percentage take from 27.4 to 53.1 percent of the entire catch for the state. For this reason, the lobstermen of Stonington are getting rich, while those of Boothbay Harbor, farther south, are just holding their own.

On a larger scale, the range of the entire species of American lobster has shifted north by 215 miles during the last fifty years. The first forty years (1968–2008) were documented by Malin Pinsky and a team from Princeton University. They found the center point of the range moving from New Jersey to Massachusetts, a distance of 172 miles. The last ten years registers perhaps another 43 miles in migration, totaling 215 miles for the half century. Pinsky's hypothesis is that marine species like lobster follow the exact rate and direction, or "climate velocity," that temperature regimes travel through space. In other words, lobsters chase the cool water at the speed that warming seas nip them from behind. Most other marine animals flee the heat, as well. And they do so fast—an average of half a mile north per year. In the ocean, climate velocities are up to ten times higher than on land.

Migrating lobsters are as clear a symbol of climate change as are the melting glaciers of Montana.

Extreme events like the heat wave in Long Island Sound in 1999, which precipitated the southern lobster's decline, or the warm winter of 2012 in Maine, which launched the northern lobster's bonanza, are critical mileposts of warming. Some show a dominolike cascade of effects. The heat of 2012 prompted an explosion of green crabs, a nonnative predatory species, which in turn forced a collapse of edible mussels and a decline in soft-shell clams. Those years are outliers. Yet the steady, incremental increases in yearly and seasonal temperatures are the most telling. Over thirty years, this gradual pace has added up to the Gulf of Maine's singular distinction on the world stage: The Gulf has warmed up faster than 99.85 percent of the planet's oceans. Such alacrity is a good reason to watch the American lobster's reactions closely.

Sea surface temperatures are expected to climb by 3° C in the next seventy-five years, perhaps more so in the ultrasensitive Gulf of Maine. This elevation is based on atmospheric carbon dioxide concentrations increasing at 1 percent per year, the anticipated rate for business as usual. Such a warming would likely cause more shifts in fish and shellfish populations—northward off the eastern seaboard. The center point of Maine's lobster population—now just 120 miles or so southwest of the Canadian border—will likely move closer to Nova Scotia in the years ahead. The consequences for Maine could be catastrophic. Meanwhile, the southern mortality zone could shift, too, into the Gulf of Maine. With the population center point moving to Canada and the disease zone coming north, one might wonder about the future date for the last lobster harvest in Maine.

Another question appears: How is ocean warming influencing the boom in lobster numbers right now off Maine? To find an answer, says Robert "Bob" Steneck, professor at the University of Maine's Darling Marine Center, we must examine the biology of the lobster. Bob briefed me on lobster science on a couple of visits to his research laboratory on the Pemaquid Peninsula. It happens that, throughout its life history, temperature cues prompt the lobster to act—to feed, to molt, to breed. Steneck says lobsters react to the seasons more dependably than do we.

Lobsters begin their lives as floating larvae, or plankton, bouncing around in the first meter of the water surface for two to six weeks. During their journey from larvae to breeding adult, lobsters move through several postlarval stages and adolescent phases, molting each time they have a growth spurt. Molting, or shedding, the act of tearing loose from its shell and growing a new, larger one when its inner body demands it, may happen up to twenty-five times before the lobster reaches legal size. One might think that lobsters would have a lot of hand-me-downs available on the ocean floor. And they do. Lobsters eat one another's and their own discarded shells to recycle calcium into a new, larger shell.

Throughout the lobster's life cycle—from floating eggs and larvae to crawling postlarvae to adolescents and adults—water temperature is critical, making the species finely tuned to warming seas. As July approaches and surface temperatures exceed 50° F, young lobsters get ready to molt. They have been growing since the previous summer and need a new outer skin. Some of these shedders will jump one size, to the predicament of legal dimensions. They will be fair game for lobstermen. But the females will molt for a secondary reason—in preparation for mating. Only soft-bodied females can breed.

The lobster is a quick-change artist, slipping loose from its exoskeleton in a couple of hours. First, the old shell weakens as the crustacean absorbs some of the calcium that will be transferred to the new shell. The old shell cracks along a joint between the carapace (dorsal shell) and the abdomen. Next, the lobster turns on its side and flexes its body to extract itself from the split shell. The lobster pulls its body through first, then plucks its claws, legs, and tail (abdomen) free. The discarded shell is a perfect replica of the lobster, right down to the claws, the mouth, and the coverings of its eyeballs. Without resting, the naked lobster consumes the old carapace. Much of the weight of the emerging lobster (up to 50 percent larger now) is water, a disappointing discovery for diners who otherwise enjoy a shedder's tender, sweet flesh.

Upon molting, Steneck says, the naked lobster resembles a rubber toy. Approximately a month is required for the carapace to harden completely. During that time, the shedder is vulnerable to predators, not to mention fishermen. When ocean warming brings on two molts in a single summer, the lobster matures faster. It is more protected (from natural predators) and able to breed faster.

Bob Steneck, who resembles a handsome red-bearded pirate, points out to me that molting, feeding, and reproduction are the central themes of a lobster's life. The most spectacular behavior, by far, is deployed during courtship and mating.

High summer temperatures stimulate the female to molt and mate. An elaborate courtship ritual protects the hen when she is bare and most vulnerable. When she is prepared to molt, the female approaches a male's den—amid cobble and boulders—and releases a pheromone, or sex perfume, in his direction. Unlike a female butterfly, whose sex pheromone may attract a platoon of random suitors, the female lobster selects her mate first, choosing his apartment among many. She typically picks the largest entrance (and male) in the neighborhood. The hen stands outside the male's retreat, squirting her scent in a stream of urine from apertures in her head. He obliges by fanning the water with his swimmerets, imbuing his condo with her perfume. Aroused, the male emerges from his lair with his claws raised aggressively above his head. Will he cannibalize her or cuddle? She often responds with a brief boxing match, claw to claw, jaw to jaw. Or she simply turns away, the passive partner. Either move seems to mollify the male's aggression. The hen lifts her claws and puts them on his head to assert her willingness to mate. They enter the den together, and eventually—in hours or days—the female molts. At this juncture, the male must choose his appetites again—to eat or reproduce— but he always chooses lovemaking. He flips her jellylike body, and once she is on her back, the male climbs on top, inserts his first pair of swimmerets, which are grooved and rigid, and passes his sperm into a cavity, the seminal receptacle, in the female's abdomen. (With brains the size of grasshoppers', it's remarkable the pair have such amorous designs on each other.) The hen remains in the apartment for about a week for protection, while her new shell partially hardens. By then, the male has had his fill of companionship. The hen has also grown tired of the memories of her one-night stand. She steps out of the den with hardly a backward glance, and is gone.

After several months (up to a year), the female lays her eggs. The internal eggs become external. At that point, the eggs are fertilized from stored sperm and attached under the tail with a sticky substance like glue. The hen carries the fertilized eggs externally like this for another year. A young adult can lay 8,000 eggs, but a nine-pound female can carry more than 100,000 eggs. Fewer than five of those eggs will survive to become an adult lobster.

When the eggs hatch (June through August), the female releases them by fanning her swimmerets. Thousands of lobster larvae float to the surface of the water. Lobster larvae resemble tiny shrimp more than adult lobsters. As plankton, they go through three molts before transforming into postlarvae, which do resemble adults. This metamorphosis takes between three and twelve weeks after hatching, depending on water temperatures. The higher the heat, the faster the molts. The postlarvae settle to the ocean bottom in search of a secure hiding place. They keep hidden, avoiding predators like cod and black sea bass, exiting the lair only at night to feed or to find a larger shelter as they grow. In the benthos, they go through at least four stages—cryptic, emerging, vagile, and adolescent—on their way to adulthood, a journey taking from six to eight years.

Recent high temperatures in the Gulf of Maine may reduce the time to adulthood by one or two years. In 2012, surface temperatures were nearly 4° F warmer than usual. That record heat increased the speed of the lobster molt and enhanced the population of legal-size lobsters. This combination prompted a record harvest that year. In the wild, faster-growing lobsters mean that more reach adulthood overall, since they spend less time in vulnerable stages. They bypass the gauntlet of predators to a size and shell of safety. The population grows, suggesting climate change influenced the boom.

Yet it does not stop there. When females mature faster—some now achieve breeding age well before they are legal size—they bear eggs earlier in life. Lobstermen have been spotting these ripe females all over the Gulf in the last two years. Early sexual maturity means earlier spawning. This dynamic vastly improves the lobster's reproductive success.

Imagine if all five-year-old humans bred successfully. We'd have a global population far in excess of ten billion, and quickly. There are nearly 250 million lobsters in the Gulf of Maine, approximately five times the population of twenty years ago. How did it explode so fast? The population explosion is likely due, in part, to early maturation in the warming seas.

Suddenly, this revelation provides more evidence, suggesting that ocean warming may have induced the glut.

Besides reproduction and molting, Steneck suggests, there may be many other aspects of lobster biology affected by temperature. Researchers are just beginning to identify a few. Jessica Waller, a lobster scientist at the University of Maine, believes that high ocean temperatures may be having an impact on the lobster internally, tampering with its ability to breathe correctly with its gills. Situated in the thorax region, the lobster's gills pick up oxygen from seawater and pass it to the heart, which circulates the oxygen in clear blood to body and limb. At high temperatures, such as those found in Long Island Sound, respiration rates, as a measure of metabolism, may actually decrease. Waller has tested lobsters in the hotter water conditions expected eighty years from now, due to climate change, and found that lobster larvae grow more slowly. The ability to catch prey and feed may be hindered in larvae by poor respiration. So, while modest temperature elevations may speed up metabolism and growth, higher temperatures may retard them.

The water is also working against them. Cold water holds more oxygen than warm water. When temperatures top 68° F, the amount of dissolved oxygen in the water has decreased sufficiently that breathing is "labored." At the same time, the amount of oxygen required by the lobsters increases, causing physiological stress and even death.

It is possible that by midcentury, temperatures in the southern latitudes of the lobster's range, including Long Island Sound, will surpass the lobster-friendly temperature zone, making the southern reaches inhospitable.

On the flip side, warming in northern regions like the Gulf of Saint Lawrence could boost stocks there by providing additional temperature-appropriate nursery grounds, an earlier hatch, a prolonged growing season, and faster development. Predators and conservation measures may play a role, but ocean warming is clearly a major player. Other factors will become apparent during my stay in Stonington. Meanwhile, Steneck has convinced me that water temperature is critical to the success and survival of the lobster. The irony is that the same force in play may be helping or hindering lobsters, depending on whether it's a northerly or southerly locale, a modest temperature increase or a major lethal spike.

Since eggs and larvae like all lobster life stages are sensitive to temperature, scientists have been monitoring the population for clues to the origins and duration of the current boom. When he was a graduate student in 1989, Richard Wahle, now a professor of marine biology at the University of Maine, devised a way to count the baby lobsters that settle onto the ocean floor each summer. Those babies are considered "young-of-year," which mature to adult (legal) lobsters in five to nine years in the Gulf of Maine. Wahle thought their abundance might be an early measure, or predictor, of future landings. In that way, newly settled young-of-year lobsters could prove to be an early warning signal of a coming boom or bust.

Wahle's tracking of young-of-year lobsters over thirty years has produced the American Lobster Settlement Index (ALSI). In hindsight, the survey levels show a correlation with the size of landings six to eight years later. Larger harvests generally follow high levels of settlement. Most intriguing, the recent boom in the eastern Gulf of Maine follows a trend of heavy lobster settlement from the mid-2000s.

Wahle says, "The risk is now reasonably high for a downturn in landings. The sixty-four-thousand-dollar question is, When will the drop come? Can the ALSI survey forecast any crash in the fishery?"

The ALSI tracks twenty-five settlement areas from Newfoundland to Rhode Island with shipboard sampling. By far, the densest sampling—fourteen areas—occurs in the Gulf of Maine. Wahle's team or its successors return every autumn to count the young-of-year lobsters. Since 2007, they have seen a sharp decline in settlement on the nursery grounds.

How could we have a bonanza in adult lobsters—and presumed egg production—at the same time settlement is depressed? I visited Rick Wahle to find out.

Wahle told me about one trip to Casco Bay to inspect one of the fourteen sampling areas along the Maine coast. Lobsterman Steve Train captained his own boat, *Hattie Rose,* chartered by the university for the day. Aboard were four divers (including Rick) and a deckhand. Their sampling method was tried-and-true.

The process took three steps.

First, they used GPS to find the right location—a cobble and boulder field at a shallow depth of twenty feet. The water temperature was 64° F (18° C), about as warm as it gets. (Below 12° C, larval development slows down and settlement is curtailed.)

With the boat sequestered offsite, the divers donned scuba tanks, masks, and fins. Teaming up in pairs, they rolled off the rail of the boat into the cool water. Then the deckhand passed a PVC pipe frame, among other gear, to each pair of divers. This frame, resembling a gigantic picture frame, would delineate a half-square-meter "quadrat" on the bottom. Each pair of divers would work six quadrats at each of the five sites in Casco Bay that day. Diving swiftly to the shallows was like training for scuba certification in a turbulent, cloudy pool. Placing the frame on the bottom, the pair of divers would be careful to contain all sea life in that sample. A mesh apron around the frame minimized escape. Quickly, they employed a suction sampler—essentially an underwater vacuum cleaner—to collect all the young-of-year and other life, as well as small rocks and rubble, within the frame. The vacuum deposited the contents in one of six collection bags. In turn, these bags were placed in a catch duffel that was floated to the surface. The entire operation, harvesting six quadrats, took twenty-five minutes.

Back at the lab for the third step, the contents of the bags were identified and counted. Young-of-year lobsters are as small as the last joint of Rick's thumb—about one inch long. The ALSI is a calculation of population density. For each sampling site, Rick takes the counts of young-of-year, averages them for twelve quadrats, and doubles the number to produce an average population per square meter of bottom. The index is that population measure.

In 2003, sampling in Casco Bay showed a peak index of nearly two young-of-year lobsters per square meter. By 2007, that reading had dropped 25 percent, to an index of 1.5 young-of-year lobsters per square meter. It then fell rapidly to an index of 0.5 and below over the past eight years—a decline of 75 percent or more. Lobsters from those years are now entering the fishery.

Most sampling sites have shown a similar collapse in the index. In fact, most monitoring areas from Jonesport to Cape Cod Bay have reported the lowest settlement levels on record. The only exception has been Beaver Harbour, New Brunswick, which showed a slight increase in settlement from 2013 to 2015. The widespread downturn is troubling, leading Rick to wonder how long the boom can last.

The drop in the ALSI indices suggests the answer is just around the corner.

Yet the answer to why the settlement rate has declined at a time of record adult abundance—and presumed prodigious breeding—may take many more years to unravel. There is no shortage of theories to explain the conundrum.

First, physical conditions could be changing. Shifting ocean currents could carry young-of-year into waters too cold and deep for the young lobsters to survive. This theory requires a change in ocean circulation, a departure from historical currents, as yet unproven.

Rick also wonders whether atmospheric drivers, such as temperature and wind, may also be in play. While elevated temperatures promote molting, growth, and maturation in older lobsters, perhaps the young-of-year ones are negatively impacted. A third inquiry into chemical science involves ocean acidification. Could the greater acidity in the ocean—from loading of carbon dioxide—make it more difficult for young lobsters to build their shells?

Other theories speak to discoveries made for various life stages. Scientists ask whether, in the wake of ocean warming, lobster egg production may be in decline. This drop in egg production, or fecundity, seems contrary to our understanding that warming may be stimulating population growth, but the findings are startling. Heather Koopman, a biologist at the University of North Carolina, spent five years sampling 1,370 brooding female lobsters—mostly big specimens—in Nova Scotia's Bay of Fundy. Over that time, she found a 31 percent decline in fecundity. The most likely cause, she hypothesizes, is the rapid hike in water temperature. Although some warming can be favorable to lobster populations, too much could be problematic. During those five years, water temperatures never fell lower than 41° F, below which a female lobster's ovaries mature. If that is true for the Bay of Fundy, it spells even more trouble for the warmer southern Gulf of Maine.

Another inquiry looks at reduction in the young-of-year in what has been termed the "deepwater settlement hypothesis." As the temperatures rise, the acreage of bottom habitat suitable for settlement expands. More deepwater nursery areas qualify above the threshold of 53.6° F (12° C), where young-of-year can settle successfully. Because this suspected new reservoir of nursery sites is offshore, Rick Wahle and his team may have overlooked them in their survey, giving a false ALSI profile. The inshore sites, like Casco Bay, may show a low reading, but the total universe of sites—offshore included—may show appropriate settlement if surveyed. This is like discovering a stash of groceries in the garage when the kitchen was nearly bare. A whole new habitat opens up. In 2016, a Maine Sea Grant initiative began monitoring potential deepwater sites (up to 240 feet down) in outer Casco Bay and Down East. Preliminary results point to low settlement there, as well. A possible culprit for mortality to the lobster larvae is a decline in food supply (zooplankton). It will take a few years to analyze any pattern and improve the ALSI as a diagnostic tool. Meanwhile, the shallow-water ALSI indices, alone and perhaps skewed, predict a downturn in future landings. Fishermen like Ketch disagree. Time will tell whether either forecast is correct.

If and when the bust does begin, a downturn predicted by most scientists, it will likely come in two waves. The first wave, the biological one, will be a direct result of poor settlement six to eight years before. Reduced settlement and landings will probably come from environmental factors, principally ocean warming.

The second wave, comprising harvest pressure, will add insult to injury. Due to inertia, it is possible fishermen will be slow to act upon the downturn. Instead, they may continue to fish at full throttle. When 3,822 active lobstermen each take eight hundred traps out on the Gulf of Maine, approximately three million traps splash into the water. While this level of fishing pressure has perhaps squared with a fishery posting landings of 120 million pounds, the same harvest pressure may overwhelm a reduced fishery of 60 to 90 million pounds (50 to 75 percent of the 2015 catch). Overfishing may ensue and the already depressed population may go into a tailspin. Admittedly, landings are a poor measure of population abundance. As the resource becomes rarer, the price per pound increases, fishing intensifies, and the fishery moves closer to a tipping point. This is what happened in Long Island Sound: A boom was tripped up by biological (and ocean-warming) forces, and then overfishing provided the coup de grâce.

Maine also has seen this duality before, though usually in reverse order. For both cod and northern shrimp, overfishing brought the stocks down to a crisis point first; then ocean warming kept them low.

"This may be the story of many modern fisheries," says Bob Steneck in his office at Darling Marine Center. Like 98 percent of scientists globally, Steneck recognizes the seriousness of climate change.

"In the Gulf of Maine," echoes Rick Wahle in the next room, "marine species are feeling the heat, so to speak. We can't control ocean warming, except globally. However, fishermen can control the level of exploitation, if they choose. Typically, only a minor cut or limitation is put in place. The irony is that this might not be enough to stop local extinction of a fishery. Ocean warming coupled with insufficient catch limits may be too big a combined threat."

One wonders whether, during the early days of the decimation of cod or hake or pollock, or northern shrimp or sea urchins, the fishermen saw it coming. Did Ketch and Ed anticipate the end of the line? Were there early telltale signs of the crash? Were captains observant? Or did fishermen just wake one day to empty nets?

To be certain, it will take prescient and enlightened minds to manage Maine's last great fishery correctly. Right now, during the boom, little management is required. There are plenty of lobsters to fish. Yet the bonanza has a mind of its own. The day of reckoning may be coming.

4

<hr />

Autumn, Goose Rocks

In the center of Deer Isle, six miles north of Stonington, a bedroom alarm goes off—silently but brightly. A digital display, backlit by a floodlight, projects numerals onto the ceiling of the bedroom. The time, 4:45 A.M., appears overhead in yellow light, the hue of a sunrise.

Julie and Sid Eaton, fifty-four and seventy-four, respectively, are instantly awake. Eyelids flutter at the bright light. Sid throws off the blanket, letting in the cool air of this September morning. He clears his throat, ready to brag about the coming day. Yet Julie, the island photographer, is the first to boast this morning. "It may be yer bottom out thar across the water," she says, "but I'm gonna land more lobster today than you ever imagined."

Julie and Sid are both lobster captains—she at the helm of the thirty-foot *Cat Sass* and he at the wheel of the twenty-eight-foot *Kimberly Belle*. They compete. Having two separate boats, however, has saved their marriage. "Thar's only room on my boat for one captain," says Julie. "I've got three knives aboard to cut the yingies off anyone who tries to muscle in. Now, Sid is my hero. I respect him more than anyone in the world. But he's got his boat and I've got mine."

The Eatons also have two bathrooms, where husband and wife wash up—separate but equal. They feed their three cats—Cole, Nicholas, and Tori—but don't make breakfast for themselves. Julie and Sid are both prone to seasickness, and a morning meal can aggravate that ordeal. Instead, Julie pours a cup of coffee from the automatic Mr. Coffee, and Sid chugs a glass of water, the first of many for the day—all he gets by on. They don't pack a lunch. Julie and Sid will each tend only two hundred traps today and be back before noon. Then they'll dine at a restaurant or their dealer's barbecue.

They have money to spend, but their slim waists disprove it. Neither of them drinks alcohol. Julie, the auburn one, is a hot-blooded woman. She speaks her mind. Like Julie, Sid can be a stitch. Laughter is the glue in this marriage. Sid is a kind soul, but something in his eye warns you not to cross him. You don't want to fuck with Sid Eaton.

At 5:30 A.M., their two sternmen arrive at the house for coffee and more boasting. The kitchen is large for a double-wide, big enough for four. Derrick Gray, Julie's helper, is twenty-six and apprenticing with her to become a captain in his own right. He must log fifteen hundred hours with Julie to claim it. Dan Fiveland, twenty-eight, has worked as a sternman for Sid for only a year but wants to continue until the older man retires. But Sid, bald as a billiard ball, is a die-hard lobsterman and the winningest captain at the boat races. Like Popeye, whom he resembles, he has a secret to his prowess and longevity. Water is his spinach.

Julie raises the ante. "Dan, you look tired. You don't think you can possibly haul as many traps, as fast, as Derrick can?"

"I've got my Red Bull," says Dan.

"I brought two cans," says Derrick.

"Well, that settles that," says Sid. "We'll see if some extra caffeine can give you an edge, Julie. Didn't yesterday."

"Thar's always another day," she says to her husband. Sid beat her last year by a thousand pounds, and she aims to reverse the tide. "I've just got to beat you one day this week to bring it even."

"Last week," says Sid, "I made thirteen thousand dollars and you made almost as much. We're beating our average. Isn't that enough?"

"Nope. I gotta win."

Today is Friday, the twenty-fifth of September. The week has been a hassle for Julie. Last Friday, the pump to the fuel injector on her boat's diesel engine broke, and while it was being fixed, she was off the water, high and dry. This put her in a nasty mood.

"She was a raving bitch," says Sid. "Of course, all she needed was to be hauling her traps again. I think it calms her down."

"I'm addicted to the water," says Julie. "I need it like a drug."

After a second cup of coffee, the conversation of boast and swagger starts to give way to a restlessness to get on the road, down to the water. Outside, the sternmen, carrying their Red Bulls, climb into the passenger seats of the Eatons' trucks. Ten minutes later, Julie and Sid pull their pickups onto the Fish Pier in Stonington.

It is already dawn—just past 6:00 A.M.—and Julie is anxious about getting under way. She is an hour behind Frank and most of the others in the fleet, who leave the dock promptly at five o'clock each morning. Julie has a smaller boat and half the traps (only four hundred out of the permissible eight hundred), as she works fewer hours. Today, she will haul 200, on a two-day rotation, as opposed to Frank's 250, on a three-day turnover, or "set." Even with a lighter gang of traps, she toils hard and lands her fair share of lobster. The men have nothing on her.

Julie is always wary that she may have to move her traps to capitalize on the migration of lobsters. "With cold weather coming, lobsters have moved out of the shallows," she announces this morning. "Let's get to them before they get too deep."

The first two waves of shedders—those in July and August—have come and gone. Both were in shoal water, which is the warmest area in summer but the coldest in other seasons. The summer sun heats the shallows, but the autumn chill cools them down fast. Now, as lobsters migrate to deeper, relatively warmer waters in September, the challenge is to anticipate the next shed and to set one's traps just ahead of the lobsters' arrival. Too often a lobsterman will be late, only to catch the tail end of a shed. "We don't want to arrive at the station just as the caboose is pulling in," Julie said yesterday at the dock.

As I walk the hundred yards from my cottage to the pier, Johnnie Furlong races his pickup down Main Street, squealing his wheels. His high school sweetheart must have given birth to that baby boy. A patch of rubber left behind on the asphalt is cheaper than handing out cigars.

I am now waiting for Julie and Derrick on the pier. The sun is peering over the shoulder of Mount Desert Island, blinking across the harbor. Slivers of fog dangle around the necks of the islands like collars of lace. When captain and crew arrive, we quickly board the skiff that will take the three of us a few hundred yards out to Julie's boat. Derrick runs the outboard, I sit backward in the bow, and Julie sits amidships. After two years of apprenticeship, Derrick can run both boats and troubleshoot just about anything. "He's a fast learner," says Julie, "and smart, aren't you, darling boy? I'm worried about him growing up. I've made him promise he'll still stern for me when he gets his license, while he's in the waiting line for entry to Zone C, the lobster area off Stonington. He can haul his own traps after work, but I need him each morning. We've got a well-oiled machine."

Derrick is loyal to Julie. The only time he went astray was when he told her four years ago that he wanted to work on a bigger boat. He thought he could make more money. Begrudgingly, she let him go. After a year, Derrick knocked on her door one morning and sheepishly asked to come back. "I had another sternman by then," says Julie, "but he wasn't so bright. I had to order him around. Derrick and I work by telepathy. So I made one more announcement. That evening, I fired the dim-witted son of a bitch." Derrick was working her stern again the next morning.

Just now, Derrick throttles down the outboard, slowing the tender to a crawl.

"You okay back thar, sweet pea?" Julie calls to Derrick over her shoulder.

"Yep." Derrick revs the engine a bit, just to answer more forcefully. Julie considers Derrick the son she never had, and she mothers him. He resists enough to keep his independent standing and his pride. He is nearly six feet tall and has bright red hair. All her tender endearments roll right off his back. Julie missed having children. In her recent years, she was too busy fishing. In her early years, she was too busy surviving.

Julie's first love was not the ocean, but the sky. She grew up in Surry, a Maine boatbuilding town, but her gaze always drifted above the horizon. She soloed in a private plane at age sixteen, before she could drive a car. She earned her commercial pilot's license when she was twenty. Her dream was to fly planes for the state police—to be of service. That dream was dashed within days of her twenty-third birthday, when a cement truck plowed over her car.

The 1987 crash left Julie in a coma for several months as a result of massive head injuries. The doctor's prognosis was poor, and if she did survive, she might not walk again, feed herself, or work. For her parents, the days passed slowly and with little hope. One day, against all odds, she began to stir.

When she woke up, she could not remember anything before the accident. She was a blank slate. However, nothing had erased her will. She spent months in physical therapy, learning to walk, talk, think again. "There is no underestimating the power of the human spirit," she says, looking back.

"My accident was the biggest blessing of my life, because I suddenly saw what was important. Finally. Not a new dress or a bigger home or truck. But breath. Just a simple breath—on my own, without a respirator. That really hit home. For a few days, I asked, Why me? Big pity party. Then I thought, Why not me? I can handle this. Let's go. Let's get it done."

Part of Julie's recovery was to go out on a boat to experience the calming effect of water. A smile lit up her face. She had forgotten how to fly but gained a new passion for the sea.

After some scallopers dared her to learn how to dive, Julie passed her scuba certification. She became a fisherman and dived for scallops for fourteen winters. "I was full throttle then," she says. "Nothing was stopping me now."

When Julie decided to try fishing full-time, year-round, she moved to Vinalhaven Island to learn lobstering from some pros. At that point, Stonington was the away team, but she collected some legendary stories of Vinalhaven's rival. Some of those legends featured Sid Eaton, her future husband—unbeknownst to her.

In 1993, at twenty-nine, she bought her first boat, the twenty-three-foot *Family Julez,* and began lobstering on her own out of Stonington. There were challenges as an outsider, both in Vinalhaven and Stonington, but she persevered. Her buoy lines were often cut by other lobstermen, yet somehow she made money. Not bad for a single woman with no exclusive territory, the prized lobster bottom that local families claim.

Ten years later, she married Sid Eaton, patriarch of the biggest family on Deer Isle. Now they are one of Stonington's power couples, making a neat $250,000 or so each year between them.

About her journey, Julie is forthright. "If you wish for something long enough—like being a lobsterman—you figure out how to do it. I'm fast on the uptake. Life is short. I'm always on the go—full out. Get it done."

Derrick depresses the throttle again and swings the skiff in a wide arc, stopping alongside *Cat Sass,* Julie's newest boat. He grabs his two Red Bulls and jumps into the lobster boat. Julie follows, clutching three packs of Pall Malls. She fires up the engine. It's a short ride to her buyer's float, Damon Seafood, lashed to a tug at the edge of the channel.

Three huge men, the size of beefy Highlanders, stand on the Damon float. They catch Julie's lines as we come alongside. One of them is shirtless, muscle-bound, looking ready for the Highland games. The biggest Scot is John Hovey, the foreman, who asks Julie about her engine problems.

"The fuel pump is replaced—that was two thousand dollars," she says. "Heaven knows what the labor charges will be. My catch yesterday will pay for the parts but not the labor."

"You landed eight hundred pounds yesterday," says Hovey. "Just do it again, Julie."

"Well, those traps had been soaking for five days. Plenty of time for six hundred lobsters to get caught. But today, I'm on a one-night soak. Takes more than one tide to make a killing."

John Hovey throws out his hands, palms spread, knowingly. Anything's possible, his hands seem to say.

"Here, take ahold of this," says Julie. "I've got two racks of baby back ribs." She passes the racks to Hovey's waiting hands.

"We'll barbecue these for lunch while you're hauling," he says. "You gonna eat all these ribs?"

"No, half is for you and the dock boys. You look like you're losing weight."

Bill Damon, owner of the float, will arrive at midday to fire up the grill. All his captains—a good sixty or so—are welcome to feast if they drop off some grilling meat in the morning. "I like to keep my captains happy," he is known to say.

John Hovey loads two barrels of bait—salted herring—into *Cat Sass* with a winch. Derrick pours the fragrant bait into boxes, scooping out the last bits with his gloved hand. Then we're off.

Julie heads west toward Vinalhaven, eight miles away. Three white windmills tower above the island, their disks like the billboard eyes of Dr. T. J. Eckleburg staring across the Valley of Ashes. Over 120 feet above the ground, the whirring blades are the island's concession to climate change, the need to acknowledge, and adapt to, a changing world. Lobstermen like Julie stare back at the "eyes" of the windmills and wonder what the future will bring—boom or bust, the eternal swing of the American dream.

We pass by Billings Diesel and Marine, the local boatyard where *Cat Sass* was repaired this week. The shoal water off the marina is McDonald family territory, so it is not surprising that we see Cory McDonald, Jason's first cousin, hauling traps in the shallows. Farther along, near Mark Island, we come upon Captain Genevieve McDonald, Cory's young wife, on *Hello Darlin' II*. Our wakes entwine and overlap.

Genevieve, thirty, is the first woman to be appointed to the governor's Lobster Advisory Council, which troubleshoots ideas such as the state's draft lobster management plan. A month before, I joined Genevieve for a day of lobstering. She wears her long auburn hair tied in a bun, a tank top, and a tattoo on her shoulder burned into her skin during a "wild weekend" in Fort Lauderdale. She says it signifies nothing—the weekend and the tattoo. She pulled an impressive 240 traps on a four-night set in forty feet of water. This haul took her all over the shoal water at the entrance to Penobscot Bay. Her sternman, Ami Carver, baited the traps while Genevieve pulled and picked. Her plum-and-orange buoys stood out next to the purple nails on her hands. This millennial pushes the limits of Maine fashion at sea level.

Genevieve has a sense of style and design. She has lobbied Grundéns USA, the leading producer of clothing for commercial fishermen, to make outfits more suitable for women—for example, waterproof bib overalls that accommodate a woman's shape. For female fishermen, men's gear is uncomfortable and unsafe.

She dubbed this campaign "Chix Who Fish." Grundéns responded and has been developing a women's line. Genevieve is testing prototypes and polling other women for preferences. The campaign has expanded on social media into a support community for female fishermen around the world.

More and more women are becoming captains and crew members. Only 4 percent of the 4,900 active and inactive lobster licenses in Maine are owned by women. But of those 196 women, 73 are under the age of thirty-five. More are coming along every year. Even a larger share are sternmen, like Ami and Alyssa, apprenticing to become captains someday. As Genevieve says, "It's not just a man's ocean anymore."

Many of the older women, like Julie, started in other established fisheries—scallops, shrimp, clams—before moving into lobsters. Millennials like Genevieve, on the other hand, began harvesting alternative stocks, such as Jonah crabs, whelks, periwinkles, eel, and sea cucumbers. As it happened, Genevieve began harvesting sea urchins for the Japanese.

The year was 2001, and the urchin harvest topped twelve million dollars. However, this was down from a peak of $35 million in 1995, just six years before. Urchin landings were in a nosedive. The urchin bonanza began in 1987, thanks to a nascent Asian demand for urchin roe. Now, less than fifteen years later, it was crashing. The verdict is unanimous: overharvesting, with many perpetrators coming from Stonington.

The urchin story actually begins with cod. When cod populations were decimated by overfishing in the 1990s, their prey rebounded throughout the Gulf of Maine, particularly sea urchins. Those same green sea urchins began overgrazing kelp. Habitat declined. Soon came the fishermen with their bounties on sea urchins, posted by the Japanese. The fishermen cleaned up: They achieved a 90 percent decline in urchin biomass across the state in fifteen years (1986–2001). The kelp grew back. A tipping point was crossed, an ecosystem shift from an urchin-dominated kelp forest, patchy in profile, to a dense kelp forest teeming with lobsters and crabs. The species lineup changed. Lobster populations are highest in areas with significant kelp cover, perhaps providing shelter and camouflage.

The Gulf of Maine changed forever, and the first domino was cod. As John Muir, the father of American conservation, said, "When we try to pick out anything by itself, we find it hitched to everything else in the universe."

Genevieve spent only a few weeks in the urchin fishery and left just past its peak. She tried sea cucumbers next, another Japanese delicacy, which was soon to crash. Like urchins, it is a typical boom-and-bust story, with little government scrutiny and no comanagement in place.

"Sea urchins are all but gone," Genevieve says. "Cucumbers and shrimp are waning. So the future is lobster. I need to double my traps. That'll cost forty thousand dollars." Compared to some, Genevieve is conservative, building her gear as money, rather than debt, becomes available. "But I've gotta do it when I can," she continues. "Someday, I'm gonna hit it big."

Julie peels away from Genevieve at Mark Island Light and sets her sights on another lighthouse, Goose Rocks Light, halfway across East Penobscot Bay at the confluence of the Big and Little Thoroughfares. The byways separate Vinalhaven and North Haven Islands. Both islands are inhabited throughout the year, and host fishing fleets. Goose Rocks is the hub of Sid Eaton's family bottom, even though he lives across the water near Stonington. These are enviable fishing grounds. Julie lobsters there all season long.

"Good bottom is very coveted among the island fleets," says Julie. "When I was engaged to Sid, I realized it was extremely important that I become familiar with my future husband's bottom." She giggles, eyes straight ahead, turning west by southwest. "Was it prime bottom or saggy bottom? Was it hard in a crunch? So I admit I sampled some and married him for his wicked good bottom." She turns to me with a wink.

Sid and his extended family are able to work valuable bottom ten miles from their home because Sid Eaton's father claimed it, and the family has fought to hold on to it for ninety years.

Family territories have been in force within Penobscot Bay—East and West—for as long as anyone can remember. The theory is quite simple: Family networks claim, mark, and defend specific lobstering grounds, where available; the government does not interfere. This is unique in

North America, turning a blind eye to partitioning a public resource. So much for the freedom of the seas. No other Maine fishery exhibits territoriality. But here, within the territories, we see an elaborate dance: Cooperation waltzes with competition, altruism steps in rhythm with greed, and closed access spins around freedom.

Bands of extended kin, some broadened to include close friends, set traps with colored buoys and patrol them in exclusive areas like native tribes. Outsiders, like Frank Gotwals, can gain admission to these lobstering tribes only through unanimous consent.

The tribes are armed at a minimum with knives, which they use to sever the buoy lines of anyone invading their territory. The act of slicing the warp effectively causes the trap to founder on the bottom, making it irretrievable. So-called trap cuttings are common, a warning to the trespasser and a loss of $120 of gear. Full-scale "cut wars," in which hundreds of traps are vandalized, erupt from time to time. The molestation has expanded to the burning and sinking of boats, even gunplay. On the positive side, this vigilance and violence has preserved lobster grounds by keeping trespassers away. It is a homegrown form of limited entry.

One famous territory is Head Harbor, a cove on the south side of Isle au Haut, the large island just south of Stonington. Dickie Bridges is chief of its tribe. The whole band comprises ten cousins, but he is the spokesman. The men are protective of their lucrative bottom, known for its prime lobster stock, he says, and have retaliated when unwelcome visitors have trespassed. Like other tribes, Dickie's brethren limit the lobster catch in their waters. Moreover, the existence of their territory fosters a sense of pride that preserves other conservation efforts like V-notching females.

Closer to Julie's world is the story of the Eaton Bottom along the shores of North Haven and Vinalhaven. It took a year for Sid Eaton to open up to me about it; he revealed the secret one morning on Bill Damon's float.

"During the 1930s, my father lobstered along Eggemoggin Reach, at the head of Deer Isle. But when he heard nobody was working North Haven, he steamed over thar and took over. My brothers and I helped him clean out any new competition. We had North Haven pretty much to ourselves. There were no fishermen living on the island then. When we got to Vinalhaven, that's a different story.

"Oh yeah, we had problems on Vinalhaven. I knew I was crowding the bottom. I was practically the only one working right with them boys. They didn't like it, of course. So they put it on me. They cut my lines, emptied my traps. It got violent. We fired bullets at each other. I hit a boat, I think, but missed the captain.

"Oh yeah, it got heavy. Twice, I lost my license over that mess. Comes with the territory. When I'm hit hard, I hit back harder."

Julie will stop short of Goose Rocks Light today, but a month ago, she went beyond it. There along the shore of Vinalhaven during the last days of summer, I discovered what makes a proper bottom. Lobstermen work certain bottoms at specific times of the year. As lobsters migrate shoal-ward in spring and summer, then return to deeper areas in fall and winter, they encounter different bottoms. Inshore areas, like Penobscot Bay and its islands, are muddy, which lobsters occupy when shedding, provided there are some rocky crevices nearby. Alternatively, in winter, lobsters roam over sand on the continental shelf. It's a mixed bag in between. I searched the shoreline of the islands for signs of what was lurking below the waves around Goose Rocks Light. I saw rocks and mud, the full significance of which became clear on our voyage.

Under a blue moon, still barely night, we skirted the lighthouse, which fishermen call "the Sparkplug," a fifty-foot-high steel cylinder crowned with a dome of glass. To the right (northwest) was North Haven; to the left (southwest) was Vinalhaven. Julie announced that she would have to wait until high tide to service her North Haven traps.

"We're playing the tide game," she said. "Those traps are nearly exposed at low tide. My boat has too much draft. Well have to wait until nine o'clock. Lobsters naturally come on a high tide; the shedders sneak out of the rocks. We've got a full moon this morning—disappearing now to the west. So much the better."

The shoal bottom around Vinalhaven and North Haven, I learned, is mostly mud. We could see this on Julie's depth sounder: muddy bottom giving off a weaker echo than rocky ground. The mud comes from

silt deposited over thousands of years from the eroding force of the Penobscot River. Penobscot Bay is the southern reach of the original river,
flooded twelve thousand years ago by the retreat of glaciers. The ebbing
ice also left behind boulders, rocks, and other debris in its wake, which
can be seen peeking out of the mud. This debris field happens to furnish
perfect habitat and protection for lobsters (read wicked good bottom).

While waiting on the tide, Julie ducked into Carver Cove, a pocket
in the Vinalhaven shoreline. She hauled three strings—fifteen traps—in
just under forty minutes. Julie considers a string to be five buoys and,
with singles, that makes five traps on a string.

"Derrick does most of the heavy lifting, but I do the heavy thinking,"
she said. Actually, Julie put in an equal share of physical labor: She
hauled, broke traps over the rail, and picked lobsters. Meanwhile, Derrick baited the bags, sorted and banded, and tossed the traps overboard.

"I'm not a female lobsterman," said Julie. "Nor a lobsterwoman. I'm
a lobsterman. I do everything on a boat that the guys do. I've been working
it for twenty years, and I've earned my stripes. Out here, I'm just one
of the family trying to beat Sid's tally. But I'll tell you, when I get home
each day, I'm happy to take a shower, sit in my easy chair, and just be Sid
Eaton's wife."

After Carver Cove, Julie worked her way along the Vinalhaven shoreline, landing lobster and killing time.

However, her big bets were placed on North Haven. Around 8:30 A.M.,
she headed north, passing the Sparkplug, to the Little Thoroughfare. She
stopped along the way to haul a string of traps just fifty feet off a vertical granite wall trickling with green and yellow lichen. The water is ten
feet deep here. Julie said, "I can see my traps on the bottom." Remarkably, the visibility is even deeper than that, which speaks to the lack of
pollution in the Gulf of Maine, unless you consider temperature a pol-
lutant.

Suddenly, an adult bald eagle dive-bombed the boat and flew circles
around us. "That's Majestic!" Julie screamed. "He's mine." Derrick tossed
the big male some salted herring, a ritual enjoyed on many lobstering
days. Julie grabbed her Canon camera and clicked a few images of Majestic in midflight. A white-headed eagle takes the place of the vanished
blue moon.

If the lobsters disappear, we lose both the Eatons and the eagle. Ocean warming is inhospitable to both.

We motored north to Kent Cove on North Haven to take advantage of the high tide. The water was "boiling" at the confluence of the channels, as the tides were out of sync, confused. Derrick picked only half a dozen lobsters from the entire string. Julie was disappointed. The lobsters had dried up—unusual for that time of year.

"I may have to move these traps to deeper water," she said. "Autumn is coming. Besides, it may just be too warm for the lobsters to shed in these shallows, baked by the sun. It's either too cool or too warm. Climate change is on my radar. Lobstermen are just starting to get our heads around this whole global warming thing. If it *is* warming, we're out of luck.

"What the lobsterman fears most is coming out here one morning and finding no lobsters in his traps. No one talks about it. But that's what we worry about."

After some consideration, Julie spent the rest of the day moving traps to the outside—at the edge of Penobscot Bay. Even with shifting gears, she landed 540 pounds for the day, or 2.7 pounds per trap, about half her expectation. Volume was down from earlier August—by about four million pounds statewide—but after a lull, prices were rebounding.

Now it is late September, colorful and cool. The sugar maples are orange along the shoreline; the cranberries are bright red in every bog. The summer people have flown south with the birds, taking their money with them. Only the lobstermen remain.

It is 7:00 A.M., and Julie is making her first haul of the morning, gaffing one of her buoys—yellow and teal. We are on the outer Thoroughfare, at the entrance to East Penobscot Bay, perhaps a mile outside Goose Rocks Light. Julie is fishing between Black Ledge and Channel Rock, two perilous obstructions. At high tide, they are hidden, marked only by buoys; at low tide, they rise above the water like huge jagged teeth. Sid has a kinder and gentler bottom, but this is the choice for the day. The water is forty to fifty feet deep around and between the hazards. This is where the 12° C thermocline extends in September, the limit of waters suitable for shedding. But Julie doesn't take the temperature of the water. She measures its suitability by hauling her traps and counting the shedders.

Derrick picks three keepers from the first trap and tosses the old bait to the seagulls. He bands two shedders and places one hard-shell lobster in a separate, "select" basket. He rebaits and tosses the trap overboard.

"Thank you, darling!" the captain calls out from the helm. She is still fishing "singles," one trap to a buoy, not doubling up the traps as Frank prefers. She is slower with singles, but "it's habit," she says. I stand next to her and learn.

A few more traps produce nearly the same result: two or three keepers. After thirty traps, we have seventy-five lobsters. Julie was hoping for more. "We're too slow," she yells. "We should do better than three strings an hour. We're falling behind. That's the sternman's fault."

Derrick shakes his head in disbelief. She would—half-jokingly—blame her crew for every setback, every misstep, this morning. It was only partially true, but Julie lets off steam this way, deflecting the weight from her shoulders.

"There's a corollary to that," Julie says. "If the sternman's always wrong, the captain is always right."

"Always," agrees Derrick. "You betcha."

The sun has now risen out of the fog enough to cast a bright runway across the water. The photons sparkle. "Look at that sunrise," says Julie. "It's delivering a million diamonds, dancing in the light."

We are still on Sid's bottom. His ground encompasses all the shoal water from Calderwood Neck and Carver Cove on the northwest side of Vinalhaven to the east side of North Haven from Kent Cove and Indian Point through the islands between the Big and Little Thoroughfares. This is some of the best lobster territory in Maine. Today, on the outer edge of that territory, is a family affair. Julie points out Meredith Oliver, captain of one boat, and Cathy Rhineberg, another captain. Both young women are Sid's nieces. "And there's Sid on *Kimberly Belle,* right next to his son," she says, pointing. "That third boat is Sid's other son's, Mitchell's."

I ask her about a green-hulled boat, just to the east of us.

"Oh, that's just a cousin."

The Eaton family represents the largest lineage on Deer Isle—actually comprising three extended branches. Sid is the patriarch of the largest branch. He has six children (from two previous marriages), nineteen grandchildren, nine great-grandchildren, and countless nieces and nephews. Each is entitled to a slice of Sid's bottom.

Derrick picks six beautiful lobsters from a trap. All large males—no need to measure. He sets them on the counting table to be banded later. His next priority is to bait the trap as it sits on the rail. He looks at the captain.

"Go ahead, hon."

Derrick tosses the forty-pound trap into the dark sea.

"Thank you, dear." Derrick laughs uncomfortably. This much praise cannot be good.

On the next buoy, Julie accidentally drops her boat hook into the water. Completely her mistake. "Looky thar," she says, "that's the sternman's fault."

"Absolutely." Derrick smiles as he reaches over the rail to retrieve the floating stick of wood. He hands the boat hook to Julie without an apology.

"I can't afford another mishap," says Julie. "I already lost a week because of engine trouble. We have sixteen weeks—July to October—to make a living for the year. Now I'm down to fifteen weeks, 'cause of that engine, with only five weeks left. And we're coming into the season of bad weather. Autumn storms can creep up on you out of nowhere. You lose the catch for a day or more."

Julie keeps hauling traps while she tells the story of the worst storm on her watch. "It was a beautiful day, hauling pots in northwest Penobscot Bay—maybe ten miles from home. Out of the blue, a National Weather Service alert comes over the radio for severe thunderstorms right where I'm fishing. I look around, see there isn't a cloud in the sky, and keep hauling. Then another National Weather Service alert comes through. I look around—the sun is shining—and I figure those boys at the Weather Service must be smoking something funny. Next thing, the sky goes black, like you locked yourself in a closet. It starts to blow—howling wind. Waves rise up to fifteen feet. I'm going up the waves, teetering on top, and shimmying down the other side. I'm not afraid yet. I'm too busy keeping straight. I try to run for home. Meanwhile, back in Stonington, Sid tells his brother I'm smart enough to duck into a cove and ride her out. But I'm not that smart. I'm trying to run for home, where it's safe. Waves are now at sixteen feet and the sky is pitch-black. But I'm headed home. That's what I keep telling myself: I'm headed home! I bucked those waves for two hours. Finally, I rounded the corner into the harbor and I was safe." She pauses to wrap a line around the pot hauler.

"Of course," she continues, "when I did get in, there are some fishermen on the dock and they say, 'You were out in that black?' 'Oh yeah,' I say, 'no big deal. Oh yeah, nothing to it. What's the matter with you guys?'

"It's the bravado, you know. If you show a weakness, they'll eat you alive."

In an emergency, Julie will use the marine radio, but she doesn't consider it a recreational outlet as do some captains. Even when Sid and Julie are in sight of each other, like now, they are not tempted to chit-chat.

"We're too busy to gossip," she says. "We've got work to do out here. Five weeks left."

Julie pushes the throttle forward and speeds to the next string, far enough to allow some more conversation along the way.

"She works hard," says Derrick. "I'm half her age and I have trouble keeping up with her. She's got some kinda secret."

"I run on pure adrenaline—that's my drug. I'm an addict, just like any other fisherman. I mainline the stuff six days a week."

"This must be our last string for the first half of the day," says Derrick.

"That's right. One hundred traps hauled, one hundred more to go."

On course to the second location—farther northeast along the edge of Penobscot Bay—we encounter two seals playing amid the kelp. The pair are not chocolate brown or black, so they are not the common harbor seal, but the much larger, more formidable gray seal, a rarity in these parts.

"That's Fred and Ginger," says Julie. "They're good friends of mine. I'm responsible for them."

Ever since her accident, Julie has been more drawn to nature, particularly animals, and they have been drawn to her. "The trauma I suffered has made me so thankful for my life," she says. "From the moment of my recovery, I swore I'd live every day fully, take in the view, and love all the creatures. I'm a steward of the resource—from lobsters to wildlife. They are my friends."

Julie's friends adorn her photographs. The marine mammals—porpoises and seals—and birds of prey look like they've been shot with a telephoto lens, but she has a simple lens. The seals and eagles come right up to her. Right now, she lingers only long enough for one photograph, not wanting to disturb Fred and Ginger's dance.

"We are visiting someone's home," she says, gently nosing the *Cat Sass* away. "It's a holy place." At each one of these encounters, Julie shows Derrick and me the magic of the Maine coast.

"You loving it yet, sweet pea?"

Derrick allows a slight smile.

Immediately, at the new locale, we come upon a partially cut warp—caused by either friction or man. The first buoy comes up cleanly, but the line to it is sliced halfway through, close to the trap. Above the cut, the fifty feet of line to the buoy is unblemished. Round up the usual suspects. Luckily, the trap is not lost.

"It better not be someone molesting my traps. I know who might try." She's careful not to name names. She's uncertain of motive. Julie grabs a short rope and splices it across the cut. The new mend will be stronger than the original line. She does this in two minutes flat, like a surgeon who has done the same operation dozens of times before.

At the end of the string, after hauling four traps, Julie is having difficulty spotting the fifth buoy. "I don't see the other one, hon," she says. Derrick points out the buoy, camouflaged by the sparkling sunlight on the water. Julie seems relieved. She puts vandalism out of her mind.

However, when a V-notched female comes aboard, she launches into a rant about thievery. "These egg-bearing females are our future. Along with oversize males, they are our breeding stock. And yet, some lobstahmen—mostly young lobstahmen—keep both aboard. Sell them to market. Sid and I look out for these guys. I'll turn them in. We don't like thieves. If you steal from the resource—taking small lobstahs or eggahs—you're stealing from everyone. That's our future. We don't like a thief."

Like the Amish, the Stonington community will shun a fisherman who breaks the rules. The buyers will refuse to sell bait to him or refuse his lobsters. A shunned man is set adrift, as if on a boat with no engine, no sails, no oars. He can't launch from the waterfront or come into shore. He loses his harbor. Without the community, a fisherman is lost. It's worse than prison—shut outside, with no way to get in.

"If you give a dog a bad name," says Derrick, "you might as well shoot him." On the Maine coast, a bad reputation lasts a lifetime.

In the next string, Julie and Derrick are picking a meager one or two lobsters per trap. This is fewer than last week, when they averaged two and a half legal lobsters per trap for the day, or six hundred pounds. Yesterday, her big catch of eight hundred pounds averaged four pounds per trap.

"The lobsters may already be dropping off at this depth," says Julie. "I don't set traps any deeper, any farther out. I leave that to the big boats. So it won't be long before Sid and I pull our traps and head home for the winter."

Derrick is having no trouble keeping up. In fact, he wishes he were busier. Yesterday, when they landed eight hundred pounds after a five-day soak, Derrick was overwhelmed with lobsters. Leaving traps in the water for five days, rather then two or three, assured more lobsters. As soon as he finished banding one batch, another flood came aboard. He was exhausted. At one point, Derrick turned to Julie and said, "Is it tomorrow yet?"

Well, now it is tomorrow, and Derrick wishes it was yesterday. He paces the deck. "You okay, darling?" his captain calls.

Julie spots a tremendous commotion over by a channel marker. Water is splashing onto the marker. Behind it, an adult bald eagle (not Majestic, but another large eagle) is trying to haul a seal carcass out of the water. Call her Sisyphus. The weight is too much for her, and she eventually lets go. But her talons have punctured the bloating carcass, which now is less buoyant and starts to sink. The eagle flies away. Julie figures the seal carcass will settle on the bottom and become food for lobsters and crabs.

Julie has her own Sisyphean challenge on the next-to-last string of the day. One of her traps has caught upon a rock in fifty feet of water. It will not budge. When she puts the warp in the pot hauler, the line simply stretches and twists. The pot hauler whines. Julie steers *Cat Sass* in a circle to try to release the impediment. After one circle, she reverses and navigates the rock counterclockwise. It works. The trap springs free.

I realize that Julie has handled her life in the same way. Her accident was life-threatening and totally bewildering to a twenty-three-year-old who could not speak or walk. The coma and its aftermath were a boulder in her way. Yet she simply circled it one way, then the next, until she found a way around it. She never gave up. Scalloping was the same: She wanted to scallop, so she learned how to dive. Lobstering? No problem. Build a trap. Let's go. Let's get it done.

Even in the face of such obstacles and challenges, she has kept her sense of humor. "Derrick, that rock was your fault."

He shakes his head, but there is the glimmer of a smile at the corner of his mouth.

"No, sweet pea. It's nobody's fault. It's just life—the cards that you're dealt—that's all." Julie has let go of her anger at losing a couple of years of her life, but the shadow sometimes trips her up.

"One more string, darling." They motor over to the last five traps of the day. The string produces seven lobsters, or one and a half lobsters per trap. That's the story of the day. Julie, showering Derrick with more endearments, sets a course for Stonington—to Damon Seafood's float. She is headed home.

Derrick does some quick arithmetic with an erasable pen. "I figure we caught three hundred and four lobsters," he says to his captain. "That's three hundred and sixty pounds, give or take."

September landings are down everywhere. All over Maine. You can tell because, with the limited supply, the price is up to $3.25 per pound.

Surprisingly, Julie is not disappointed. She takes the bad with the good. Seasons come and go, but today she has a different yardstick in mind. "Three hundred and sixty pounds, you say? Better than Sid, I bet," she says, her white teeth showing in a wide smile. "I know I've got my old man beat."

At the float, owner Bill Damon has arrived, a big boy himself, joining John Hovey, the foreman, and the other XXLs in his employ to weigh the harvest. Julie's catch comes in at 355 pounds—less than half of yesterday's.

"Five pounds shy," she says. "That's the sternman's fault." All the men laugh, Derrick the loudest. Any sign of weakness, I recall, would be like chum in the water.

However, the only feeding frenzy on the float this afternoon is the chomping down on barbecue ribs. Hovey passes out soft drinks and beer and paper plates, a half rack on each.

"Our barbecue grill is just one way to keep fishermen happy," says Damon. "I've got sixty captains who want ribs today. Here's another way to keep them smiling." He hands Julie a check for over $2,400, her net proceeds—after bait, diesel, and paying her sternman—from yesterday's bonanza.

"Oh, you're making me happy today, Bill!" She shakes Damon's hand, which is as big as a baseball mitt next to Julie's modest paw.

The other men gather round, giving Julie high fives. It looks like a huddle of linebackers and one diminutive female coach. Everyone joins in the pleasure of a good catch, and the success of a good captain. To them, Julie is just one of the boys.

5

To Market

At barely 4:30 A.M. on an October morning, I descend the metal ramp to the float at the Stonington Lobster Co-op. The aluminum railings and steps are coated with condensation. Though not freezing, the night air dipped below the dew point. The float's wooden deck is slick. I'm careful. A single boat, *Seahawk,* is tied to the float. Captain Jason McDonald, Frank Gotwals's stepson, is waiting on his sternman. I tip my hat at the captain.

"If you're waiting for Frank," Jason says, "he may be late. He's not an early riser." This is a running joke between them. Frank says Jason is too early, and Jason says Frank is too late. Time is relative and only dependent upon the tides.

Chris "Kit" Bruce, the sternman, arrives at the top of the ramp and slides down, the railings in his armpits. When he reaches the wet float, he promptly takes a header, falling backward on his shoulders and skull. Pride overrides the pain. He jumps to his feet and boards *Seahawk.*

"Moving too fast, partner," says Jason.

"The faster I go, the behinder I get," says Kit, placing his cigarettes in a cubbyhole by the cabin.

Jason wastes no more time, casting off his lines and winging the boat swiftly around to access the bait shed. *Seahawk* is the first boat to buy bait this morning—she always is—but two other boats are now hovering behind *Seahawk,* waiting their turns. On the other side of the float, yesterday's lobsters wait for market. They reside in ninety-four blue-and-gray crates, tied to the float and to one another in "boxcars." The floating crates are awash in seawater, keeping the lobsters alive.

Across the harbor, Damon Seafood, Julie's buyer, does not bother with floating boxcars or any other overnight storage. Instead, Bill Damon loads his fresh lobster onto Ready Seafood trucks, bound for Portland every evening, thereby getting them to market more quickly.

Here at the Co-op float, a more classic operation is under way. Yesterday's lobsters will be picked up this morning by a truck owned by Garbo Lobster Corporation and wheeled away. Right now, the live lobsters have spent very little time out of the water. But that's about to change. It will take the better part of the morning to load them into the truck, scheduled to arrive at seven o'clock. Then it is an hour drive to their initial destination, the first of many, a sorting facility in Hancock.

Twenty minutes later, I step into the office of the Stonington Lobster Co-op to repay a loan. I'm carrying Frank's insulated work boots, dry but heavy with insulation, as if they were filled with sand. After borrowing them for weeks, I have finally bought my own pair. The office lobby is half-full, with seven or eight men queuing up for coffee. They pay me no notice. The room is divided into halves: lobby to the right, where the men mill about, and to the left, on the other side of a low counter, are four desks. In between is a bulletin board, pinned with five handwritten notices from sternmen seeking jobs on lobster boats. In a corner is a coffeemaker and a sign: STILL 25¢ PER CUP. A typical office, except the sun has not yet come up.

A man and three women are shuffling papers. One of the women comes to the counter to ask me if I want to buy some lobster. I tell her I never buy seafood in the dark; I'll wait until dawn. "Be my guest," she says. "I'm Shirley. If you need anything, just whistle."

Shirley goes back to her desk to count receipts, hundreds from yesterday afternoon. The Stonington Co-op is the biggest seafood co-op in Maine, with annual sales in excess of ten million dollars, half of the lobster commerce in Stonington.

"Looks like you're carrying Frank's better half," says the man at the desk, scanning my boots. He rises to his feet, says he is Ron Trundy, the Co-op's manager. He inspects the boots again and nods his head in confirmation.

"A loan from July," I say. "Does Frank usually stop by in the morning?"

"So yer the green hand. Hope you can swim."

"Just trying to earn my stripes."

"You can set those boots in Frank's truck when he pulls up." He glances at the wall clock; it is just shy of five o'clock. "Should be a minute or two. No more than three."

"I want to thank him personally."

Ron Trundy nods his head and rushes out the door. On the landing, he encounters three more lobstermen—one tall, one short, and one size that fits all. They're standing under a sign that says FOUL LANGUAGE SPOKEN HERE. After a few words, Ron lets them pass.

They enter in midsentence: ". . . that union is a wicked good deal," says the short one. "I think I'll join. With enough people, we could keep the dealers from lowering prices. You know they'll try squeezing us again."

"I'm already out two hundred bucks to the Lobstermen's Association," says the tall guy. "I'd hate to pay union dues, too—what is it, three hundred and sixty bucks?—on top of that."

"It's worth it," says the one with the average build. "A union has power that lobstermen never had." Point taken. Maine lobstermen have rarely had collective bargaining power. The International Association of Machinists and Aerospace Workers (IAM) is backing the brand-new Maine Lobstering Union with all its might. It provides structure, lawyers, and communications. Still, it's an oxymoron to think the independent, wayward lobstermen would join a group that demands consensus.

I scrutinize the faces of the three union sympathizers, searching for something that would distinguish them from rank-and-file lobstermen, the sort that join the Co-op and the probusiness Maine Lobstermen's Association, pay their dues, and keep quiet. Their tanned, rugged faces look to be from the same gene pool. Stepping under the full fluorescent light of the lobby, they quit the union banter. The room fills with complaints about some lobster buoys that have gone missing.

"Cutting traps loose is what it is," announces the tall lobsterman. "Somebody over to Isle au Haut has a sharp knife."

"It's revenge over one of our Stonington men fishing Isle au Haut waters," says a fourth man.

"Not worth it to me to set any buoys around that island," says the tall guy. "If they cut me loose, I lose more than one hundred and twenty dollars for each trap. I think I'll stick to our side of the channel."

"Hey, Bud," says the short one, "here you are too tight to pay union dues and yet you spend a fortune on gear. Somebody's charging you too much for a trap. That's if you ever get round to paying the bill."

A ripple of laughter spreads across the room, does an about-face, and washes over the men once more. In slow motion, Bud stuffs his wallet deeper in his trousers, admitting he's tight. There are no secrets in Stonington, so no one bothers to hide.

I inch toward the window, outside of which a bright floodlight illuminates the path to the lobster wharf. A lone worker, called a "wharf rat," stands in the semidark, monitoring the floating crates of lobster— over 8,500 pounds caught yesterday and spending the night.

I see Frank's GMC pickup pull into the parking lot. My watch says 5:03.

Ron Trundy returns. "Frank's here," he says.

"Thanks. Can I take these back stairs all the way down to the wharf?" I realize my mistake right away.

"You can't take them anywhere," he says, repeating an old Maine joke.

"Right." I think about taking Frank a cup of coffee, a small repayment for the boot loan. "Would you say Frank takes his coffee black?" I ask the woman behind the counter.

"I wouldn't say a thing," says Shirley.

I'm drowning in dry humor.

From the landing, I do not see Frank. He must have rounded the corner of the boathouse. Stepping across the gravel in the parking area, I secure Frank's boots in the well of his truck and tiptoe down the gangway again to the floating dock. I spy Frank in his rowboat, already hugging the mooring line of *Seasong*. I shout, "Good morning."

"Hello." He waves back across 150 feet of black water.

"Brought your boots back. I invested in my own pair."

"Thanks."

"I appreciate the loan."

"You been here long?"

"Early enough to see Jason."

"He's always early. Even as a child, he woke up way before dawn."

"He catches the first lobster, though."

"That he does. Oh, you wanted to know. I got three dollars and seventy-five cents per pound yesterday." He ambles into the cockpit of *Seasong* and starts the engine.

I drink Frank's black coffee in one gulp. So, for 750 pounds, he grossed $2,800 for the day. Further along the distribution chain, those same lobsters will be worth $16,875 at the Fisherman's Friend Restaurant down the street—that is, $22.50 per pound, or six times the boat price. Somebody is pocketing the difference. There can be many middlemen, each clearing a dollar or so per lobster on each trade. You can bet the union men—all lobstermen, in fact—want a better slice of the profits.

A wooden shack stands next to me on the floating dock, essentially a weighing station. It appears as though a stiff breeze could carry it out to sea. On the side of the shack is a green chalkboard, carrying messages for the benefit of lobster captains pulling up to the dock. Richard "Poochie" Nevells, the wharf foreman and head of the wharf rats, is erasing yesterday's price from the board. He does this with the heel of his hand and a little spit. When he is done, the ghost of the "$3.75" in chalk is barely visible, but the message is clear: The dock price could change today. Anybody's guess—it could spike or bottom out. Lobstermen can tell you stories of each happening over the years.

Like any resource value, the price of lobster is determined by a balance between production (supply) and the desires of consumers (demand). The law of supply and demand defines the effect of these two seesawing factors on price. When there is excessive supply, prices fall because people will not pay for easily found items. A luxury good like lobster becomes commonplace and has less value. When the supply gets tight, however, the price climbs. If the ascent is brisk enough, demand can outstrip supply. Low production and high demand spell big profits. That's when people pay a premium, like FedEx prices, for lobster at Christmas. The factors at work, especially demand, are not always quantifiable. But a short history of lobster prices and landings reveals the tug-of-war between supply and demand over the years.

Americans were harvesting lobster for over one hundred years before records were kept. In Colonial times, Maine lobster was fed to prisoners—a limit of three times a week, the quota an act of mercy in light of such a poor meal valued at a penny a pound. But as late as 1880, when the Maine lobster catch was fourteen million pounds, the price was two cents per pound. The entire fishery was valued at $300,000. That year, there were 2,763 captains and 100,000 traps in the water. The price continued in the single digits until 1905, when the supply dropped to eleven million pounds, spiking the price to thirteen cents per pound. Even though the abundance had dropped 22 percent, the effort had increased to 250,000 traps on the bottom. Low supply and steady demand boosted the price. The supply retreated further in the 1920s, by another 50 percent, to 5.5 million pounds. Consequently, the price bounced higher—to thirty-three cents in 1924. Demand nearly dried up during the Depression, bringing prices to a new low of fifteen cents per pound in 1939. Despite poor demand and poor prices, out-of-work laborers tried lobstering, elevating the number of license holders to 3,700 men. In the 1920s and 1930s, the only confirmed overharvesting took place. After World War II, the supply bounced back—in the twenty-million-pound range—for the thirty-nine years from 1950 to 1989. During this period, prices climbed from thirty-five cents to two and a half dollars as demand rebounded with the growth of the middle class. Inflation had an impact. The high prices attracted more fishermen to lobstering, with over six thousand licenses and two million traps in the water by 1989. The annual harvest was now over fifty million dollars. This was the end of a long run of modest but (at the time) impressive catches. Maine lobstering was declared the best in New England.

During the 1990s, a new round of superlatives had to be invented to describe the harvest. The number of license holders increased 15 percent, to 5,836. A rush of boatbuilders produced a new fleet of bigger lobster boats. Over three million lobster pots were now in the water. The attraction for the fishermen—old and new—was the dockside price, peaking at $3.45 in 1999, the year the Maine harvest nearly topped $185 million for a harvest of 53.5 million pounds. Frank Gotwals remembers these years as "tremendous, thrilling really." Scientists warned about overfishing again. Could this high harvest level be sustained?

The next decade saw prices climb due to demand, despite an apparent oversupply, to above the four-dollar-per-pound level. The Maine lobster touched the all-time record of $4.63 in 2005. Then the economy faltered. With the 2008–2009 recession, Americans did not have the discretionary income for luxury foods like lobster. Few people ordered surf and turf in restaurants. Without the demand, the lobster price plummeted. By 2009, the dock price was below three dollars per pound. Lobstermen waited for a remedy. Then out of left field came a solution few could afford.

It began with a mild, short winter and a warm spring in 2012. Water temperatures climbed 6.2° F to 54.3° F at a depth of sixty-six feet. The relative heat induced lobsters to molt in June, rather than in July, bringing a new legal-age class into the fishery—in abundance. Early shedding was the prominent cause of oversupply, which depressed prices overnight. Early molting also placed the peak summer catch in a June time frame, when there was only modest demand. Furthermore, the Canadians dumped millions of lobsters onto the American market at the same time. Tourists do not come looking for lobster in Maine until July and August. The boat price hit a low of $1.25 and averaged $2.69 for the year. Meanwhile, with higher modern overhead, lobstermen could only expect to break even at four dollars per pound or better. They were $1.31 short. (If a lobstermen grosses 100,000 pounds for the year, that's $131,000 missing from his pocket.) After 2012, some hung up their spurs. Some tied up their boats in protest. Others worked harder, trying to make up in volume what they lacked in price. Over 127 million pounds of lobster were landed.

Another warm winter and spring in 2013 brought on a repeat early molt in the Gulf of Maine. Shedders appeared in great abundance again, caught in near-record numbers. The total annual landings were 500,000 pounds over 2012's previous gold standard. Lobstermen, on average, earned twenty-one cents more than the previous year, so they made more money—$370 million. Either the protests or better demand did the trick.

Besides annual fluctuations in price, the cost of lobster varies seasonally, as well. For example, the dockside price is typically low in early autumn, when supply is high but demand has trailed off after the lucrative summer market. Then the price climbs in winter, when few lobsters are caught but people want seafood for the holidays. The influence of a low supply continues into spring, when prices can double. In April 2007, the boat price peaked at ten dollars per pound. Still, these predictable seasonal patterns can be disrupted. In May 2012, just before the glut hit, Maine prices dipped to $2.25 for shedders, despite a low supply, since Canadian hard-shell lobsters flooded the market. Like Maine, Canadian landings have doubled since 2000. They now tally the most—225 million pounds—and dominate the market. Market dynamics in New England and Canada are forever intertwined.

While there is no perfect formula to determine price levels from season to season, lobstermen rely on basic economics to gauge where price is going to move generally. Supply is monitored at each buyer's station and compared to previous years. This gives a sense of how the season is coming along, relative to historic landings. Demand is more guesswork. Dealers measure demand by the volume of orders, but they cannot put a hard number on it. Lobstermen "feel" the demand for lobster as a trend, as it moves, as it shifts up or down.

Just when it looked like a warmer ocean might push the fishery into its third year of heavy harvests and light prices, a cold winter steamrolled over New England, producing more typical, average ocean temperatures for the summer of 2014. Molting began late—actually on a normal clock— with shedders appearing in traps in bulk in mid-July. Demand was up, thanks to a boom in exports. The boat price climbed to $3.70 for shedders and $5.00 for hard-shell lobsters, plus an end-of-the-year bonus of eighty cents. The overall harvest was 124 million pounds, down 3 percent from the previous record year. Yet, thanks to the higher boat price, the catch achieved a record overall value of $459.5 million, a 24 percent gain in value. The big surprise was how the poundage stayed so high, even with a colder spring.

What was going on?

Scientists are hard-pressed to explain it. Many seasons may have to pass before these patterns and their causes become clear.

For the next couple of years, I am in Stonington for the summer seasons. In 2015, the shedders appear a week late; in 2016, they will appear a week early. Those small deviations are not enough to disrupt sales for either season. By autumn of both years, it is clear the boom is still in force.

The challenge for lobstermen is how to respond to the glut and the accompanying lower prices. How will they adapt to climate change and other environmental forces?

Yesterday's catch was typical of October 2015: hardening shedders and a mess of selects, large lobsters. Jason McDonald, forty-three, brought the *Seahawk* to port around noon, ahead of the rest of the fleet. He tied up on the east side of the Co-op float, and immediately Kit and he transferred lobsters, two at a time, one in each hand, from the water tanks to an empty crate. In a few minutes, close to seventy-five lobsters filled the first crate, or around ninety pounds.

Two wharf rats lifted the crate and carried it to the electronic scales. They removed three lobsters so that they had *exactly* ninety pounds. The three extra were set aside for padding any crate bearing a light load. The rats recorded the original weight on Jason's account sheet.

While Jason and Kit filled a second crate, another pair of workmen tied the first crate to a string of boxcars on the west side of the float and lowered the catch into the drink. In this fashion, the lobsters were out of the water for less than ten minutes. They would remain in the ocean until ready to be loaded onto trucks.

Once Jason had another crate of seventy-five lobsters ready, the same two teams of wharf rats handled the weighing and the reimmersion in the boxcars. Each of the six men played his peculiar part of the dance. Meanwhile, Poochie stood watch, ready to weld any weak link in the chain.

Occasionally, Jason or Kit came upon a double-banded lobster, which meant it was a hard-shell or a select one. These premium picks were placed in a basket, to be weighed separately at the end of the operation. Yesterday, hard-shell and select lobsters earned $5.50 per pound, over two dollars more than the shedders. The basket would be lowered through a trapdoor in the float, a holding zone for special customers, like restaurants.

The boxcars and special orders floated overnight, waiting for a complex distribution network to be set in motion. Everything hinged on the lobsters surviving. Jason and the rest of the captains had no other catch in their traps or nets, no other species to weather a storm or a dip in the lobster harvest.

Jason said only yesterday, "We are vulnerable to the rise and fall of lobster numbers, to the vacillation of prices. All we can do is buckle up and hold on for the ride." Jason is done for the day.

Yet the cost to the community of any drop in overall value in the catch would be substantial. Typically, lobstermen have two mortgages—one on the house, one on the boat—as well as truck payments. All are a burden during hard times. The bank could end up owning all three. As captains know, the financial outlook can change as quickly as the weather. Too many lobsters coming at the wrong time—early summer—can swamp the distribution network. In 2012, there were a few weeks in June when buyers could not move the product. So the dealers dropped the price even more, and lobstermen were left holding the short end of the line.

Peter Miller, a lobsterman in Tenants Harbor, said that same year, "My catch is ahead of last season, in terms of volume, but my checkbook says I'm not doing as well." If the price drops below two dollars again, Miller may tie his lobster boat to the dock, quitting early for the season.

While Miller's desperate act may be a last resort, other lobstermen are tying up for a few days to make an interim protest. In mid-June 2012, as prices began to fall with a rise in landings, lobster boats sat idle in harbors up and down the coast. With dockside prices as low as $1.35 per pound for the month—roughly 53 percent below the yearly average—lobstermen could not turn a profit. Thus the protest—a refusal to work. In Winter Harbor, thirty boats stayed in port for a week. Reports circulated that some lobstermen were coercing others to tie up next to the first thirty. The action had two effects: One, it lowered supplies, thus raising prices a bit; and, two, it directly worried dealers about the dependability of the product. Yet before the buyers reacted, over four hundred boats had tied up along the Mid-Coast, where only one thousand captains are licensed. It would seem the bullying had worked. Patrick Keliher, the commissioner of the Maine Department of Marine Resources, was concerned that the coercion, which included threats of cutting loose the traps of anyone who resisted the action, could spread statewide. He promised "swift enforcement," adding that any attempts to impose a wider fishing ban "may be in violation of antitrust laws."

A statewide tie-up—essentially constituting an unofficial strike—could be illegal, mainly thanks to a sixty-year-old court decision that favored lobster buyers after lobstermen protested prices. In this case, the lobstermen were viewed as "price-fixers," rather than the usual case of that moniker being nailed to wholesalers. A federal consent decree concluded the trial. It prohibited lobstermen from negotiating—or even discussing—price in any organized way. Strictly speaking, policemen could arrest captains for doing so in public.

For this reason, when contemplating a protest, lobstermen speak only of a "tie-up" or of "not hauling today," rather than using the *s*-word. Interestingly, the word *strike* first appeared in 1768, when British sailors, in support of wage demonstrations in London, "struck" the topgallant sails of merchant ships—that is, removed the highest sails to cripple the ships in port. Men of the sea are still fighting over a decent wage. The waterfront had not changed.

After the 2012 tie-up, Vinalhaven lobstermen contacted the International Association of Machinists and Aerospace Workers to get pointers on establishing a local lobstering union. Besides helping with lobbying the legislature, acquiring health insurance, and establishing retirement plans, affiliating with the IAM potentially gives them the right to discuss dockside prices. The jury is still out on that one. Yet the lobstermen are motivated. Lobstermen have been slowly losing their livelihood thanks to poor prices, skyrocketing costs, and regulations that favor wholesalers. The Vinalhaven fishermen look at unionization as their salvation. Over six hundred people have joined.

Others are not so sure. Captain Genevieve McDonald of Stonington says, "Workers join unions to negotiate with employers, but lobstermen are independent businessmen, not employees, so it's uncertain whom they'd bargain with. What's more, the big unions have no experience in the lobster business."

Nevertheless, it has worked elsewhere. The Seattle-based Deep Sea Fishermen's Union of the Pacific represents fishermen on crab, halibut, and sablefish boats off the Pacific Northwest. In Nova Scotia and New Brunswick, lobstermen are protected by the Maritime Fishermen's Union. In Labrador and Newfoundland, the Fish, Food and Allied Workers Union represents ten thousand fishermen, including lobstermen. The Newfoundland union negotiates the prices lobstermen get for their seafood. When the prices are not agreeable, Canadian fishermen go on strike. "We take our strikes seriously here," says Bill Broderick, a union director in St. John's. "That's the best way to deliver a message."

So, at first blush, it would seem the only possible protection for a strike action among Maine lobstermen might be to join the newly founded spin-off of the IAM. But that's not true. There is one other loophole: An exemption under the Maine Fisheries Cooperative Marketing Act of June 1934 gives any co-op member the right to discuss prices. Less than 20 percent of Maine lobstermen are members of co-ops. All are free to talk and protest. In June 2012, while others pushed the limits of the law, Dropping Springs, the Chebeague Island lobster co-op, organized an overt strike, perfectly legal for them. In less than forty-eight hours, the Chebeague Islanders made their point with dealers and were back on the water in pursuit of their prey.

The sky to the east is now streaked with yellow light. The wooden ramp to the dock shifts in its tracks and creaks as Ron Trundy, the Stonington Co-op manager, makes his way to the float. Frank and Alyssa are long gone, but other lobstermen motor to the float to pick up their sternmen. One, just now, hesitates to catch a glimpse of what Ron is up to. With a deft hand, for a gloved one, Ron grabs a piece of chalk and scribbles today's price on the blackboard: $3.90. Another fifteen cents for today's fishermen. If today has the volume Jason saw yesterday, this amounts to over $110 more in the boat's corner. Every little bit counts. And it does not end there.

As members of a co-op, Jason and his comrades are entitled to a bonus at the end of the season for all their poundage during the year. This tip typically ranges between sixty and ninety cents per pound. The pennies add up to tens of thousands of dollars for each man. In total, Maine lobster co-ops distributed over $15.3 million in their bonus programs at the end of 2015. It's difficult to compete with the dividend from a well-run co-op.

"Nice to get a few thousand dollars at Christmas," says Jason, who has taken over Frank's role as president of the Co-op. Members voted for the family's honesty.

The earliest cooperatives date from the first days of the Industrial Revolution in Europe. As workers migrated from farm to city, they had to rely on groceries to feed their families, since they no longer had acreage to feed themselves. Many decided to pool their money and purchase groceries together at a discount. These "consumer co-ops" served as models for American farmers who pooled resources to make joint purchases of equipment, feed, tools, seed, and other supplies. Some of these became "producer co-ops" by also seeing to marketing, helping farmers obtain the best price for their crops. The first seafood co-ops performed both these functions—buying cheaper supplies like fuel and bait while selling the harvest in bulk at a better price than the lone fisherman could negotiate for himself. In return, the wholesale buyer gained a steady, dependable supply. Established in 1948, the Stonington Co-op is owned and democratically controlled by its worker-owners. A board of directors is elected by the members. Before Jason took the reins, Frank had been president for most of the past twenty years.

The Co-op has pursued various side ventures over the years, dabbling in scallops, mussels, finfish, crabmeat, shrimp, clams, and Irish sea moss, but has always returned to its core business: lobster. In addition to diesel fuel, the main commodity that fishermen buy here is bait—frozen and salted herring, menhaden, and redfish. A captain's purchases are simply deducted from his catch. It's all written down in the company's books. Today, with over eighty active members, the Stonington Co-op, selling in excess of six million pounds per year, is the largest of Maine's dozen or so lobster co-ops.

The Garbo eighteen-wheeler rolls into the Co-op wharf at seven o'clock sharp. Danny, the truck driver, backs up so that the tailgate is directly beneath the back end of the conveyor. Like an airport baggage carrier, the conveyor will lift the crates—in this case, out of the water—and deliver them to the truck. The crew of six swiftly falls into action, the next step in shuttling lobster from dock to dinner plate.

Ron Trundy stands on the float, directing crate traffic with a boat hook. Two of his wharf rats are in a skiff, untying a boxcar so the first crate can ascend the one-hundred-foot-long conveyor. Crates float easily into position. Then they're off. Once the train of crates is under way, it takes less than thirty seconds for each crate to be ferried into the truck. Poochie and his two rats, standing inside the truck, are nearly overwhelmed, stacking the crates as fast as they come off the rollers. It takes forty-five minutes to load the ninety-four crates.

Ron yells, "That's all the new shell," meaning the shedders are loaded.

"All right, fellas," says Poochie to his rats, "you can relax."

"The children are barely out of breath," says Danny, the Garbo driver.

"That was a slick operation," says Ron. "Four and a quarter tons of hardening shedders in less than fifty minutes. We'll see even more lobsters today at Co-op Two." The newer facility is the Co-op's second buying station in downtown Stonington.

In the early summer, the main Co-op has the most boats (landing the majority of the Co-op's lobsters), since they're working the eastern bay, or Jericho, where shedders arrive first. Later in summer and fall, Co-op II has the majority of boats working the western bay.

Today, Co-op II delivers 124 crates, or five and a half tons of lobster. The truck's capacity is eighteen tons, so with nine and three-quarter tons today, Danny is carrying a half load.

The drive to Hancock, Maine, the lobsters' first stop, takes less than an hour, so the truck is not refrigerated. No need to ice the crates down. (On longer legs of their journey, the lobsters will be bathed in crushed ice.) An enormous storage and distribution facility awaits them in Hancock. They are graded for size and quality—hardiness, that is. Sorters determine if a given lobster likely has the stamina for a long plane ride, halfway around the globe. The lobsters must arrive alive and kicking. Any excess select and hard-shell lobsters not already bound for local restaurants are measured, too. These will fetch a premium price in Beijing.

Once sorted by size and shell type, all are weighed. Then they are placed in a large storage pool of salt water, chilled to 38° F. This frigid bath retards the instinct to feed or to prey on one another. At this point, Co-op lobsters have been mixed with lobsters from other deliveries. Further travel has been scheduled. For lobster, Hancock is Grand Central Terminal, and Garbo Lobster is the largest lobster travel agent in Maine.

Within hours or days, Co-op lobsters are farmed out to three destinations: Groton (Connecticut), Canada, or Prospect Harbor (Maine). The Connecticut facility serves as a cargo lounge for JFK airport. Lobsters bathe in another frigid pool, awaiting their flights to Europe or Asia. Meanwhile, the Canada-bound crustaceans endure several hours in a truck before arriving at a processing plant in Deer Island, New Brunswick. Until recently, 70 percent of Maine lobster was trucked to Canada for processing. Construction of new lobster plants in Maine in just the past six years has increased domestic capacity to the extent that this figure is closer to 60 percent. One of these new facilities is in Prospect Harbor, just twenty miles from Hancock.

A thirty-foot-tall wooden lobsterman, wearing a yellow sou'wester hat and oilskins, clutching an outsize lobster trap, announces the processing plant in Prospect Harbor. The facility, called Maine Fair Trade Lobster, is a joint venture of Garbo Lobster and East Coast Seafood, based in Lynn, Massachusetts. Forum Capital is a third financial backer. The oversize sign once depicted a sardine fisherman, but the sardine factory went bust. The new owners, having painted over the sardines, are hoping for better luck.

Fair Trade has been operating since 2013. It expects to process more than nine million pounds this year (2018), a 15 percent increase in production. To realize this, they are expanding their workforce from 150 to 225 employees. Prospect Harbor is a tiny village, so they are building worker housing on a hill overlooking the plant, just like the mining boomtowns of old.

Dave Garbo, president of Garbo Lobster, said recently, "A key component of our [expansion] plan includes strengthening our existing vertical network." Garbo and East Coast Seafood have a combined purchasing reach of thirty million pounds of lobster, one-fourth the current Maine yield. And they're growing. In the seafood business, vertical integration means owning operations from dockside buyers to processors to distribution networks—from sea to the supermarket shelf. The Garbo–East Coast venture does not own boats—in the United States at least—or stock in Whole Foods, but they have a piece of everything else.

All aspects of the venture are bigger than life. The giant lobsterman outside the facility is emblematic. The 100,000-square-foot plant originally processed sardines, a cannery founded by E. T. Russell & Co. in 1906. After nearly one hundred years of operation, Bumble Bee Foods acquired the plant in 2004, only to close the cannery in 2010, the last sardine factory to shut its doors in the United States. Bumble Bee sold the facility to Live Lobster in 2010, but the start-up went bust in 2012. At that point, Garbo and East Coast Seafood purchased the huge corrugated-steel building for $900,000 in September 2012 and began processing lobsters the following year.

The cooperative effort between the two seafood companies took many observers by surprise. The pair are rivals for market share in the lobster industry. So the collaboration seemed as far-fetched as the thought of Coke and Pepsi getting into bed together. Yet a few point to a shrewd maneuver: Together, they will control more of the dock-to-dinner-table chain. Moreover, the industry has been rocked lately by wide swings in supplies and prices. "The marriage will cut waste and reduce overlap," said Mike Tourkistas, president of East Coast Seafood, recently, "saving money for both of us in the long run."

On the day I arrive at Maine Free Trade Lobster, two Garbo eighteen-wheel trucks roll into the parking lot. Around back, workers unload a third semitruck under the cover of a roofed bay. They are in a hurry. Seventeen thousand lobsters must be resubmerged in seawater before they expire.

The challenge of moving lobster has always been that the lobster must be alive when it gets to the kitchen. Otherwise, the decaying muscle tissue exudes toxins that can make a human sick. For this reason, boats with water tanks, called "smacks," still crisscross Penobscot Bay. Yet, today, lobsters are mostly transported to market by trucks. The trucks sometimes carry ice on their crates, but always a ticking clock.

I was first introduced to the processing at Prospect Harbor via a company video. Garbo is too cautious to allow observers. The operation is pretty much the same throughout Maine. From the receiving area, workers wheel the lobsters—still in their plastic crates, ninety pounds at a time—on dollies to the holding tanks. Four tanks can hold 100,000 pounds each—a ten-day backlog. Each tank is a shallow pool, the size of a large swimming pool. Gray and blue crates float in the pools, half-submerged, covered with crushed ice to keep the lobsters comfortable.

As needed, crates are extracted from the tanks and taken to the grading area, where large lobsters (over one-and-a-half pounds) are separated from chicken lobsters (one-pound size). Shedders are segregated from hard-shell lobsters. Then, according to the kind and intensity of the pending wholesale orders, the lobsters are either cooked or shucked raw. While most orders are typically placed for cooked and picked meat, there is a growing market for raw produce, particularly tails, sold in grocery stores—often for grilling. Raw claw meat is sometimes sautéed for gourmet dishes, like seafood ravioli. The nonlive-lobster trade exceeds $250 million in the United States.

Processing is the often forgotten link in the chain from dock to dinner table. First, lobsters are cooked in huge steamers—twelve minutes for each one. All the hues of thousands of varicolored shells turn bright red.

Scientists have been hard put to explain the chemistry beneath this mysterious change in color. Only recently, a team from the University of Manchester (UK) may have deciphered its alchemy. They discovered a chemical called astaxanthin, which has a red hue that is located in both raw and cooked lobsters. However, in raw lobsters, the redness of astaxanthin is obscured by the dark blue color of crustacyanin, another chemical present in the shell. When we cook a lobster, the blue crustacyanin molecules become denatured, losing parts of their chemical structure. This permits the red astaxanthin to radiate through. The morphing color of a lobster shell, it turns out, is related to the changing colors of autumn leaves. Summer leaves harbor the pigments that make them red and orange, but those bright pigments are masked by the green color of chlorophyll. Only in autumn does the chlorophyll wane enough to make the red pigments visible. Lobsters are the maple leaves of the seas.

After cooking, the lobster meat is picked by a line of workers in white coats and hairnets. They have a curious term for the picking: They say they're "making mincemeat." In its classical definition, mincemeat is a fruit and meat filling for pies, but the British speak of "making mincemeat" as cutting meat into little pieces. Indeed, lobster is often reduced to bite-size morsels.

Whole tails and mincemeat, once cooked and cooled, are set in

Styrofoam trays, wrapped in plastic, and frozen. The freezing allows transportation of the produce over long distances, as far as California and overseas. Before freezing and canning were invented, lobster customers were restricted to New Englanders. It was essentially a live-lobster trade within the radius of a truck ride. Today, jet transport has broadened the live trade, as well. Lobsters can just barely survive the thirty-six-hour combined flights and layovers to Hong Kong or Seoul.

But I'm getting ahead of the game. Back to the frozen lobster at Prospect Harbor: Once placed in appropriate packaging, the tails and claws are stacked in freezers. Now they are reliant upon refrigeration for the rest of their journey.

The roster of frozen lobster products shipped from Prospect Harbor is considered to be proprietary information by East Coast Seafood. However, it is safe to assume the items are similar to what East Coast produces at its Paturel plant in Deer Island, New Brunswick, including cooked whole lobsters, frozen (and raw) tails, cocktail claws, and vacuum-sealed picked lobster meat. *The Ellsworth American,* the closest daily newspaper to Prospect Harbor and Stonington, reports that Maine Fair Trade's customers include Costco and Legal Seafood. Frozen lobster is on the verge of entering the market in China, as well.

Meanwhile, from Groton's holding tanks, live whole lobsters are already being shipped out of JFK airport to Asian destinations. Commerce by airfreight has become commonplace for not only Garbo and East Coast Seafood but also Calendar Island Lobster, Ready Seafood, and Stonington's biggest dealer, Greenhead Lobster. They all compete intensely, with minimal transparency and maximal distrust, but a few owners like Hugh Reynolds of Greenhead are forthcoming when discussing their greatest passion—lobsters.

Hugh is not a native of Stonington but has a loyal following of 110 lobster boats, about one-third of the town's fleet. "The best margin is the live trade," he says, explaining why Greenhead trades exclusively in live whole lobsters. He does not dabble in frozen product, other than eventual sales from his excess stock, which he sends to processors in New Brunswick. "Live lobster has half the market share, both domestically and for export," he continues. "It's growing all the time." Between 2007

Frank Gotwals, Stonington lobsterman and captain of the *Seasong,* holds a two-pound lobster, known as a "select." In 2016, Maine lobstermen caught more than 130 million pounds of lobster, totaling more than $533 million dockside. That harvest is six times the typical catch from the 1980s, an enigma that scientists are trying to solve. *(Photograph © Donna K. Grosvenor)*

The lobster fleet moors off Stonington Harbor in winter. *(Photograph © Julie Eaton)*

In summer, a lobster bake attracts everyone in town. *(Photograph © Robert F. Bukaty/AP)*

A lobster boat, laden with traps, passes by sea cliffs on Monhegan Island. *(Photograph © Peter Ralston)*

A sternman tosses back a small lobster, called a "short," as part of the conservation efforts of the Maine lobster fleet. *(Photograph © Robert F. Bukaty/AP)*

Frank Gotwals, sixty-two, strumming one of his folk songs at the Church of the Morning After. *(Photograph © Donna K. Grosvenor)*

The rest of the band, led by lobsterman Steve Robbins, playing their favorites at the same venue. *(Photograph © Donna K. Grosvenor)*

Jason McDonald, forty-four, stepson of Frank Gotwals, selling the day's catch, nearly a thousand pounds. The claws of each lobster are protected with a rubber band. *(Photograph © Donna K. Grosvenor)*

Julie and Sid Eaton, at fifty-four and seventy-four years, respectively, are the senior husband and wife lobster captains in Stonington at the helms of *Cat Sass* and *Kimberly Belle. (Photograph © Donna K. Grosvenor)*

A lobster boat arrives at the Great Bait Shack in the early hours of the morning to load up with herring, the most common lobster bait in Maine. Each captain uses three hundred or more pounds of bait each day. *(Photograph © Peter Ralston)*

A dockhand maneuvers a load of herring into place. *(Photograph © Peter Ralston)*

After weighing the day's catch, lobsters are placed in crates, called "cars," which are semisubmerged in water to keep the lobsters wet, cool, and oxygenated. The next day, trucks will whisk the lobsters off to airports or processors. (*Photograph © Donna K. Grosvenor*)

Alyssa LaPointe, sternman on *Seasong*, sorts lobsters into crates of shedders (new-shell), hard-shells, and large selects. (*Photograph © Donna K. Grosvenor*)

Jill McDonald, nine, hoists a lobster of five pounds, a record for her father's *Seahawk*. Now fifteen, she remembers saying of the lobster, "Wow, that's big!" Today, Jill sterns for her father in the summer. Despite the reserve of large lobsters and females in the Gulf of Maine, scientists predict the current boom will likely go bust in the next few years. (*Photograph © Jason McDonald*)

and 2016, Maine lobster exports jumped 175 percent, from $145 million to $397.8 million.

"Our biggest markets are Italy, France, China, and South Korea," says Hugh. "There was a time we only sold to Europe."

The growth of lobster exports to China has been especially impressive. Sales to China climbed from zero in 2007 to $40.9 million in 2016. Sales to South Korea jumped from two million dollars in 2012 to fifteen million dollars in 2016. These two countries lead the Asian stampede, a full 14 percent of all exports.

"The export demand has definitely shifted from the traditional market in Europe to Asia," says Hugh, who started selling lobsters to China in 2009. The demand is fueled by China's expanding middle class and a new free trade agreement with South Korea. Red (as in the hue of a boiled lobster) is a lucky color for both countries. Thus, live lobster is the number-one choice for celebrating weddings or New Year's.

"Getting them there is the tricky part," says Hugh. "I would say that keeping the lobsters alive for a twelve-thousand-mile flight to Shanghai is my biggest challenge in this business. I'll tell you there's nothing worse than getting a call that we have forty thousand pounds of live lobster on the hot tarmac in Dubai—a delay on the way to Singapore—and it's one hundred and twenty degrees Fahrenheit in the shade. That's when I sweat a little."

The worst fear of every dealer is "shrinkage," or loss of lobster. The Chinese customers, for one, like to keep the deaths from the rigors of travel to under 5 percent of the shipment. Each stage of transport is a race against the stopwatch.

Back at the Stonington Co-op, I am in time for the first boat to "put out," or off-load her lobster, for the afternoon. Early to bed, early to rise, first to come in. Jason McDonald steers *Seahawk* in a wide arc, bringing her gently alongside the float. Poochie catches the two lines tossed by Jason and Kit, then passes two crates to them to begin the weighing process. All routine, performed in silence like long-practiced mime.

But a shrill voice suddenly cuts through the quiet. "Daddy," calls

Jason's thirteen-year-old daughter, Jillian, from the ramp. Her sister Adeline, fifteen and less blond, follows closely. Behind them are two girl-friends about the same ages. Middle-school brunettes. The companions carry two white bags, each imprinted with a red lobster.

Poochie says to the girlfriends, "So you wanna buy some lobster?"

"Yes," says their father, Charles, traipsing slightly behind. "How much?"

"Only five dollars and fifty cents per pound," says Poochie, holding up two pound-and-a-half lobsters. "These will cost you eight dollars and twenty-five cents each."

"Lobsters are so cheap, they may lose their cachet," says Charles.

"Cheap enough to feed prisoners four times a week," says Poochie.

"Well, lock me up," says the girls' father. "Make it five times a week and you can throw away the key."

"I can see the headline," says Poochie. "'Demand in Jail Climbs Forty Percent.'"

"I guess I'll have to haul some more traps in the morning to keep pace," says Jason from his boat.

"Daddy," says Jillian, "you were going anyway. Soon I'll be able to go with you, too, right?"

"I'll be your sternman," says Adeline.

"Of course, you'll both be captains someday."

The men smile. The chance of succession has doubled with the ascension of daughters—to become lobstermen.

The four girls walk up the ramp, two with live lobsters, two carrying their dreams.

6

Lobster Wars

At ten o'clock on a November morning, Stonington Harbor is quiet. The silence runs from bank to bank, wharf to wharf, as if the majority of captains had overslept. A few boats motored to the lobster grounds at dawn, then quit, returning home. At least two hundred boats now sit idle, their engines silent. A northeast wind has dragged the tethered boats southwest of their moorings, a conspiracy of near unanimous consent.

Captains and crew have retreated to the Harbor Café for their third cup of coffee of the day. But not to discuss strategy. The tie-up, an unofficial strike, will send a clear message to the lobster dealers: Offer a better price for our catch or we won't fish. Words are unnecessary. What's more, they're a little dangerous. The federal court put a gag order on Maine lobstermen sixty years ago, a story Julie Eaton would eventually share. A federal consent decree demands compliance. Whenever fishermen gather, such as at the monthly board meeting of the Maine Lobstermen's Association (MLA), they cannot discuss prices or any hint of rebellion or coercion against dealers. In public, they've been silenced. In private, however, lobstermen suspect buyers themselves of price-fixing all the time. Meanwhile, dealers distrust lobstermen. Like kids on a scrimmage line, the accusations go back and forth. Only recently is it coming to a truce.

Julie Eaton sniffs, fighting back a persistent cold, and tastes her

French toast. She leaves her bacon till the end. She coughs and worries she may have pneumonia. She sips her tea, an herbal remedy. Due to her ailment, Julie missed most of last week. She acknowledges that there are a few Eaton family boats idle today, but she will not say any more on the subject.

Ever buoyant, Julie does have another story to tell. "Chris," she says, "I always told you the Eatons were the largest family on this island. Well, it's not true. Sid corrected me just the other day. It's the Head family, clearly the biggest. We were driving around in his truck, and each pickup we passed, I asked, 'Who's that?'

"Sid says, 'Oh, that's Shit Head.' I think, What an unfortunate name. Another pickup comes by, and I ask, 'Who's that?'

"Sid says, 'Oh, that's Fuck Head,' And it goes on like that all afternoon. Shit Head, Fuck Head, Mother-F Head . . . I counted fifteen members of the Head family that way and never left the truck."

Julie Eaton is outspoken this morning, as always, but not about the tie-up. All over Maine, lobstermen are mute about prices. Besides the Harbor Café, I already tried my luck at the MLA board meeting in Belfast the week before. I arrived at Darby's Restaurant in Belfast in time to take in the spectacular view of upper Penobscot Bay, while the board members began trickling into the private meeting room. The conference table was shaped like a horseshoe. At the head, Dave Cousens, MLA president, and executive director Patrice McCarron held court. On either arm of the horseshoe, lobstermen Genevieve McDonald and John Williams (Sid Eaton's nephew) represented Stonington. Twelve other board members filled the ranks.

Dave Cousens, late sixties but still blond, welcomed the board but made no acknowledgment of any price crisis. Instead Patrice McCarron introduced Kathy Mills, a guest speaker and scientist from the Gulf of Maine Research Institute. The GMRI had recently initiated a lobster-forecasting project to predict when, in a given year, the first shed would appear in summer. By utilizing water temperature data, Kathy explained, a computer model pinpoints that date for the entire Gulf of Maine. There was much skepticism in the room.

"What's the purpose of this?" asked John Williams, a large man of big appetites. He had dark hair and a ruddy complexion—*weather-beaten* is the word. "As fishermen," he continued, "we're already good at predicting the shed. And if we're wrong, it doesn't matter."

"Our goal," said Kathy, "is to enable the industry to be more prepared for the coming lobster season with advance notice of its expected timing."

"The forecasting is most useful for extremes," added Patrice, shepherding her two small children to a corner table. "In 2012, it would have been helpful if we could have prepared for the big early catches. As it was, the buyers couldn't move the product."

Patrice then warned Kathy about using the forecasting tool as a predictor of price in the marketplace. Ever cautious about discussions of money, she urged the GMRI to focus on volume and timing.

Even with the admonition, there was more dissent among the troops.

"You say this is a tool for fishermen," said Genevieve, "but you're telling us what we already know. It's really just a tool for scientists—an average shed for all of Maine. But we work locally."

"The shed may have happened during the week of July tenth to seventeenth in eastern Penobscot Bay," says Cousens, "but it was two weeks later in Beal's Island. In Thomaston, where I live, the shed has always been July seventeenth to twentieth. That's typical. You need to break the forecast into three regions. Make a computer model for Down East, Mid-Coast, and Southern Maine."

Kathy promised to take everyone's suggestions back to her boss in Portland. At the mention of the big city, so far "away" from Belfast, a few eyes rolled around the room.

Dave Cousens shifted the conversation to child labor laws, the second item on the agenda. "The U.S. Department of Labor is suddenly scrutinizing the Apprenticeship Program," he said, "after a storm off Matinicus Island claimed the life of a fifteen-year-old sternman."

In 2014, on the first Saturday of November, Captain Christopher Hutchinson and two crewmen were on their way back to port after hauling traps, when winds and seas grew fierce, prompting the forty-five-foot *No Limits* to flip. Hutchinson managed to climb out of the inverted wheelhouse and swim to the surface, but Tyler Sawyer, the young teenager, and his costernman, Tom Hammond, twenty-seven, disappeared under ten-foot waves. The emergency position indicating radio beacon (EPIRB) and life raft popped to the surface. The captain kept yelling for Tyler and Tom, but when the Coast Guard helicopter arrived, they were nowhere to be found.

Tyler Sawyer had dropped out of high school that fall, but child labor laws still applied. On school days, fourteen- and fifteen-year-olds can work for only three hours; they can work eight hours on nonschool days. In any case, Captain Hutchinson had been employing the boy for over ten hours. Hutchinson was fined sixty thousand dollars, but the fallout from the tragedy had cast a wider net. Teenagers must start the three-year Apprenticeship Program at fifteen in order to acquire their captain's licenses by eighteen. Twelve-hour days are not uncommon. Apparently, the Department of Labor had never noticed that fact before. There's the rub: One of the most successful fishermen's programs in Maine—apprenticeship—is now in jeopardy.

"We'll keep an eye on this," Cousens said, "and keep you posted. The case is compounded by the fact that the captain, who had marijuana and oxycodone in his bloodstream, is now charged with two counts of manslaughter. Now we turn to the bait situation. It's a mess, too. We only have enough herring fish for a couple more weeks. And it's getting scarcer."

What's more, the shortage had driven the bait price up nine dollars a bushel. The problem began when one of the herring-management areas off the coast, known as Area 1A, was expected to exceed its catch quota for June to September, a limit of fifty million pounds. As a result, the National Marine Fisheries Service (NMFS) closed the fishery in that area in early September. The temporary shortfall elevated the bait price for dealers and fishermen alike. Fishing continued in areas farther offshore, but that didn't help. Tapping other sources required trucking frozen herring from Canada and Massachusetts. Wherever lobstermen turned, the price was higher. A forty-dollar bushel was suddenly close to sixty.

The boardroom erupted into epithets, a unified dissent.

"What is the lobster fishery without fucking bait?" said Genevieve. "It's nothing."

"What is a damn fishery without lobstermen?" John Williams asked, rhetorically. "We can only operate with reasonable costs."

But no one mentioned dealers, the ones who sell the bait, the third spoke in the wheel. Instead, the meeting wound down. Prices—of both bait and lobster—were on everyone's lips, but no one was breathing a word.

Herring is still on the lobstermen's minds the next Monday at the Harbor Café. Julie finishes her bacon and, though avoiding discussion of the tie-up, tells the rest of the bait story.

"It seems a computer glitch at the—you guessed it—National Marine Fisheries Service led operators to miscalculate the quota," she says. "That caused an abrupt cap on herring fishing with no warning at all. That's why bait prices spiked all over Maine." Julie takes a long drag on her herbal tea. "Too bad we cannot sue NMFS for the difference."

"It's a domino effect," says our waitress, Judy, a lobsterman's wife and thus one of the most informed and opinionated people in the room. "Costly bait jacks up my husband's overhead. That's less for groceries at home. But that doesn't mean dealers will raise the lobster price. The lobstermen get squeezed."

"Meanwhile," says Julie, "herring is in such short supply, so says the computer, that we'll be baiting our traps with seabirds by the end of the week."

"I'll tell you what," says Judy, "if you want to know why nobody at the Maine Lobstermen's Association will talk about dealers and prices, just track down the consent decree from federal court. The year was 1958, I think."

The story began a couple of years before that. In 1956, a group of lobstermen from Vinalhaven banded together to form the fledgling MLA. The initial purpose of the organization was to bargain with wholesale dealers who had set prices for lobster at dockside. The relationship between lobster catchers and dealers had long been based on distrust. While the dockside price, or "boat price," as it is sometimes known, supposedly followed the laws of the marketplace, lobstermen long suspected buyers of "setting" the price tag on a whim—that is, fixing the price. For generations, lobstermen had been at the mercy of arbitrary dockside prices—often below a living wage. The wholesale buyers, it was alleged, took more than their fair share. Yet the U.S. Department of Justice did not initially go after the dealers for price-fixing, a violation of the Sherman Antitrust Act. (Section 1 of the act pertains to conspiracies in restraint of trade, which include manipulation of price in the marketplace.) Instead, when the MLA organized a strike of eight hundred lobstermen up and down the Maine coast in 1957, government prosecutors came after the lobstermen, the little guys. All for an attempted ten-cent hike in the price of lobster.

The problem was that the MLA did not simply negotiate with buyers over a *daily* price while they were striking. They demanded a permanent *minimum* price of thirty-five cents per pound. (In those days, lobstermen often received as little as twenty-five cents per pound.) That threw up a flare. Furthermore, when promoting the strike, the MLA threatened violence against dissenting fishermen—violence against bodies, boats, and gear—reminiscent of the bullying of scabs in the film *On the Waterfront*. These tactics inevitably placed lobstermen on a collision course with the Justice Department.

The 1957 strike did not succeed, but the mere acts of revolt and intimidation brought the government case swiftly upon the lobstermen. On August 9, 1957, the day the strike ended, four Justice Department attorneys from New York began interviewing lobster dealers and lobstermen in Portland. Within two months, they indicted the MLA and Leslie Dyer, its president, for conspiracy "to fix, stabilize and maintain the prices for live Maine lobsters in unreasonable restraint of interstate trade and commerce. . . ." The federal attorneys far outnumbered the defense attorneys. Meanwhile, the press and public opinion were overwhelmingly in favor of the lobstermen.

The Portland trial was well attended. John J. Galgay, the lead antitrust attorney, revealed to the press that he didn't like the taste of lobster, which did not help his standing with the public. Nonetheless, the trial proceeded. After five months and hundreds of witnesses, many of whom admitted to seeking a minimum price, the judge instructed the jury: "You need to decide whether the [strike] last summer was the result of a mutual agreement to refrain from hauling traps until a better price could be obtained; or whether the [strike] represented individual actions, individually arrived at by each individual concerned."

In other words, were the parties responsible for an organized strike, created to influence and tamper with prices?

After four hours, the jury returned with their verdict: "Guilty."

Fines of five thousand dollars and one thousand dollars against the MLA and Leslie Dyer, respectively, were handed down with a flourish, then suspended by the judge. Leslie Dyer delivered a case of live lobsters to federal attorney John Galgay, in thanks. Galgay, though known as unflappable, not bribable, and unacquainted with seafood, accepted the gift. Perhaps the trial had given Galgay a taste for lobsters after all.

Of lasting value has been the consent decree that the judge wrote at the conclusion of the trial. In it, the MLA was instructed to limit the scope of its mandate, restricting its organization to that of a cooperative, rather than a trade group. For fifty-six years, the MLA could not advocate on behalf of its twelve hundred members. No lobbying the state legislature. No negotiating with lobster dealers to influence supply or price. The organization has been still in the water, unable to reach out to either shore—governmental or commercial.

Yet, in reversing the judgment recently, Judge Brock Hornby called the consent decree "outdated" in U.S. District Court in Portland. Mary Ann Mason, attorney for the MLA, said the decree had outlived its purpose and was no longer needed to protect market competition. The MLA is now free to reorganize as a nonprofit trade association that can lobby for issues such as a state lobster-management plan.

The fear of God, however, is more than skin-deep. Even with the repeal of the consent decree, the MLA has signaled its intention not to engage in discussions about price. "We do not fish for lobsters; lobstermen do. We do not buy lobsters; dealers do. We really have no involvement in [price] issues at all," says Patrice McCarron. The lobstermen see no daylight in a return match with the feds.

On Tuesday, the stragglers in the Stonington fleet return to work. The small boats try the inshore waters one more time. Julie and Genevieve tend their traps on either side of East Penobscot Bay. The midsize boats haul in deeper waters outside Spoon Island. Frank and Jason hit some lobsters that have migrated there. The biggest boats, like John Williams's forty-five-foot *Khristy Michelle,* head for the wide-open ocean and strike it rich there, as well.

It is not clear whether Monday's protest had been heard. Yet the dealers raised the lobster price by ten cents per pound today, not a paltry sum. The increase could have been stimulated by the shortage of bait, a curtailment in the supply of lobsters, a pulse in demand, or other market forces. Or by the silent fleet. Whatever the cause, lobstermen welcome the new rate. For a lobsterman who lands 150,000 pounds, the ten-cent hike amounts to fifteen thousand dollars more in his pocket. Dimes add up.

Shortly afterward, the MLA released an "Antitrust Policy Statement," in anticipation of the Justice Department lifting the 1958 consent decree. The statement, in part, reads:

> *It is the policy of the "MLA" to comply fully with both the letter and spirit of all federal and state antitrust laws . . . because antitrust violation can have serious consequences. . . . In particular, members are reminded it is inappropriate . . . to engage in communications or conduct that could lead to . . . an agreement on the price . . . of lobster landings, except with respect to the business of an individual cooperative.*

So, even with the judge lifting the ban on lobbying the government, the MLA and its members must have zero tolerance with regard to influencing the market. In fear of consequences, no one seems to be demanding that dealers meet the same standard.

"Communications or conduct," of course, means not talking and not tying up. Yet there is plenty of precedent for not showing up at work in protest. You just cannot organize it or discuss it. A tie-up must be magically spontaneous. Just do not claim it is your idea. Most important of all, you cannot refer to it as a "strike." When prices fell to $1.25 a pound in 2012, 70 percent below normal, roughly two hundred boats sat out the week in Friendship, Maine. They said they were "idle," not that it was a strike.

Earlier, in 1988, fishermen staged a tie-up in Tenants Harbor for ten days in hopes of raising the price from $2.10 per pound to $2.25, the level enjoyed by lobstermen north and south of St. George. The negotiations with dealers played out in the press. It worked, but with the Justice Department more vigilant now, that level of pricing pressure is a thing of the past. Or, at least, it has gone underground.

A separate proceeding in the MLA's encounter with the federal government dealt with the other side of the coin: price-fixing by dealers. Lobstermen presume the wholesalers call one another in the afternoon to set the daily price. In their words, the dealers "get their heads together."

During the MLA trial, the judge refused to allow lobstermen to use previous price-fixing by dealers as an excuse for their own indiscretions. But then the same judge brought five Portland lobster dealers to task. There were 125 major dealers in Maine at the time, far more than now, thanks to consolidation. The court prosecuted 4 percent of them. Four pleaded no contest and were fined. Fines ranged from $250, paid by John E. Willard, Jr., to $1,000, paid by Willard-Daggett Company, the latter a bargain for controlling the price of lobster. The Maine Lobster Company and Benson Lobster paid five hundred dollars each. The fifth dealer was acquitted. The press questioned whether the minimal fines would discourage price-fixing by dealers in the future. Thirty-five years later, in 1993, Les Dyer's son Bert was asked if price-fixing continues. "Hell, of course them dealers [are] price-fixing," he replied. "They still do."

More recently, in 2009, fifty lobstermen from Washington County sent a written complaint to Maine's attorney general, accusing local dealers of price-fixing. This was nothing new. Before and after the consent decree, lobstermen had accused buyers of colluding to set low boat prices in an effort to control the market. But this time, the lobstermen signed a written complaint. In response, the attorney general's office opened an investigation into the allegations.

The probe discovered that while dealers regularly pay less than three dollars dockside for a pound of lobster, the same product might retail for anywhere between ten and twenty-five dollars a pound. "Market forces aren't working," said one lobsterman. "The boat price is artificially low. Dealers talk amongst themselves and set the price. That's illegal. Allegedly. It violates the state's antitrust laws."

Several Washington County dealers were subpoenaed and required to submit their records. After several months of poring through ledgers, phone records, and emails, the Maine attorney general's office concluded that there was not enough evidence to prosecute anyone.

Four years later, in July 2013, angry lobstermen assembled at a state lobster forum in Ellsworth to voice the same protest. Patrick Keliher, Maine's Marine Resources commissioner, discouraged a formal complaint. He reminded the lobstermen that the 2009 investigation did not find any evidence of price-fixing. "Frankly," he said, "it's very difficult to prove."

Outright theft is easier. Robert Thompson, the dock manager of Spruce Head Fishermans Co-op, was arrested and accused of stealing more than one million dollars' worth of lobster from co-op members and selling them on the side to J. P.'s Shellfish. He had been the wharf manager for twenty years but did not have a seafood dealer's license. In December 2014, Thompson pleaded guilty in U.S. District Court to federal income tax evasion and to illegally selling lobsters. Later, he was sentenced to eight months in jail and $65,000 in restitution. The owner of J. P.'s Shellfish, who bought the illegal lobsters, received forty-five days and was fined $100,000.

Tensions between lobster harvesters and buyers will likely continue for the rest of the century, or until the lobsters run out. It's an open wound. Not surprisingly, the harvesters' distrust of dealers gives way to a general antipathy toward anyone in the lobster-distribution business—retailers and restaurants included. The Maine waterfront is colorful.

My partner, Donna, and I owe Julie and Sid a dinner—a return engagement—so we show up at Fisherman's Friend (recently renamed Stonecutters Kitchen), the local seafood emporium, at five o'clock sharp.

Outside the restaurant is a hand-lettered sign in red and black:

NATIONAL MARINE FISHERIES SERVICE

DESTROYING FISHERMEN AND THEIR FAMILIES

SINCE 1976

On the way into town, Julie and Sid stopped off at Buxton Boatyard, where Frank's *Seasong* and Jason's *Seahawk* had been built. Julie handed over some of her photographs of *Seasong* under construction to Peter Buxton, the builder. Chitchat ensued, as it always does, so they are a little late getting to the restaurant.

At half past five, we assemble in the big dining room, which is anointed with lobster paintings and photographs.

Julie sits down, then stands up again. She is wound up like a watch. Sid and she have just finished pulling up their gear for the winter—a bittersweet five days and the last electrifying week of the year. Julie feels wired after operating her boat, the feel of the diesel engine vibrating through her body. She paces for a minute, makes no apologies, then sits down.

"We spend more time with our boats than with our spouses," says Sid. "Those workboats are our way to work, our livelihood, our constant companion, so it's no wonder we're finely attuned to them. I've got a grumpy boat right now, so I figure it's time to haul her for the winter."

The waitress, Kristen Hutchins, passes out menus, which Sid and Julie set aside. She pours water. Julie takes a deep swig to recharge her batteries, even though she has enough wattage to light up the room. "You can tell it's about over for the year," she says, "when we catch mostly selects, pistols, punched females. All week we caught everyone's leftovers— what they've caught once already and culled overboard."

"It's a case of diminishing returns," says Sid. "We put out more and more bait, but the shedders bury in the mud or migrate to deep water. Or just don't trap."

"So you're done?" asks Donna.

"Yep, time for Sam's Club." Julie explains how she and her husband stock up on groceries for the year. "Most of the restaurants close for the winter. Only one—Harbor Café—stays open, so I'm forced to cook. We drive our two pickups to Sam's Club in Ellsworth, an hour away, and spend three thousand dollars in one day. That fills our three freezers and our back room that's set up as a pantry. Sid used to shoot a buck, and then we'd have venison all winter. But he just feeds the deer now." Julie waves her menu at Sid. "Prime rib tonight?" she says, then turns back to us. "We also freeze a lot of our own lobster. Nothing like lobster chowder in January."

Kristen takes our orders. Two prime ribs—one medium, one well-done. Donna gives in to lobster scampi, and I buckle at the sight of steamed clams. The clams are sold at "market price"; Kristen promises to find out the price tag. Not surprisingly, fishermen do not order seafood in restaurants. They get it for free at home. Out on the town, it's red meat all the way down.

"So we go shopping on Monday," Julie continues, "when the aisles are fairly free for our six carts. Of course, we can only do this since the lobsters have been good to us this year. With a better dockside price, we could check out eight carts and never return till spring."

When the appetizer arrives—broiled mushrooms stuffed with crab—the conversation on prices switches to the Maine Lobstering Union. Julie Eaton was secretary/treasurer in 2013, during the union's inaugural year.

"We have six hundred and fifty members now," says Julie. "We never expected so big a turnout, so fast." Like the MLA's recruitment, the hefty union enrollment comes as a surprise to many: a collective groundswell from the ranks of self-reliant, independent lobstermen. Yet with fishermen now getting rock-bottom prices, they are adapting again.

In just a few years, the Maine Lobstering Union has racked up an impressive list of achievements—from outlawing lobsters caught by draggers (in some areas) to securing affordable insurance for members. In its first legislative season, the union drafted a law allowing military personnel to maintain their lobster licenses while on active duty.

"For the first time," says Julie, "we feel like we have a voice. For the first time, we can protect our way of life."

Others are mystified by the rapid ascent of the union, questioning whether a machinists' union should represent lobstermen. For its part, the MLA launched a campaign to question the union's agenda. Whom are they representing? What are they trying to do? "My frustration is they aren't answering the basic questions," says Patrice McCarron, the MLA's executive director. The union takes a big scoop out of the MLA's potential membership pool.

While the union must give a wide berth to the Sherman Antitrust Act, Julie suggests there may be measures it can take to protect the financial interests of its members. "We're the ones who catch the lobster," says union president Rocky Alley, "so we should be able to control the price. If we're united, you can't just beat us down with a low dollar."

At dinner, Julie shares with us one way union members might stabilize prices—by purchasing a buying station. In this way, the union would really act like a cooperative and perhaps be exempt from price-negotiating rules. The union captains would be selling their lobsters to a buyer they control and could share in the profits. The prospective location is on Mount Desert Island. The price: four million dollars, which the union can easily raise. The wholesale operation will ship live lobsters domestically and overseas. That places Julie more directly in the Chinese trade. "The move is going to change the lobster industry in Maine," she says.

At the most basic level, the quest to create a group that can champion the marketplace—legally or not—is a reaction to the price volatility brought on by climate change and other factors. In the future, ocean warming will affect our pocketbooks even more than now.

From my blind side, a man in his forties, looking like a pirate—bald and tattooed—approaches our table. More than just a friend of the Eatons, he introduces himself to Donna and me as Tony Bray, owner and chef of Fisherman's Friend. "That's Jonah crab in those mushrooms," he says. "A resurgent fishery since the ocean began to warm." We all agree it's tasty crab. Tony seems pleased. He invites me to step back to the kitchen.

I realize I've seen Tony before, at the helm of *Intuition,* one of the lobster boats at the Stonington Co-op. He and his wife, Katie, started the restaurant in 2002, but he could not give up lobstering, so he returned to the water. "By nature, I'm a fisherman," he tells me as we pass through the kitchen's swinging double doors, right next to the restaurant's bar. I'm overwhelmed by the aroma of melted butter and garlic. "I hauled two hundred traps today," he continues, "took a shower, and came to the restaurant to work lunch."

First stop on the kitchen tour is the walk-in refrigerator, just beyond the three Vulcan ranges. As big as a semi, the walk-in is where the lobsters are stored. Six crates are teeming with live crustaceans. Tony buys these wholesale from the Co-op at $4.50 per pound. Today's market price for a one-and-a-quarter-pound lobster at the restaurant is $22.50. Tony explains that this is a fourfold markup. He has a bigger margin on whole lobster than other dishes at the restaurant. The typical menu markup nationwide for an item is threefold.

With at least 325 patrons a day (up to 10,000 per month), Tony goes through a lot of lobster—at least a hundred whole lobsters a day. In addition, his prep staff picks a hundred pounds of lobster from the shell to make gourmet entrées. These dishes include Lobster Mediterranean (with summer vegetables), Lobster Pillows (in puff pastry), Lobster Alfredo (in cream sauce), Lobster Scampi (in garlic butter), Lobster Pie (in pastry crust), and Lazy Man's Lobster (a whole lobster picked for the patron). In all, Fisherman's Friend cooks lobster sixteen ways. The most popular is Lobster Mediterranean, thanks to the vegetables, olive oil, and feta cheese.

Tony says, "You should try our hard shedder." An oxymoron, it seems, this specialty is a shedder that appeared in July but wasn't caught until September, October, or November. Its shell has hardened somewhat but not completely. "That's when we get them—in the fall. The hard shedder is the best-tasting lobster of the year," he says.

I watch his main cook, Elizabeth Barbados, make Donna's lobster scampi. Heaped on the stainless-steel counter are seven ounces of lobster meat (the reward from picking a chicken lobster, just barely legal). Elizabeth, a native of Barbados, sautés the lobster meat in diced garlic and butter for two minutes, flipping the contents of the pan in the air halfway through. One more flip and it's done. The trick is to cook it minimally at low heat and, for the flipping, to have a supple wrist. She arranges the scampi on a bed of rice pilaf and—voilà—a legend is born.

Departing the kitchen, I run into Genevieve McDonald at the bar. She is visiting with some of her lobstermen friends, their voices high and their boasts louder. We chat for a moment. Then, looking across the room to our table, she says, "I see the union is out on the town tonight." Genevieve shakes her head. "Well, I'm outta here."

Just then, Kristen exits the kitchen with a huge platter poised on her fingertips. I follow Donna's scampi to the table. Next come the steamed clams and prime rib. Julie scans the table to her left, where two couples from New Jersey are digging into four large lobsters, brick red from steaming and accessorized with melted butter. Each lobster, they say, is a pound and a half and costs them twenty-six dollars, a point of pride for them—the highest price at the restaurant.

Julie turns back to us and mouths the words, "From away."

Sid adds, "We have a dealer here in Maine who is selling picked lobster meat for a hundred dollars a pound at his restaurant in Texas."

"Now," says Julie, picking up the story, "he's paying four dollars a pound for the lobsters. The lobster meat comes from perhaps three one-pound lobsters to produce that one pound of meat. So maybe it costs him twelve dollars for the lobster. What are his other costs? How much, exactly, does it cost to fly that lobster meat to Texas? Does it fly first-class? Whatever the cost is, it's not going to the lobstermen."

Julie cuts into her nicely marbled prime rib and takes her first bite. "Local restaurants are boosting the prices, too," she continues. "I'm not saying who, but there are several on this island. From four dollars at the dock, that local lobster is suddenly worth twenty-five dollars." She swallows and sips some water. "Come on now, how expensive are those baked potatoes? I can't see any other costs. Harbor Café only charges sixteen dollars for a lobster dinner, a fair price, but right across the street, they hit you for twenty-seven dollars, and no baked potato. No corn on the cob.

"That's not supporting the local fishermen, when restaurants pocket most of the profits. They're doing it up and down the coast. You've got a town full of people from away who come here to eat lobster. Why not make a little less, sell a little more?"

Sid urges Julie to stop talking and eat by aiming his fork and knife at her plate. He says, "There are two ways to make a profit: charging big prices and making one sale, or charging reasonable prices and making many sales. Seafood restaurants should try selling volume."

Julie has a couple of bites and is ready to jump back into the fight. "If the restaurants understood you could make more money," she says, collecting her thoughts, "if they saw you could get more people eating lobster by pricing a fifteen-dollar dinner, they'd still make a profit and their customers would come back for more."

Kristen appears, offering dessert, which we decline. She also has some bad news: "The market price of your clams doubled overnight to thirty-six dollars a pint." We are all stunned. Kristen tells the story.

"Steamers just hit an all-time high," she says. "And once they go higher, they never seem to back down. Clams are scarce, thanks to overharvest-ing, and demand is outstripping the catch."

"That's the law of supply and demand in action," says Sid, pushing away his empty plate. "Summer people want their clams and they're will-ing to pay for them."

"Fair competition is all we ask for," Julie says. "Fishermen selling and dealers keeping a fair share but not the whole store."

"We have enough competition at home," says Sid, merriment in his eyes. "No need for a battle at the buyers'. Two years ago, Julie beat me by five hundred pounds harvested—that's lobster—for the year."

"Yeah," she says, "but last year he beat me by a thousand pounds. Sid's my hero."

"She's come a long way. At the beginning, it was 'Don't mess with her—she's Sid Eaton's wife.' You know, I have a reputation. Then she earned her stripes, along with a few bruises. Now, it's 'Don't mess with her—she's Julie Eaton.'"

"I take it some people are criticizing the union," I say.

"What are they saying?"

"'A machinists' union has no experience in the lobster industry.'"

"Anything else?"

"Someone said, 'It would be foolish to give up a fisherman's indepen-dence to join a union with no background in the fishery.' I heard it at the bar tonight."

"Oh, her? Pay that no mind."

From our table, Julie scans the bar, now teeming with the second shift—the after-dinner crowd. Young lobstermen—millennials—building up courage to fish in the morning.

"You cannot drink like a fish," she says, "and expect to catch lobster. It's dangerous enough out there without the shakes."

Over coffee, Julie delivers the news of the day. The bait fiasco is old hat, but the tourists have made the gossip circles again, committing a priceless faux pas.

"The people from away," says Julie, "have complained about the foghorn from Mark Island Lighthouse, which, upon a certain wind, can be heard in town." The siren warns boats off Mark Island and the other islands, which are a hazard in the fog. "They want it turned off," she continues. "It must interfere with the music on their SUV stereos."

"How long has the lighthouse been there?" Donna asks.

"Since 1858," Julie says. "The lighthouse was blaring before the summer people arrived and it will be blaring long after they're gone."

As we exit the restaurant, Julie has a parting shot for people from away. "The flatlanders got it all wrong about lobstermen. We don't smell bad because we're lazy; we smell bad 'cause we work with fish all day."

Sid and Julie walk off to their truck and drive slowly home, slowly enough to recognize any of the Head family they might pass along the way.

Maybe I've gone native or the odor has saturated more than my clothes, but walking home tonight, I no longer smell the bait on the wharves or the rising tide.

7

Winter, Gulf of Maine

Come December, the weather in Maine turns temperamental, the opportunities for venturing to sea infrequent. Storms and surface ice allow entrance to the ocean only by a unique kind of lottery. On any given week, one day out of six may be calm enough to set sail. That leaves five weekdays ashore. So, with blustery winds at the top of the week—just before Christmas—it is not surprising that Frank Gotwals cancels each day through Thursday. Alyssa, his ace sternman, is happy to have the holiday time with her children. But come Friday morning, all bets are back on. The wind has subsided to ten knots. Frank and Alyssa and every lobsterman in Stonington rise with their boots on. Whatever the temperature, they're ready to go.

Nevertheless, December has been unusually mild, the twelfth month in a row of record high temperatures worldwide. Frank, who typically retires his boat for the season by Christmas, plans to continue lobstering into January if the weather holds up. Even with weekly winter storms, he may get in one lobstering day each week. The draw for him: In winter, lobster prices are at their highest.

At 4:30 A.M. sharp, Frank pulls his GMC pickup into the second parking lot beside my cottage on Pink Street. He has offered me a lift. While I gather my gloves and new boots in the dark, Frank talks to my neighbor, J.B., the bait fisherman. Only the gibbous moon illuminates their faces. From my front stairs, their voices are too distant to discern.

Afterward, in the truck, Frank says, "Good news: Herring supplies are back up. That should bring the price back down. I hate to have to stretch my bait."

When we reach the intersection of Pink and Main, I spy some activity around a school bus perched on the town fish pier. Sure enough, it is the Skippers Class from the local high school setting up their Sternmen's Olympics for the day, an annual rite of passage. The students will compete in a lobster-trap race and a banding contest to see who can seal the claws of ten lobsters the fastest. The competition will help prepare the teenagers in applying for their student lobster licenses this summer. Among them are Elliott Nevells, now fifteen, and Caleb Hardie, sixteen, who have eyes on lobstering as a future profession. Motivated like no others, they will tie in the trap race today.

We turn left, heading east toward the Co-op. I anguish over caffeine withdrawal. Frank sympathizes. He tells me he has time to stop at the store. For the holidays, it is lit up in green and red, like a Christmas tree. Three pickups are idling out front.

Adrienne, the remarkably thin girl of doughboy fame, unlocked the front door to the Harborview General Store at exactly 3:00 A.M., ushering in the first wave of customers. Ninety minutes later, Genevieve and Cory McDonald elbow their way in, followed closely by Jason McDonald, their cousin, but better known as Frank's stepson. Genevieve ambles to the back of the store to order a cold-cut submarine for her lunch six hours from now. She is crewing on a big winter boat; her small *Hello Darlin' II* is not hardy enough for winter lobstering. Cory stops short for a Styrofoam cup of coffee; he works for Billings Diesel all winter long. Jason muscles past him to get to the coffee machine first, pouring a rancid blend of thin "dark roast." On the water, anything hot tastes pretty good in late December. Caffeine is a plus.

Frank is still in his truck, speaking with Donna on his cell phone. She is just now rising to let out the dogs.

Lobstermen make way earlier in the winter. After November first, they can haul traps before sunrise. And the shorter days allow less time to haul in good light. These factors add up to an early start for any fisherman with ambition.

Two young bucks, barely twenty, march though the entrance and join Genevieve at the sandwich counter. She is turning thirty, so there is some affinity. One of the boys, Sawyer, says he just bought a new house. "I own the mothah-fuckah," he says.

"The bank owns part of it," says Genevieve.

"Not if I catch every lobster in this ocean," Sawyer says.

"Not if I catch 'em first," says his buddy, an acne-faced kid named Rex.

"Leave some for us," says Cory, who has strolled over to the counter, coffee in hand. "We all want the house on the hill."

"I'm planning on six hundred traps this summer," says Genevieve. "Up from four hundred last year. Next year, it'll be eight hundred. Then I can compete with the big boys. Buy myself a new truck."

"I've got a new truck," says Rex, selecting one of the ready-made submarines from the cooler. (Genevieve had hers custom-made.)

"I wanna buy a house when we're ready," says Genevieve now, bitten by the boys. "Renting is getting old."

"I'm taking it one step at a time," says Cory. "We have a pretty good life right now."

Finished with real estate for the day, the four millennials saunter out of the Harborview General Store, their subs and colas and coffees in tow.

By now, Frank has finished his call and is pouring a cup of dark roast. Jason looks on. "I've got something a little stronger on my boat," Frank says.

"Yeah, I've got some good Kenyan beans," Jason says.

"Well, you should try my Rwandan coffee from that roaster over near Blue Hill. It'll pop open your eyes in the morning."

Next to arrive at the coffee counter is John Williams, Sid Eaton's nephew and captain of the *Khristy Michelle,* a wooden boat of forty-five feet, capable of fishing in the open ocean—twenty-five miles out or more. Ever since the Maine Lobstermen's Association board meeting, John has slowly moved his gear, following the lobsters as they move toward deep overwintering sites in the ocean. Unlike Frank and Jason, who tend to work fewer traps in winter, John keeps pushing his gear to the maximum eight hundred traps.

When he sees Frank and Jason, fellow Co-op members, he decides to size up the competition.

"How many traps have you got, Jason?"

"I'm setting five hundred traps off Spoon Island, less than three miles out, down from eight hundred this past summer."

"I'm working four fifty or so," says Frank. "Deep water—three hundred feet. That's all I can get to in a week with this bad weather."

"If we all cut back thirty percent," says Jason, "we might lower the landings of lobsters and force up the price."

"Fat chance of anyone cutting back," says Frank.

"Fat chance is right," says John. "I'm still working seven hundred fifty traps. Seventy-five trawls of ten traps each. With my big boat—and three sternmen—I can turn them over in a day."

"I'm happy with fewer," says Jason. "I'll quit for the season next week anyways."

That winter abstention takes pressure off the fishery, too. The smaller boats do not drive hard through the winter. Surprisingly, the new, larger boats are owned by the younger crowd. Ocean lobstering is a young man's game.

Outside, the lobstermen mount their trucks for the three-minute drive to the Co-op. On the way, snowflakes fall on their windshields. The moon shines through the tumbling snow, giving the appearance of backlit lace. Ephemeral. The temperature is just above freezing. When the snowflakes touch the pavement, they vanish.

At the Co-op, Frank maneuvers *Seasong* from her mooring to the bait shack. She is second in line. Jason has already loaded up with herring and is now racing through the islands into Jericho Bay. Meanwhile, Frank and Alyssa order four crates of salted herring and pogies (menhaden), the latter a treat for the lobsters—like a T-bone for Frank's dogs. (A second sternman, required for deep water, is expected shortly.) The lobsters prefer the more expensive pogies, and they last longer in the trap. Never frozen, both herring and menhaden are considered "fresh bait," albeit an oxymoron appreciated only by lobstermen and their wives.

Poochie lowers four crates—three herring and one pogie—to the deck of *Seasong,* which, at low tide, sits ten feet below the station. Each crate holds a bushel and a half of fish. The bait is salted down to delay spoilage and can last a week out of the hot sun. Still, according to lobstermen, the fresher the better. For that reason, Frank always picks up his bait the morning of his haul. The freshest bait, if you can get it, can double your catch of lobsters.

The winch cries out, as if in pain. Each crate weighs 120 pounds and will service eighty traps. The herring costs forty to forty-five dollars per crate; in normal times, the pogies run five dollars more. Each has dropped twenty dollars from their highs during the bait shortage of October. Stocks have bounced back. The new surplus allows a savings of 30 percent, totaling thousands of dollars for the season.

If Maine is dependent on lobster, it is doubly dependent on herring. The source was once routine. Herring bits and chunks were obtained from the old sardine cannery at the end of Main Street. The cannery closed its doors in the 1970s. Since then, fishermen have actively netted herring. Since the demand for bait is easily ten times what it was in the old cannery days, heavy pressure bears down on the fishery. However, Frank is nonchalant about the inevitable shortages. He simply switches to different bait—pogies, redfish, tuna heads—all available for a price. Yet, by far, herring is the most popular.

Maine fishermen landed over 104 million pounds of Atlantic herring last year, valued at $16.3 million. Historically, about 70 percent of those fish are used for lobster bait. (The balance becomes canned or otherwise-edible fish—smoked, pickled, or salted.) On top of that 73 million pounds of herring bait, Maine lobstermen may buy out-of-state bait, as well. The New England herring landings double what is caught in Maine. Not surprisingly, Stonington is one of the largest herring ports in the state, ranking third after Portland and Rockland.

In Stonington, the largest purveyor of herring is J.B. Throughout the Northeast, herring is mostly caught with either midwater trawlers or purse seiners, which encircle a school of fish with a single net, then close off the bottom with a drawstring. A third method, employed by J.B., is to cut off a cove with a net and then reel them in. This shoreline method is called stop seining. Only purse seiners are allowed in federal waters (from three to two hundred miles offshore), where Frank will be baiting lobster traps with J.B.'s herring today.

Baiting complete, *Seasong* tears through the chop and snow, weaving through the islands of Jericho Bay. Frank's destination is twenty miles out in the Atlantic Ocean, in the middle of the Gulf of Maine. He stands at the helm, wedded to the wheel. The spokes seem to be an extension of his hand, like a bat to a slugger. His eyes are on the lookout for familiar ledges and rocks. In six months, I have never seen the captain peek at a marine chart of the islands. He knows his children's faces almost as well.

Despite the generous moon, the sea is still ebony black. Up ahead, the running lights of Jason's *Seahawk* give us some purchase on the night. Behind us, three other lobster boats have departed the Co-op—red and green, port and starboard, bow lights leading the way. The winter fleet is only a third the size of the summer fleet. Less than one hundred boats now work out of Stonington in December. With their smaller boats, Julie and Sid are tied up till spring.

Frank's *Seasong,* at thirty-eight feet, is a medium-size boat, but small in the spectrum of the winter fleet. By December, the lobsters have migrated from shore to ocean depths of three hundred to four hundred feet (where the water is relatively warm). Because of climate change, lobsters may be found even farther out than before. Seas are rougher on the open ocean, especially at this time of year. The lobster boats that follow them there tend to be the larger vessels, over forty feet. These boats can best withstand fierce winter storms and seas—what the lobstermen call "mad winter winds." They can also carry the necessary gear—traps and buoys and warps—to distances exceeding twenty-five miles from shore. To lobster beyond the three-mile state limit requires a special federal permit. Frank has one of these; Jason does not. For safety and convenience, Frank restricts his ocean exposure to twenty-five miles tops.

One of the larger boats, with a commensurate overcharged engine, steams past us now. It is the *Khristy Michelle,* the name framed in the stern lights, with John Williams at the helm. Seven feet is a big advantage in boating. The forty-five-foot boat is broader (beamier) than *Seasong,* too.

The formidable width will allow John to shift one hundred traps today from two hundred feet of water to a depth of four hundred feet, in search of a mother lode of lobsters. By contrast, Frank can move only eighty traps at a time. He also bucks wildly in the swells.

Just now, rounding Fog Island, the first spray catches Alyssa unawares. Luckily, she has already climbed into her oilskins, her yellow jacket with the hood up. A second sternman is below in the galley.

Passing Spoon Island, the last of the Jericho islands, Frank makes for open water. He flips on the GPS, which will take him to his first buoy, an hour away. The course is east-southeast. As he reaches federal waters, the three-mile line, the sun comes up. The snow ceases. Frank can now just barely see Spoon Island and Isle au Haut behind him. This tangible security will vanish in a matter of minutes. The commitment to the day is nearly complete.

Somewhere beyond the federal line, say fifteen miles out, all horizons become seamless: The sky fuses with the water, with land no longer in view. Later, Frank reminds me of André Gide's famous words: "If you want to discover new oceans, you must have the courage to lose sight of the shore."

Frank's first buoy is at mile twenty. When there are five miles to go, the captain breaks away from the helm to brew some coffee and to speak with Alyssa and Dan Larrabee, the second sternman, about the plan for the day. Dan, a native of Stonington, is twenty-five, tall, and thin. He could be Alyssa's twin. Frank steps below to microwave some water in the galley. Then, back at the wheel, he places two scoops of Rwandan coffee in his French press. Voilà: coffee for him and the crew.

Blowing the steam off his coffee mug, Frank pats the GPS plotter with his free hand. "We'll reach our first buoy in fifteen minutes or so."

"That was quick," says Alyssa. She sips her java carefully. With her hair in a ponytail, Alyssa looks especially fine today—pretty, or "cunning," as the lobstermen say.

"We made good time coming out of the harbor," says Frank. "No ice barricading us this month. Last year was a different story."

"Yeah, I could walk across the harbor last Christmas. And it wasn't 'cause of Jesus slippers."

During the winter of 2014–2015, the harbor surface froze into blocks of ice, permitting passage only when the wind was right—a land breeze.

Few mornings were suitable for lobstering, even though the ocean, if one could get to it, was always free of ice. The Gulf of Maine is too warm for freezing, except at the edges. Still, snow falling into the water dropped the temperature of the Gulf enough so that the lobster shed came two weeks late last summer. Stonington received over one hundred inches of snow the winter of the harbor freeze-up.

Maine winters can have other impacts on the coast, as well. Roads on Deer Isle can be nearly impassable. Transporting lobsters to market can be a trick. Even when the harbor is not choked with ice, the wharves and boat decks can be treacherous. Frozen lines are difficult to uncoil.

Yet the greatest nuisance to a buying station, such as the Co-op, is the ice forming around the lobster cars floating in the water. One story by Stevie Robbins's younger brother Brian has it that two fishermen—simple do and simple don't—had a go at an ice-encrusted lobster car with a maul and a hatchet. After a few minutes, they could barely open it. Next, they placed some bricks in the car to steady it and counteract the buoyancy of the ice. It was a brick too far. The car upended and gurgled its way to the bottom of the harbor. Seventy-five lobsters were lost. The lesson: Never use a hatchet or a brick to pry open a lobster or car. Simple does and simple don't.

No ice has appeared yet this year. It has been unseasonably warm. The Gulf is 47° F in December, when it's usually 44° F by January first. Many believe a heavy winter holds off waterborne diseases in the spring. Conversely, a mild winter like this one could stimulate shell disease and other maladies in lobsters.

It is not unusual for a lobsterman to become lost in winter storms off the Maine coast. In the words of one fisherman, "It happens either year."

One infamous drowning happened at the mouth of the Damariscotta River in late November 2003, in bucking waves. Captain Roy Bickford, seventy-seven, was lobstering alone when he disappeared from his boat, *Sharon Marie,* slipping overboard without a lifeline. Yet what was remarkable about the tragedy was what had happened sixty-seven years before. At the age of ten, young Roy was sterning for his mentor, Harry McLain, when the older man got caught in the anchor line and nearly drowned. Young Roy released the anchor and saved his captain's life. In another twist of fate, Roy's two older brothers, Bussy and Kenneth, also lost their lives at sea. More recently, in February 2014, nineteen-year-old Devin Pesce of Lisbon Falls was pulled overboard when his ankle got tangled in the lines as the crew was setting a trap. Like young Roy, the crew saved the teenager's life.

Sid Eaton tells the story of a January storm that hit fifty-six-foot *Stacy V.*, captained by Stevie Robbins, off the edge of Georges Bank. He had four crew, including a cook and Sid. They were over one hundred miles out when the storm descended, turning the sky black, blowing hard. Waves as big as a house. This was no day trip. In those days, twenty-five years ago, they stayed out for a week, hauling four hundred traps a day. Forty-four trap trawls. Stevie and the crew kept hauling right through the storm.

The crew members were hard rollers. For refreshment, all they had aboard was a case of Crown Royal and a few mixers. No water. To conserve soft drinks, the cook would wave a Pepsi over the liquor to give it just a hint of sugar.

Everyone got seasick. Sid felt so ill, he could not eat. He was dehydrated and lost thirty pounds in that one week. The worst bout was the fifth day, just when the crew thought it was over. The ocean suddenly churned up with eighty-foot seas. The steel-hulled boat simply buried into the next wave. Somehow, they came out of it and headed for shore. Sid calls the experience "an imperfect storm—imperfect 'cause a perfect storm would have killed us."

On the sixth day, they motored into Portsmouth, New Hampshire, to sell their catch: 25,000 pounds of lobster. "I was happy to see dry land," says Sid. "Steve bought us pizza and beer, but I only had a sandwich. That was my last winter trip. I was done."

Contemplating my first winter voyage, I am happy to see space blankets and a first-aid kit nestled against the bulkhead. Provided by the Island Fishermen's Wives Association, these safety measures furnish some relief. Life jackets are hidden from view, as if too much precaution brings bad luck.

Why risk it all? The attraction to big bucks—high winter volume and high price—draws many lobstermen to the high seas.

Amid the gentle swells, less than ten feet high, *Seasong* rocks fore and aft. Frank spots his first buoy in a trough between the waves. In one motion, he spins the wheel to port and grasps the boat hook with his left hand. Leaning far over the rail, he lifts the red-white-and-blue buoy and puts the hauling process in motion. Haul, rail, pick, band, bait, set. Frank could follow the steps in his sleep.

Just before the first trap surfaces, the captain says, "Working once a week or so in winter keeps the supply of lobsters low and prices high—up to six dollars per pound. Yet other forces are at work. I'm . . ." His voice trails off; he is preoccupied with the hauling sequence and the dangers it brings. A foot caught in a coil of rope has drowned many a captain and crew. This morning, Frank has prices on his mind yet speaks about them in non sequiturs in between hauls.

The pot hauler reels in five traps, each separated by about one hundred feet of line. This is called a five-trap trawl, Frank's preferred arrangement for deepwater fishing. Beyond three miles, by law, he must have at least a three-trap rig, in part because multiple trawls are safer for whales. With fewer buoy lines dangling in the water, the whales are less likely to get entangled. The bottom lines between the traps present no harm.

Five-trap trawls are more efficient than three-trap rigs, called "triples," and are faster to retrieve. But Frank needs two sternmen to manage them. Farther out in the ocean, the big boats employ ten- and twenty-trap trawls, or more. To handle the volume, they use up to four sternmen and stay out for a longer day. The days of overnighting on the ocean, like Stevie and Sid used to do, are rare.

The efficiency of five-trap trawls, called "fives," is all in the math. The two hundred traps that Frank hopes to haul today are suspended from forty buoys. In summer, working on pairs inshore, he would have one hundred buoys for the same number of traps. That's sixty extra to hook and haul.

Alyssa and Dan pick and band twenty-five legal lobsters from the trawl. They're all hard-shells, or what Frank calls hard soft-shells, still solidifying from last summer's molt. Another thirty-six shorts and females are tossed back into the ocean. The sternmen band the lobsters and bait the traps, resetting them in the ocean at the captain's command. Frank throws the throttle forward and *Seasong* bucks into motion, beginning the search for another buoy.

Alyssa is pleased, though she skips her customary dance. At forty trawls, she says, they could catch one thousand lobsters today—if the pace keeps up. Hope is a gambler's first bet of the day.

The captain agrees. "Somewhere between a thousand to fifteen hundred pounds is typical for us out here." He rummages in his yellow oilskin jacket for something. "We have a good market for them," he says.

Frank pulls a *Boston Globe* clipping from his pocket. The headline reads: "CHINA'S APPETITE FOR NEW ENGLAND LOBSTER BOOSTS INDUSTRY."

Frank stares at the breaking news, then looks up to say, "Imagine dinnertime today in Shanghai. Somewhere in the city a Chinese family is feasting on Maine lobster. Maybe caught on my boat a few days ago. Chinese imports of our lobsters will top thirty million dollars this year. That's nearly eight percent of our produce."

Driving the five-dollar price of lobster today is the prospect of the Chinese New Year, coming in late January. The winter fishery, expanding all the time, is tied to the Chinese holiday. That celebration is one of several festivals where Maine lobster, boiled to an auspicious bright red, is popular. The burgeoning middle class is China's fastest-growing market for Maine lobster.

Overhearing these words on China, Alyssa steps forward to say, "I'll tell you why they're eating so much lobster. The Asian women think it's an aphrodisiac for the men."

The captain steers clear of that one. Instead, he returns the conversation to exports. "Chinese New Year," he says, "is now Maine's second-biggest lobster-shipping week, just behind Christmas."

The Chinese demand, in part, is what is keeping Frank out on the ocean this winter.

"Supply and demand drives everything," he says, then loses his train of thought as he sights a second buoy. Frank buttons it up while he maneuvers *Seasong* into striking distance of his mark.

Once he has the buoy aboard and the warp is whining through the pot hauler, Frank and Alyssa rekindle their conversation about price. Stimulating demand through building exports, they say, is not the first chance to influence price. After the 2012 glut upset the price balance, driving the market below two dollars per pound, the initial idea among many lobstermen like Frank was to curb the supply—that is, catch fewer lobsters, in the hope their relative rarity would double the price.

There are a couple of ways to limit the supply: Harvesting over fewer days or months is one avenue. Reducing the number of traps is another. In terms of management, these methods address effort, the number of hours worked or gear turned over. In Maine, there are precedents for such a campaign.

Frank fills us in on history. The seven Lobster Zone Councils, which oversee management areas, have had the authority to reduce effort for over twenty years. During that time, however, they have reduced the eight-hundred-trap limit only once. In Zone E, a reduction to six hundred traps was an isolated success. Other trap-reduction proposals have lost in a vote. This year, the councils would not even entertain the motion.

In 2005, another experiment was launched outside the councils. The initiative began with the state government. Trap reduction was seen as having myriad benefits in terms of saving costs and protecting species. "It's promising and necessary," said George LaPointe, the former commissioner of Maine's Department of Marine Resources. "If there is anything we've learned in fisheries, it is do not wait until you are in trouble to do something. And trap curtailment could mean less money spent on gear, bait, and fuel."

Another advantage of scaling down the three million traps in state waters would be to lessen the danger posed by end lines to endangered right whales and other cetacean species.

In a state-run experiment on Monhegan Island, lobster scientists found that 150 traps caught nearly the same number of lobsters, within 15 percent, as 500 traps did, presumably because more lobsters were caught in each one of the less densely arranged traps. In other words, in two areas of similar size, the same number of lobsters will frequent an array of traps, regardless of the number of traps.

Despite the success of the experiment, the majority of lobstermen remain opposed to trap reduction. "Fishermen always want to catch more," says Frank. "That's their nature." In that atmosphere, intentionally curbing supply to accelerate the price is unlikely in Maine. Attempts at cutting supply have not worked. Lobstermen are generally averse to joining any faction that limits their catch or does them any other favor.

To illustrate this point, Frank offers a joke. "Two lobstermen are making their way in a thick fog, without compass or radar. They seem to be lost. Older man says to younger, 'Do you know any prayers?' 'Yes.' 'Start praying.' The younger man chants feverishly. The old-timer says, 'Not too much, we don't want to be beholden.'"

So, if tightening the catch is out of the question, what are the remaining options for controlling price? Climate change and the loss of predators have perhaps brought on a glut and rock-bottom prices. How can the lobstermen adapt?

"We have another avenue," says Frank. "All of us are working together to boost demand for Maine lobster. If we're successful, that should elevate price. Today it is six dollars, with the one-dollar bonus, and the year average is close to four, but I'd sure like to push it to five."

Frank reaches out for his third buoy, almost hidden in the swells. One by one, another five traps surface. They are picked clean by Alyssa and Dan—eighteen lobsters join the other forty in the saltwater tank. It is adding up to a "stellar day," in Alyssa's lexicon. Dan keeps his thoughts to himself.

The sternmen glance at their captain. He holds his left hand up in a gesture meaning "Halt." The five traps freeze right on the rail. Despite the good haul, Frank wants to move the quintet. He has a hunch, or is curious, about a better spot.

While he motors to a new locale, Frank shares the highlights of the recent marketing initiative to stoke demand for Maine lobsters.

In 2013, in response to the glut and subsequent low prices, and at the urging of lobstermen, the state legislature created the Maine Lobster Marketing Collaborative (MLMC). Its mission: to package and push the Maine lobster brand domestically and overseas. The members meet around a conference table quarterly, but more frequently, they spread the word to chefs around the country. They encourage major restaurants to place Maine lobster—and, most important, shedders—on their menus. Recently, Frank represented the MLMC at the National Restaurant

Association Show in Chicago. He was the hit of the party, telling tall tales of lobstering in the Gulf of Maine. He has also welcomed chefs onto *Seasong* for a day hauling shedders—what the MLMC calls "new-shell" lobsters—now the hottest, or rather sweetest, seafood around. Chefs return from a day aboard the boat with their own personal adventures to go with their lobster recipes.

"When people think lobster, they think Maine," says Frank. "Americans, well, people everywhere, are fascinated with the provenance of their food. Our idea is to court a team of chef ambassadors who will experience lobstering, then broadcast the story of new-shell to other chefs and the media. The chefs deliver a Maine experience to the other forty-nine states. I won't be shy about singing a few bars from the Maine songbook, as well."

The MLMC's initial budget was $750,000 and is projected to grow to $2.2 million in 2018. By contrast, the previous Lobster Promotion Council had only $350,000 in annual funds and, thus, was hamstrung from the start. The MLMC is funded by a surcharge on licenses issued to lobstermen, processors, and dealers. In 2015, for a Class II commercial lobster license (the most common license), a fee of $220.50 went to support the MLMC. Climate change and the glut have likely made this necessary. Fishermen have invested heavily and equally, betting the marketing effort will pay off.

In turn, the MLMC has gambled on Weber Shandwick as the contractor for this endeavor. As an international marketing company, Weber Shandwick has launched new product lines and consumer campaigns for the milk industry (the "Got Milk?" campaign), Mars, Harley-Davidson, and L. L. Bean. Brand repositioning is one of its specialties. This is the company that successfully promoted tart cherries, once only known as a pie ingredient, as a year-round "super fruit," a stand-alone nutritious snack. Can they turn lobster around like that—especially summer shedders, now mostly enjoyed just locally in Maine for the month of August? Will they become a gourmet item in California?

Frank Gotwals believes so. He is the newly elected chairman of the MLMC and steers an eight-member board, composed of lobstermen, dealers, and state officials. He is the soul of the new machine.

"First we tackle restaurants in the Northeast," he says; "then next year we conquer North America. We have identified twenty-two hundred upscale restaurants between Delaware and Maine. Only four percent of those establishments currently list Maine lobster on their menus. Only twenty percent list any type of lobster, not specifying Maine. That's an enormous opportunity to increase sales. We have the lobster. It's just a matter of getting the chefs to order them. Our message is: When you order lobster, you order from Maine."

Frank arrives on a deeper contour of the continental shelf. He pulls back on the throttle, waking the sternmen from their daydreams.

"Yep," he commands.

Alyssa and Dan toss the traps overboard, doing a quick step to avoid the lines whipping across the deck.

Now for the search for the remaining buoys. On the way, Frank has a few more words on the MLMC. "I'd like to see the number of restaurants serving Maine lobster increase significantly. That would be a success. On the price front, we're already seeing some movement. The average price of lobster dockside jumped eighty cents per pound from two seasons ago [2013] to three dollars and seventy cents in 2014. This year's average may set a record. Demand is up, vanquishing oversupply." Frank and the MLMC seem to have outfoxed the glut at dockside.

In the retail arena, prices are also climbing. This week at Shaw's supermarket in Ellsworth, a large whole lobster is going for $12.99 a pound. For picked lobster, prices are four times as high. At Yankee Lobster in Boston, lobster tail meat is claiming fifty-five dollars per pound. Hugh Reynolds of Greenhead is now getting the gourmet prices he has desired.

Demand is strong. In the battle between lobstermen and climate change, the fishermen may have won the second round.

Yet the MLMC is not without criticism. Julie Eaton, speaking for the Maine Lobstering Union, claims the MLMC's efforts have had little impact on a lobsterman's bottom line. Since the MLMC's formation in 2013, the dockside price has climbed from $2.90 per pound to $4.09 (2015), an increase of 41 percent. However, not all of that growth can be attributed to the MLMC.

Lobsters are surfacing with regularity now. Frank is hauling his twentieth trawl of the day, and the count has been impressive for the last five.

"Twenty-four keepers in that last batch," says Alyssa, picking some beauties from the first trap on the rail. "I've got five more here, so we're doing about the same as that last trawl. I'm betting on twenty-five."

"Good," says the captain, "and they're pretty lobsters."

The second trap comes up, and Dan breaks it over the rail. He opens the wire cage and lifts out a big male with barnacles growing on his head. This rogue has not shed in a while.

"There's a beauty," says Dan.

"We're seeing quite a show today," says Alyssa.

Dan's next selection is a pistol—no claws. "Look's like a male," says Frank. "We might as well sell him."

"Every dollar helps," says Alyssa.

"Pretty lobster, though, even without his claws. Good size, good shell."

The pot hauler bitches and moans over the last three traps. It strains under their weight. The squeal, the pitch of it, rides high above the drone of the diesel engine.

Those next three traps produce five market lobsters each, so Alyssa makes her twenty-five. She's not dancing, though. No jig as yet. She must be going for double or nothing.

Dan and Alyssa are measuring a lot of lobsters and throwing back three for every one they keep. The shorts are right on the fence, just shy of legal.

Frank smiles at the steep ratio. "So many marginal lobsters means we'll have a good year next season," he says. "We've got plenty of young lobsters coming along. In the 1980s, this coast was in poor shape—no little ones. Then it came back. Now, we're booming. It's strong everywhere, all the way Down East." But not as robust southwest of here. Everything is headed northeast.

Frank is shy of mentioning the migration. Giving it voice may give it power.

Alyssa and Dan clean the bait bags from each trap, tossing the remnant, week-old herring over the stern. The herring gulls, which have followed *Seasong* to these distant hunting grounds, dive for the bait, snagging the snippets before they sink away. Excited by the morsels, the herring gulls make a buglelike racket, underscored by the tenor of a lone black-backed gull. Such is the chorus trailing the *Seasong* all day long.

On the afterdeck, four of us sit on the rails and transom of *Seasong*, contemplating our lunch choices. Alyssa cradles her daughter Audrey's Cinderella lunch box on her lap. She pops a grape. Frank hoists his blue-and-white cooler onto the rail, as if tailgating. He eyes some smoked salmon. Dan is new; he opens a brown paper bag and extracts a Dorito. The cuisine is commensurate with the containers.

Alyssa says, "Frank, would you like a napkin?"

"Got one, thanks."

Such are the preliminaries of *Seasong*'s movable feast.

Frank says, "Ayah, I've been looking forward to this—fresh salmon on a bagel. I traded some lobster for the hickory-smoked fish."

Not to be outdone, Alyssa says, "I've got some scallop salad—with a little Old Bay—now that's a sandwich. You want some chips, Frank?"

He does not answer. He's slicing a red onion—from his garden.

"Well, I'm fresh out of gourmet items," says Dan, the most talkative he's been all morning. "Nothing fresh in this bag. Even my old bologna here smells like bait." He sniffs, but one nostril is running. "I guess I cannot get the herring out of my nose."

Alyssa hands Dan some paper towels. Dan wipes his nose, then his mouth.

"We're into the fresh pogies now," says Alyssa. "Third box of bait. They aren't as rank as salted herring. Herring is cousin to a roadkill. You'll have a better afternoon."

"Ayah, what we do for lobster," says Dan.

"And smoked salmon," says Frank. "My this is good."

"You want some grapes, Frank?" says Alyssa. "I got plenty."

Frank shakes his head in exasperation. A lobsterman, if anything, is self-sufficient—an island unto the main.

Dan stands and steps over to the bait boxes to take a gander at the pogies. He comes back quickly.

"Them pogies are ugly fish. Eyes like black marbles staring you down."

"Lobsters like them best," says Frank.

Alyssa says, "Lord knows how many lobsters taste them before we actually pull up a few keepers to the boat."

Frank says, "I've heard that for every six lobsters we catch, ninety-four have visited the same trap, eaten a little, and left."

"They escape with ease—especially the shorts—after chewing on some herring," says Alyssa.

"They're getting a free lunch," says Dan, picking his teeth now with a hunting knife.

"Some say fifty percent of a lobster's diet is bait—served up in three million fast-food joints at the bottom of the sea."

"Maybe that's why the lobsters are booming," says Alyssa. "Maybe it's not climate or predators or kelp, but the tons of bait we bribe them with each year. Are we ranching lobsters?"

"Maybe," says Frank. "But who knows? I suppose it's possible it has an effect. Yet, how would you prove it? There are a lot of other creatures coming into those traps, eating the bait. If we cut off the bait, would the lobsters starve? Probably not. But I could be completely wrong." Frank lets his eyes drift over the water, as if fishing for something. He's quiet, lost in his thoughts.

"You wanna cookie, Frank? They're homemade."

"Hell no."

Alyssa has failed to unload a single cookie in six years.

After lunch, another trawl is quickly emptied. Dan gathers two lobsters from the third trap, one in each hand, and tries to juggle a third. A dangerous shortcut. The odd lobster slips from his grasp and drops on his foot. The lobster, a male, arches its tail—its abdomen—and raises its claws in defense. Dan sets his lobsters down to rescue the outlier. Yet the escapee defends his freedom. At last, Alyssa does a little dance to avoid the crustaceans. She's up on her toes, *en pointe*. For a minute, the two sternmen look like Woody and Diane, battling a kitchen full of angry lobsters in *Annie Hall*. But the captain is not amused.

"I don't believe in multitasking," he says. "A sternman can only concentrate on one thing at a time." It was Frank's first admonishment of the season.

So, opening the fourth trap, Alyssa does her best to march through her tasks in single file. With two hands, she selects the grand prize of the day.

"Oh my God!" she exclaims, and looks over her right shoulder at her captain. "You're not going to believe this!"

Alyssa holds a brilliant blue lobster in her hands. From claws to tail, the entire body is Mediterranean blue, like those aquamarine colors on the domes of Santorini. It is difficult to pin down the exact chances of the genetic mutation, but over the years, lobstermen and scientists have figured the odds of a blue lobster at one in two million. During the height of the glut, with landings of 100 million lobsters, chances are that 50 blues will surface with the fleet.

Yet the wild colors do not end with bright blue. Previously, Frank and Alyssa have captured a bright red lobster (one in twenty million) and a rarer bright yellow one (one in thirty million). Frank caught a second blue lobster while hauling crab pots with a friend last December. Yet the crown jewel was a calico lobster, spotted with orange, blue, and white. The odds of finding that one are one in forty million.

Rarer color morphs can also be found in the Gulf of Maine. A bicolor, or split-colored lobster, which is half orange and half brown, comes in at one in fifty million. And taking all bets is an albino lobster, which is solid white and paying 100 million to one. That phantom like any lobster may live to sixty years, reaching three feet in length. In forty years of hauling, Frank has only seen two albino lobsters. He enjoys knowing they are around.

Alyssa holds the blue lobster out over the water. "Say good-bye," she says. "There'll be no melted butter for you." The sea swallows the blue rarity; it returns to its underwater home.

"I never tire of this beauty," says Frank. "No two days are ever exactly alike. The light is always different. Summer glare. Winter haze. The fog. The mist. Every day brings something new. Look at today. We wake up to a three-quarter moon. Then all of a sudden, a blue lobster."

"A film crew is supposed to go with us tomorrow," says Alyssa. "Too bad they missed the blue one."

"You better wear your makeup," says Dan.

"I just use mascara," says Alyssa, wiping some mud off her chin. "I gave up trying to look pretty a long time ago."

Dan smiles. Alyssa does not have to try to look pretty. Even in oilskins, she's wicked cunning.

"Frank, that's two blue lobsters in a year," says Alyssa. "You're a lucky guy."

"I know I'm lucky," he says. "I think about it all the time."

"That's 'cause you're getting old—turning sixty next month. You're becoming philosophical."

"That's not age. That's fishing."

Frank makes his last haul of the day—the two-hundredth trap to the nose. He orders his sternmen to hold the final five. After picking twenty-one legal lobsters, the crew stacks the traps atop fifteen already in reserve. The twenty will be retired for the season today. In a series of relays, *Seasong* will slowly return her gear to shore. It will take a dozen trips or so. In another six weeks—early February (after the Chinese New Year)—Frank will quit for good, or at least for the rest of the winter. Until then, he keeps track in his head of the traps retired and those outstanding, as if he were calculating a virtual balance sheet. For each trap in the water, he knows how many lobsters it produced today—and last week. All this while navigating, steering, and hauling. And orchestrating two sternmen.

"It's like playing music," says Frank. "You have to juggle, but it takes a lot of concentration and coordination. Playing the guitar and singing requires doing a lot of things at once. Yet the melody holds it together. That's like lobstering. There's a rhythm to what we're doing."

"There's your one-man band," says Alyssa. "People ask me how we catch so many lobsters. 'That's easy,' I say. 'I've got the best captain in the world.'"

Frank changes the conversation by announcing that his jazz band, Isle of Jazz, will be playing tonight.

"You better clean up your shirt, then," says Alyssa. "You got mud all over the front. You want a towel?"

"No."

"You want a sponge?"

"No."

"You want some bottled water?"

"No, I don't want a damn thing."

Dan's calculation brings today's harvest to over one thousand lobsters, or over twelve hundred pounds. "That's close to six thousand dollars," he says. "Not a bad day's work."

Just now, John Williams steams past us on the *Khristy Michelle,* heading for deeper water—up to four hundred feet down. He is laden with traps, pulled from shallower seas. He likely has a larger catch aboard. The bigger boats can land from six thousand to seven thousand pounds in a long day—well over thirty thousand dollars at these prices.

With more captains able to afford them, more and more big boats are heading out to deep water. They have redefined the winter fishery, now nearly 20 percent of the annual catch.

Remarkably, Frank is not curious where John Williams has been or where he's going. Then he explains why.

"The best fishermen," he says, "are the ones who do their own thing. Set their first trap where they want and revise their plan along the way. They don't worry about other fishermen. We have any number of ways you can play it. Make it *your* choice. It's best to follow your own compass."

Frank cranks up the throttle and heads for home. Furtively, he glances over his shoulder at the *Khristy Michelle* on an opposite bearing, making for open sea.

"You have to look at your expenses," he adds. "We buy less diesel, buy less bait than him. He's bigger, but he carries a burden."

Frank's eyes are now searching the horizon for a sign of Stonington, the home port to be celebrated tonight in his songs of longing. He has one more refrain, made up on the spot. From the helm, he sings to no one in particular: "I'm happy to be playing with the band, happy to see a blue lobster, happy to catch my dinner on a boat I helped build myself."

He is surrounded by beauty and belonging, by a fisherman's code, an ancient way of navigating through his years.

8

The Chinese Bubble

An old lobsterman's lament says that, if you must visit Massachusetts, do not bring anyone back with you. Anyone living south of Maine, you see, is "from away," and is thus invited to stay away—permanently. For Mainers in the tourist business, sentiments are more complicated—they need the tourist dollars—but at least one voice in their heads is saying, Keep the pilgrims south of the state border, where they belong. Today, an exception might be made for all the lobster buyers who descend on Boston each March for the Boston Seafood Show. Just renamed Seafood Expo North America, it fills the downtown Convention Center with potential lobster buyers from fifty-one countries. The foreign dealers buy lobster for all their countrymen back home. They visit Boston, shopping for Maine lobsters, buying them by the millions. Afterward, many are curious and venture north to see the Gulf waters for themselves. Mainers welcome them begrudgingly.

The dealers come not only for lobster but for seafood caught in all the oceans on Earth. For three days, more than twelve hundred exhibitors offer nearly every commercial species, ranging from salmon and sea bass to cobia and monkfish, from scallops and squid to shrimp and Dungeness crab, from Australian rock lobster to Iranian caviar. Lucky attendees get to sample raw and cooked produce, often prepared by top chefs. The Japanese cut sushi on demand; the French shuck Belon oysters from beds of shaved ice; and Cajuns from Louisiana demonstrate how to open a boiled crawfish. It's best to fast for a few days before coming to Boston. With three mornings and afternoons, each, available to explore the culinary arts of the maritime countries, pacing is required. I find it best—to prevent a war in my stomach—to pursue the six great oceans one at a time.

When I arrive, the thirty-sixth annual festival is in high gear. Balloons and banners announce the colorful logos and countries like the opening festivities of the Olympics. Life-size stuffed animals, mostly red lobsters and white polar bears, guard chests of ice. A sea of people—over twenty thousand attendees—roam the aisles to test delicacies at the booths. The odors are enticing. I quickly pick out barbecued *unagi* (freshwater eel from Japan) and fried soft-shell crab from Maryland, my home state. Carts deliver crushed ice to each booth—snow removal turned back on itself. The walls of the Convention Center echo with multiple foreign voices. A man with a British accent announces he's here to find new markets for periwinkles. Another dialect is garbled to my ears. Is that Chinese, Korean, or Vietnamese? In the next aisle, I can distinguish the voices of Russians by the king crab and beluga caviar at their fingertips.

A Norwegian salmon-filleting demonstration catches my eye. The fishmonger introduces herself to the large crowd as Astrid. She's barely twenty, with a crown of braided blond hair, but totally in command. Amazingly, she cuts the fillets right to the bone in a couple of minutes with a long, sharp blade. She then selects another fish and repeats the procedure—chilling to see a young woman so adept with a knife.

Suddenly, there's a tap on my shoulder and a voice behind my ear: "Don't get on her bad side." It's Frank Gotwals. He holds a stack of business cards in his fist. One by one, he's handing out the website address of the Maine Lobster Marketing Collaborative. Frank has driven down from Stonington to drum up interest in Maine's new marketing initiative.

"There are hundreds of buyers here today, whole countries," he says, "that have yet to try Maine lobster. We're here to get them excited about serving the best lobster in the world."

At his first stop, Frank preaches to the choir. Emily Lane, export director, stands under the banner of Calendar Islands Seafood Company, based in Portland, Maine. She is surrounded by three South Korean gentlemen in ties and jackets. Emily is partial to the Koreans. Last week, she drove Korean chefs around Maine—in what the passengers dubbed "Emily's Go-Go Bus"—to introduce them to Maine lobster. After three days on the road, the Koreans begged, "Enough lobster. Can we go to McDonald's?"

Emily sells lobster in the form of "value-added" split lobster tails, lobster-stuffed potatoes, appetizers, and other seafood specialties all over the globe. She's also on the board of the MLMC, so she needs no schmoozing from Frank. Still, he always checks in with his compatriots.

The Koreans disperse, and Emily walks over to us. She is a lovely woman. "Another day, another won," she says. Won is the currency of Korea. Emily says she's made four sales this morning. It's impolite to ask to whom and how much, but her grin speaks volumes. Orders are usually by the multiple pounds, shipped by container, thousands of meals each.

Calendar Seafood clearly labels and markets their lobster as coming from Maine, so Frank is pleased. Emily is an ambassador for the MLMC's mission—to build demand for Maine lobster—wherever she goes. After Boston, Emily heads off to Europe in April for the Brussels Seafood Expo, the largest in the world. In a universe of cutthroat competition, Emily is lucky to represent Calendar Seafood as one of the many successful seafood companies from Maine. "There's plenty of room for all of us," she says. "Over a billion Chinese—I can't feed them all alone."

Emily regularly attends three seafood shows in Asia: Shanghai, Chengdu, and Hong Kong. As is in the West, restaurants and retailers buy from wholesalers at these markets. Meanwhile, fishermen are busy on the water. More and more, seafood caught outside China, including lobster, shows up at these festivals. Of late, there have been seafood safety scares in China, often due to rampant water pollution, so Chinese consumers prefer foreign fish and shellfish. This new demand plays right into Emily's hands.

While some European and Asian seafood shows are bigger, the Boston show is the largest in North America. In addition to selling seafood, the Boston festival features conference panels and talks. This year's themes are sustainability and traceability, the tracking of fish and shellfish from source to consumer.

Emily is besieged by potential customers. Here a new client from Spain, another one from Germany, there an old friend from Italy, where Maine lobster is popular at Christmas. So Frank decides to wander. He must cover 220,000 square feet of exhibit space—the equivalent of about 4.5 football fields—in three days. The booths appear as an archipelago of islands in the convention hall. We ease up to each atoll, banking left, then right, like two denizens of the reef.

The first pavilion we encounter spotlights Maryland companies, offering bounty from Chesapeake Bay. This is my turf, or surf, I suppose. I recognize J. M. Clayton Seafood immediately, remembering its roost in Cambridge, just upriver from Tilghman Island, where I lived for two years. Frank asks Bill Brooks of Clayton Seafood how things are going. "I'm meeting people from all over the world," Bill says, "that are interested in the Chesapeake, what she has to offer. I'm selling a ton of blue crab."

Just beyond Clayton Seafood is a row of oyster peddlers. The tenth annual oyster shucking contest is under way. We watch Jorge Hernandez of Elliott's Oyster House in Seattle defend his title. "It's all in the wrist," he says. Jorge expertly opens ten oysters in less than a minute and takes home the trophy again.

The oyster displays run the gamut from Chincoteague (Virginia) to Tamales Bay (California). A purveyor of Damariscotta oysters (from Maine) gets into an argument with a Blue Point salesman (from Long Island) about who has the best oyster. For a minute, the rhetoric is explosive. But for the most part, the exchange is friendly.

Next, we come upon some Maine lobster companies: Cozy Harbor, Island Seafood, and Ready Seafood, which ultimately handles Julie Eaton's catch. They all know of Frank's work at the MLMC. Farther along, we run into Hugh Reynolds at Greenhead Lobster, which specializes in live lobster. His is the single Stonington booth in the crowd. Hugh is branching out. He will soon sell frozen lobster tails to Asia. Emily will have to accept the new competition; she'll have to share her Chinese market.

The news propels Frank across the room. He navigates the exhibits as if their layout were hardwired into his brain like the arrangement of islands in Jericho Bay. Frank arrives quickly at Dalian Seafood, the first

Chinese company in aisle one. Three men in black suits and ties stand behind the counter. Frank passes the center man his card—with two hands, as is the custom. Everyone bows. Frank explains he is promoting Maine lobster, that the names and numbers of all Maine lobster exporters are on the website, and that they can provide free samples.

"Excellent," says the Chinese salesman. He is all smiles, missing the irony of Chinese pollution's contribution to climate change, which, in turn, has brought a glut of lobsters, lower prices, and Frank to his door.

"Brilliant," says Frank, as if he were across the Pond. "Thank you," he adds, correcting himself and nodding respectfully.

"Too many languages competing in my brain," he says under his breath as we walk away.

Frank makes the rounds of all foreign seafood companies over the next couple of days. There are forty-three Chinese companies, eight Korean, twenty-two Japanese, and five Vietnamese. There are fifty-five European distributors, as well. These two continents—Asia and Europe—are the bread and butter of Maine's overseas sales. Yet those numbers simply apply to booths, which largely sell exotic produce. Some also buy American seafood, but most of the buyers roam the festival, nomads without a tent.

At the pavilion for the Maine Lobster Marketing Collaborative, Frank replenishes his card stock. To boost demand for Maine lobster, the MLMC encourages the media to feature pertinent stories and invite chefs to try new recipes. To this end, their exhibit today has press kits and serving suggestions, as well as the ubiquitous website address.

"A perfect place to launch the initiative," says Matt Jacobson, fifty-five, executive director of the MLMC. To Frank, he offers a few words of encouragement and sets Frank on his way. According to the clock, Frank is a country or two behind.

Before departing for the evening, I witness an event rarely seen outside Japan: the butchering of a large bluefin tuna, top carnivore of the sea. This fish, stretched out on a stainless-steel table, is about four feet long, maybe four hundred pounds. A Tokyo fish cutter carves the tuna with striking precision, quickly getting to the belly meat, prized above all others for its fat content. He slices thin strips from the belly and offers them to passersby. Raw sushi. The facial expressions on those beneficiaries shifts from curiosity to delight as the bluefin literally melts in their mouths.

Yet there is something wrong with this picture. Bluefin tuna are vanishing from oceans around the world. The story of the two Atlantic populations—east and west—is one of accelerating demand, intense fishing pressure, and declining stocks. The Atlantic bluefin is an apex predator that grows to the size of a small boat, outswims just about every other fish in the sea, and commands tens of thousands of dollars each, thanks to the Japanese sushi trade. It has a high value to the ocean ecosystem as well, but this is often overlooked. This magnificent species—or at least its most vulnerable populations—are being driven toward extinction.

Before 1950, the commercial catch was virtually nonexistent. Growth in demand was explosive. By 1964, the harvest was eighteen times the 1960 level. By 1970, landings had crashed by 80 percent. The population in the western Atlantic, including just off Maine, is now less than 15 percent of pre-1950 levels. Despite the crisis, some governments have recently considered actually increasing catch quotas. Tragedy of the capitalists. For this reason, the management of Atlantic bluefin tuna has been characterized as "an international disgrace."

Meanwhile, with similar "stewardship," the Pacific bluefin tuna is already at rock-bottom levels. Closer to Japan, this species has been depleted to less than 3 percent of its estimated unfished population. One of the reasons for its spiraling descent is that most—perhaps more than 98 percent—of the Pacific bluefin that are landed are immature juveniles, which have never reproduced. This is a recipe for extinction and has prompted a petition for listing Pacific bluefin under the Endangered Species Act. Sadly, Atlantic bluefin may be next. That is, if the White House still permits an Endangered Species Act.

Some other fish marketed at the Boston show are endangered, too. The *unagi* population in Japanese streams is only 5 percent of levels found in the 1960s. The world's oceans are in trouble and so are the majority of its fisheries. These facts give me pause.

The Maine lobster, however, is considered "sustainable," that eco-friendly designation given in 2012 by the Marine Stewardship Council. This green label was awarded at the height of the recent glut, when lobster landings exceeded 125 million pounds. It was unclear at the time whether this harvest level was an aberration or not. If ocean warming or a dearth of predators was to blame for the glut, then perhaps the peak may subside into a trough—a dip in the population. How far can it fall? Is the fate of the bluefin the fate of all marine species?

The questions tumble like a cascade. Will we consider Maine lobster sustainable in ten more years? What will the harvest be? And the exports?

The growth of Maine's lobster exports is staggering. For 2016, the most recent record available, Maine's lobster exports were $397.8 million, a jump of 174 percent over 2007. That earlier year, the value was $145 million. Since overall lobster landings were $533 million in 2016, the higher, more recent export figure represents 74.6 percent of the annual catch in Maine. Most of our lobsters are shipped overseas. Lobstermen have become dependent on foreign sales. That's their meal ticket.

To obtain a country-by-country breakdown of exports, I must venture to Vinalhaven, an island off the coast of Rockland. Here is the home of Emily Lane, the wise woman and exporter for Calendar Seafood. She promises some answers if I make the crossing. Vinalhaven is second only to Stonington as a lobster port and has its own special charm. It is remote enough—an hour and a half by ferry—to resist gentrification. Emily uses the island as her base, not only to attend the Seafood Expo North America but also to launch her travel to every seafood fair from Brussels (the biggest in the world) to Shanghai (the most far-flung).

Emily and I have lunch at the Harbor Gawker, the best place on the island for lobster and crab, as well as stuffed halibut, my favorite. Like any fisherman eating out, Emily has a BLT, which she cannot get on her boat. I choose the lobster roll, the white meat picked right at the counter. The Gawker's version of the lobster roll is rated among the best in Maine.

"Calendar Island is exporting diced lobster meat now," Emily says, "but not the rolls. Our customers must find a baker on their own. The finished product is selling like wildfire. The global demand for live lobster and value-added products like claw meat and tails is escalating. Of the six top export destinations, three—China, Hong Kong, and South Korea—are driving the stampede. It's all about Asia."

According to the Food Institute, China imported $40.9 million of Maine lobster in 2016, compared to $2.1 million in 2009, a 2,000 percent increase in just seven years. So China now represents 10 percent of all Maine lobster exports; their share is growing fast. One out of every thirteen lobsters caught in Maine waters is shipped to China.

"There you are," says Emily, sipping her iced tea. "The story of China is a high-octane version of what's happening to Maine exports generally. Lobsters—and I mean all species globally, from Australian rock lobster to our local variety—move like a commodity, such as pork bellies or oil. The price has shot up this spring with booming demand."

But what about those other lobster species? I ask. Don't they dampen the demand for American lobster?

"For Chinese customers," Emily responds, "Maine lobster is a cheaper alternative to their favorite crustacean—the Australian rock lobster, a large clawless species that fetches one hundred dollars apiece in Beijing. Our lobster sells for a third the rock lobster price. Luckily, despite the price difference, both species are symbols of prestige throughout Asia— not just China, but Korea, Vietnam, and Japan, as well. Lobsters look like little dragons to them, an auspicious creature. The bigger the lobster, the better they like it." The Chinese are not known as conservationists.

The larger, select lobsters earn a premium price in Asian markets. On Alibaba.com, the Chinese version of eBay, "Soft, huge Boston lobsters" were listed in December for from thirty to one hundred dollars each, including shipping. The photograph on the site shows a bright red "cooked" lobster next to a "live" greenish one.

"We still have a brand challenge," says Emily. "Lobsters shipped from Logan International Airport are called 'Boston lobsters' upon arrival in China because that port of call is stamped on the shipping documents." Her colleague Hugh Reynolds of Greenhead Lobster believes the Maine label will come eventually. The supply of lobster in North America is ten times greater than in Australia, he says, so the Chinese must import more product from the United States to meet the demand. That means Maine, not Massachusetts. "The Chinese economy is growing and their appetite for lobster grows with it," Reynolds says. "We own the future. It's just a matter of math."

Emily tells me she puts 90 percent of her effort at Calendar Seafood into building exports—especially now with the push to market new-shell lobsters. Meanwhile, 60 percent of her current sales are overseas. Results lag only slightly behind investment. This, too, she says, will change. "The Marketing Collaborative is already stimulating domestic sales, but going after the big bucks requires an export license."

Emily is now matching every one of my lobster bites with a munch on her BLT. I think my commodity is a better pick, though three times the price of her bacon.

Emily says keeping that price competitive is one of the main challenges of exporting lobsters. "Now, Greenhead," she explains, "only sells live lobster. That's a commodity where the price changes daily. At Calendar, we don't sell live lobster. We specialize in value-added products, mostly frozen, like stuffed lobster tail and appetizers. Our prices are more stable. But if the dock price climbed one to two dollars more, it would kill the deal."

Hefty shipping and spoilage costs make margins slim. Thus any price elevation stateside could put lobsters out of reach for Asian customers. And yet domestic dealers are counting on their business. They have invested heavily in infrastructure—processing plants, freezers, trucks, airfreight facilities. It all turns on the dollar being cheap enough and on foreign demand for a crustacean that is notoriously difficult to ship. A modest Chinese tariff would scotch the deal. A trade war would unhinge it.

I tell Emily the lobster roll is fabulous. Would she like a bite? She offers me a look, as if she's seen it all. "For every lobster roll you can eat," she says, "I ship ten thousand of the fixings to Chengdu, in Sichuan Province." Nothing succeeds like excess.

I bid farewell to Emily and Vinalhaven, promising to visit Tenants Harbor, a fishing village on the mainland—home to Peter Miller, another board member of the MLMC. She suggests Peter may know a bit more about how China is changing the map of lobster sales in Maine.

Tenants Harbor is located two-thirds of the way down the St. George Peninsula, which runs sixteen miles between Rockland and Port Clyde. Just before reaching town, I came upon the old great Eastern Mussel

Farm, converted in 2012 into a state-of-the-art lobster-processing facility, Sea Hag Seafood. The nondescript white buildings have no company sign or other markings. Three dozen cars in the parking lot, however, give away the frenzy of activity inside. Around back, next to the wharf, thirty or more herring gulls dive-bomb the Dumpsters, trying to snatch lobster guts and shell.

Sea Hag, named for the owner's family lobster boat, was born of the belief that Maine needed more lobster-processing capability to compete with Canada. For years, Maine had only four large plants, whereas Canada claimed thirty-two. With the addition of Sea Hag, Ready Seafood (in Scarborough), Luke's Lobster (in Saco), Maine Fair Trade Lobster (in Prospect Harbor), and a few others, Maine now has thirteen facilities, half of them built in the past five years.

Even with the expanded capacity, less than 15 percent of Maine's catch is processed in the state. Twenty-five percent of the whole catch goes to the live trade, while 60 percent still travels to Canada for processing. Maine's facilities presently handle an estimated twelve million pounds annually. Kyle Murdoch, the owner of Sea Hag, believes Maine could eventually process 30 percent of the pie.

"If Maine could process forty million pounds, I'd be happy," he said last year at the plant. "I—well, me and my staff—plan to pick two and a half million pounds this year at Sea Hag." Kyle has fifty employees and expects to increase his workforce to sixty or seventy this summer, making Kyle Murdock the biggest employer in Tenants Harbor. He is twenty-six years old.

The day I dropped by Sea Hag, Kyle was visiting Monhegan Island, his home turf, a small island ten miles off the coast (just south of Vinalhaven). The manager gave me the grand tour—of the parking lot. The interior, I am warned, is an industrial secret. Monhegan has a year-round population of fifty and a lobster fleet of fourteen, including Kyle's father's *Sea Hag.* Kyle is an ambitious man. He plans to consolidate his interests by acting as a lobster buyer, purchasing lobster directly from fishermen. He can buy from lobstermen right at his own dock, cutting out the middleman. That's consolidation.

A second advantage to Kyle's waterfront property is his ability to cook all his lobster in seawater, a technique employed by gourmet chefs to cook a better meal. Sea Hag's products range from scored claws and whole split lobster to frozen mincemeat. In the lobster business, Emily Lane tells me, everyone has a niche.

In fact, Maine and Canada have a niche each. Canada, which has a predominantly winter-and-spring season, features mostly hard-shell lobster. Maine, which has mostly a summer season, when lobsters molt, boasts the shedder. Processors buy lobster from both countries so that they have a steady supply regardless the time of year. Formerly, there was little market overlap between Maine lobster and Canadian lobster. Yet as landings in both Maine and Canada have boomed, the two countries have competed more directly for new customers. Canada is even launching its own marketing program to compete with the MLMC.

Canada has a larger lobster fishery: $680 million (in U.S. dollars), compared to $495 million for Maine (2015). It also has higher exports. It's well known that hard-shell lobsters are more durable, with lower mortality in transport, than soft-shell lobsters. For this reason alone, the Chinese often prefer the Canadian product. But the discrepancies, north and south, do not end there.

"We know Canadian lobster is better quality than lobster from the United States," says Jack Liu of Zoneco, a huge Chinese seafood company that has just bought a stake in a Canadian processing plant. "It's firmer; the meat is fuller. The yield is high; there is more meat inside."

Nonetheless, China is escalating its purchase of Maine lobster every year. They just prefer Maine's hard-shell lobster, when available. Selling new-shell lobsters overseas may be a challenge. Shedders are tasty during the summer months, but they don't travel well. Maine lobstermen, like Frank Gotwals and Jason McDonald, may have to work longer into the winter months to meet the hard-shell demand.

The tide may turn. Canada could someday be eclipsed by China as the largest importer of Maine lobster. Right now, Canada imports $312 million worth of Maine lobster, followed by China's $40.9 million. China simply has to increase its demand eightfold. No other country is in the running. Hong Kong, at six million dollars, and South Korea, at fifteen million, are distant competitors. Italy, England, Spain, and France are buyers, but with each below five million dollars, not in the Asians' league. In all, twenty-five countries import Maine lobster.

Whether China eventually passes Canada or not, Maine has a gauntlet on its hands. It will be a challenging course for lobstermen and the Maine Lobster Marketing Collaborative to sell their brand amid steep competition and entrenched preferences.

"We're in business together," says Jason McDonald of the Maine-Canada rivalry. "But we market new-shell and they sell the Canadian brand. Often it's the same lobster. Or the same distributor anyway. Maybe we should call a truce and simply market the North American lobster—anything to halt the 'Boston lobster' name."

There is a sympathetic ear north of the border. "We've got a lot of balls in the American basket," says Geoff Irvine, executive director of the Lobster Council of Canada. "We don't have any intentions of getting into a showdown with the Americans."

And yet confrontations have erupted just recently. In June 2012, the glut of lobsters in both Maine and Canada pushed prices to the lowest level seen in decades. Maine fishermen had to settle for dockside prices hovering around two dollars per pound. In Canada, processors tracked the U.S. boat price and offered their fishermen the same wage. As a result, Canadian fishermen blocked deliveries of Maine lobster to processors, protesting that they could not compete with the bargain-basement imports. The blockade brought the Canadian industry to a standstill. Anxiety on both sides of the border climbed. The shutdown continued for days, and several shipments of lobsters spoiled. Meanwhile, in Maine, several lobstermen flew the Canadian flag upside down in protest.

Tempers cooled when the Canadians accepted the next load of American lobsters without constructing a roadblock.

Yet other skirmishes may be on the horizon. The second-largest trade relationship—that between the United States and China—may also become a love-hate affair. China has not been content just to buy seafood. Chinese companies are now acquiring processing plants in the Canadian Maritimes. Furthermore, they have an eye on U.S. properties.

In 2014, a subsidiary of Zoneco Group Corporation purchased a huge lobster-processing plant in Eastern Passage, Nova Scotia, with an annual capacity of five million pounds. Zoneco is one of China's largest seafood companies, claiming five thousand employees and four hundred retail outlets. Based in Dalian, China, it is a powerhouse worth two billion dollars. Jack Liu, president of North American operations, says, "We think we can double shipments to ten million pounds in the very near future. The challenge is not selling them there, but transporting the lobsters safely to China. Zoneco has an army of salespeople in the country. We will simply add North American lobster to their offerings."

But Jack Liu is sensitive to North America's fear of carpetbaggers. He insists that China is not here to make a quick buck. "We are here for the long term," he says. "We will become part of the community. I'm ready to sponsor hockey teams, if any are available."

South of Canada, seafood distributors are busily acquiring lobster-buying stations, but so far there have been just a few nibbles on the line from the Chinese. An exception can be found in Tenants Harbor. There, as the fishermen say, the Chinese have swallowed the hook. On my drive south, when I see the sign for Wildcat Lobster, just past Sea Hag Seafood, I hit the brakes. Local lobstermen are up in arms about the leasing of this old lobster wharf and pound by two Chinese-Americans. Well, some are up in arms, but not those selling their catch to these men from away.

The Wildcat Lobster sign has new stenciling, a new phone number, and a new coat of paint. A single naked bulb, flickering yellow, burns over the back door of the house, a dormitory for owners and workers. I discover the dock manager, Mark Farquhar, thirty-eight, on the wharf. He is a Maine native with a solid build, strong enough to lift crates of bait on his own. He stands next to the pound, a three-hundred-foot-long oval pool employed for storing live lobster. The pound is Wildcat's secret weapon.

"We put lobster here through the summer and fall," Mark tells me, "then when the price triples in winter, we sell them—ship them overseas." The pool will hold between fifty thousand and sixty thousand pounds of live lobster, which Mark feeds. The three barrels of bait a day cost him four hundred dollars. The expense is factored into his profit; he netted about $250,000 last year. Aerators keep the water charged with oxygen. When needed, they retrap the lobsters or retrieve them with the aid of scuba divers.

The system is flawless. Wildcat is able to control the price it gets for lobsters, much the way De Beers controls the diamond market by holding back inventory in its vaults in London. A three-dollar lobster becomes a nine-dollar one in four months' time.

The trick has an eighty-year history in Maine. In 1935, Augustus Heanssler was the first person to build a pound in the Sunshine area of Deer Isle. In 1947, Heanssler shipped seven hundred pounds of live lobster from his reserve to London for the wedding of Princess Elizabeth to Philip Mountbatten. Deliveries from the pound and by the pound have continued ever since.

Mark suggests I knock on the back door of the three-bedroom house next to the pound, where the owners—Peter Yee and Steven Yip—live when in town. Both are Hong Kong natives who grew up in New York City. Yee, sixty-two, answers the door and stands below the yellow lightbulb. After a career as an aircraft parts executive (and briefly as a New York fish dealer), he tells me, the Maine-China express is something he cannot pass up. "There's an opportunity here," he says, "to break into new, untapped markets. I have strong business connections in Hong Kong and Shanghai, but that's only the beginning. We have big plans for Tenants Harbor." Peter Yee races back inside to answer a phone call from China.

On the wharf, Mark says they will be packaging lobsters today for airfreight. "We have a surplus right now, so we'll also sell some of the catch to Maine Shellfish Company in Ellsworth. But, back in January, we nearly emptied the pound to fill orders for the Chinese New Year."

Yip and Yee understand the politics of coastal Maine and its fear of outsiders. They were smart to hire Mark as a local manager who could talk "Mainah" with the lobstermen. So far, he has corralled five boats into their fold, sometimes offering five cents per pound over the competition, a move that has further alienated Wildcat from local lobstermen. Yet it keeps Wildcat's small fleet happy. This gives Mark access to anywhere from 2,500 to 5,000 pounds per day, so he can fill the pound in two weeks' time, stockpiling $100,000 worth of lobster. In twenty weeks, Yee and Yip will turn over close to one million dollars gross.

"My boss—Peter—says he could market six million pounds, if we could get them," says Mark. "The trick is having a fleet big enough to meet the demand."

At present, Peter Yee and Steven Yip are leasing the Wildcat operation, but they plan to buy it soon. The asking price of $685,000 includes the house, pound, and wharf, with access to Penobscot Bay, the greatest lobster grounds in the world. (They have also acquired a buying station in Rockland and are eyeing one in Stonington.) The two Chinese-Americans could be sitting pretty.

Peter Yee says, "China consumes thirty-five percent of the world's seafood, making it the biggest importer of fish and shellfish. That's a big appetite. We plan to ride the crest of that wave."

Like Wildcat, over thirty seafood distributors in Maine would like to sell a million pounds or more. Some, like the Lobster Company in Portland, aim at ten million pounds. The expectations are high and the competition is intense. Their targets rely on a robust supply of lobsters in the Gulf of Maine—over 100 million pounds, a recent phenomenon—and a robust global demand. They need a sustainable fishery; they need customers. They are reliant on two bonanzas—supply and demand—that do not always stay at a peak. Yet everyone is riding that wave.

In the middle of town, which is spick-and-span and painted like new, I come upon the Tenants Harbor General Store, for decades a ma-and-pa establishment. Today, it has fallen into the hands of an outsider, Linda Bean, heir to a chunk of the L. L. Bean fortune.

Though it is April, Christmas lights frame the porch of the store. The season of giving is over, yet nobody is bragging about it. I enter the store, intending to buy some ice for my cooler, but, as happens to most Maine adventurers, serendipity tugs at my arm and derails my intentions.

Inside the door, a gurgling water tank holds half a dozen live lobsters. I inspect them closely. A graying man of retired age walks up to me as I lift a lobster from the water. He's a customer, not the cashier.

"You better wait to buy that one when the price drops again," he says with a Boston accent.

"Just looking." I place the lobster back in the tank.

"I saw you at Wildcat as I was driving by. That was you, right?"

"I guess," I say, rummaging through the local newspapers.

"Bad time for those two Chinamen to be investing in a lobster pound. They missed the boat."

"Why's that?" I ask, turning to him now. "Who are you anyhow?"

"I'm Whittaker. I was an import-export man in my former life.

Returned to Tenants Harbor last summer. The fear among lobstermen down here is that there may be a bubble—a Chinese bubble or a lobster balloon in general. Already, nearly ten percent of Maine lobster exports go to China. What if it was twice that? Do we want to be that dependent, that vulnerable? A bubble forms, as you probably know, when forces like credit temporarily prop up an economy, leading to wild speculation and spending. All bubbles begin with a boom—like what we have now."

Whittaker gives me a history lesson, which I don't mind at all. I shove my hands into my pockets and listen.

The pre-Depression bubble of the 1920s began as a growth boom, he says, spawned by mass production in the United States. The pattern repeats itself. Japan's bubble in the 1980s was launched by breakthroughs in electronics and manufacturing. The dot-com bubble grew out of thrilling advances in the information age. Even though these booms evolved naturally, they still formed bubbles that burst disastrously in the end.

"The Chinese bubble is following the same routine," he continues. "It began as a boom founded on positive reforms and modernization, lifting a billion people out of poverty. However, it has devolved into a frenzy of speculation, fueled by credit and an addiction to acquisition."

Whittaker goes on to tell me that an orgy of real estate speculation has led to the construction of "ghost cities," like Ordos in Inner Mongolia, which is uninhabited despite many skyscrapers and apartment buildings. The world's largest mall, New South China Mall, in Dongguan, China, is virtually vacant. Five of the world's ten tallest buildings are now under construction in China. Finally, the reckless mood has nurtured a powerful appetite for luxury goods, the more frivolous the better. Yachts, Ferraris, and Château Lafite Rothschild are now within the grasp of many Chinese, as are two-hundred-dollar rock lobsters from New Zealand. Many economists predict China will have its own Great Depression when its bubble pops.

"The burst will be heard around the world," Whittaker says, "as derivatives of its bubble—Australia, Canada, Korea, and commodities in general—also pop." Could Maine's economy also crash? If Chinese demand for Maine lobsters, now on a skyrocketing trajectory, came to a sudden end, what would be the consequences?

Whittaker offers a parallel story that is telling. Farm commodities react to China in a similar way, he says. It's not just the fear of a Chinese downturn; American farmers also fear that China's patronage is fickle. "One day last August," he says, "American corn futures sank more than five percent, the largest one-day percentage dip in two years. There was too much produce, depressing the price. Oversupply was only part of the issue. Demand was down, too. Major buyers like China have switched to other producers, such as Brazil and the Ukraine, for corn. When there's competition like that, local demand can plummet." Whittaker turns toward me with a wink. "Look out for those Australian lobster tails. They're moving faster than the American."

Whittaker has impressed me. Lobsters are not corn, but the laws of economics are the same. I reach around him to grab a jar of Maine honey off the shelf. "You know," I say, "honey never spoils; it can last three thousand years."

But Whittaker will not be distracted. He's coming into his home stretch. "Twenty years ago, Maine lost more than five thousand jobs when its lumber and paper industries failed, partly from cutthroat competition by the Chinese. The potential crash of local lobster stocks could double the impact on the economy, on coastal communities. But I'm just making predictions. Who really knows? John Kenneth Galbraith says there are two types of forecasters: those who don't know the future and those who don't know they don't know." And with that, Whittaker disappears out the front door.

I realize at that moment that a balloon of exports is a little like a burst of warming: At a low volume, sales and heat are helpful, but too much exposure to foreign markets or temperature can lead to a downdraft in productivity. Exports to China may be more precarious than I thought. If climate change prompted the glut and the glut stimulated the bubble, then indirectly warming has stoked the Chinese bubble itself, a fragile predicament for all.

I forget the bag of ice but, on impulse, snatch a soft drink as I make a beeline for the front door. The soda is parked between the Australian wine and the imported beer, both new arrivals for Tenants Harbor. Foreign taste (and investment), whether from Boston, Sydney, or Beijing, is changing the profile of the town.

Behind the store counter, the blond cashier is working on a crossword puzzle. She holds the pencil in her teeth.

I ask her if she's lived in Tenants Harbor all her life.

"Not yet," she responds, clamping down on the pencil with uncommon force.

I pay the cashier for my drink and honey, and step into the sun. I scan the street. Much of the town's modifications are hidden from my view. New construction takes place on the waterfront, far away from the frontage road.

Driving through Tenants Harbor now, I scan the facade of homes and commerce. The frame homes have not been altered, but the ownership has. This predicament is a tale of two seasons. While spring is bustling, with tourists arriving, downtown is nearly vacant in winter. Formerly, residents occupied all the homes on Main Street all year long. As in Stonington, this is no longer the case. Real estate speculation has followed. Now summer people leave their homes empty in winter, the pipes drained and the furnaces turned low—everything buttoned up. Lobstermen like Mark Farquhar and Peter Miller complain of a ghost town.

Peter Miller owns a commercial wharf and restaurant, Cod End, right in the middle of town. He is also a lobster buyer. In a harbor of forty lobster boats, Peter buys from a third. All three of his enterprises are up for sale.

I find him on his wharf, fixing lobster traps and painting buoys. His colors: bright yellow and red. Peter is sixty-six. He inherited his red hair from his father, Carlton "Red" Miller, along with the restaurant. Red and his wife, Anne, started out with a fish market, supplied with bycatch from their five sons, lobstermen all. When times were lean, Red worked in maintenance for Andrew and Betsy Wyeth on nearby Allen and Benner Islands. But most years he thrived. The Cod End Market and Cookhouse served lobster dinners, scallops, shrimp, cod, flounder, haddock, mussels, clams—all products of the fisheries Maine has loved and lost. Cod End can no longer get the fish; its doors closed in 2014, after forty years of service.

Miller's Lobster Wharf sits alongside the empty restaurant, with a beautiful pier reaching into the harbor between them. At the end of the pier is a floating dock, similar to the one at the Stonington Co-op. But lobsters are actually bought and sold at an independent floating hub, a miniature island farther out in the harbor. Ten lobstermen sell to Peter here regularly each day, plus several drop-ins. Most of these captains live farther up the St. George Peninsula. Only a handful of captains can still afford to live in town. Surging property taxes may drive the last hold-outs away. Tenants Harbor is a model of gentrification. After the center point of lobsters vacates Penobscot Bay, Stonington could be next.

Since the crest of the Maine lobster population departed the waters off Tenants Harbor in the late 1990s, the town has had twenty years outside its beneficial shadow. The town is graying at the edges. The whole place seems to be for sale.

I ask Peter right off the top if he has had any takers for the three properties.

"One," he says. "I'm a lobster dealer, but the next big distributor who purchases from me up the chain—Mainely Seafood of Owls Head—may buy me out."

At this point, Peter's sternman, John Alden, joins us. He's thirty and plays short to Peter's tall. "Mainely wants to consolidate," Peter continues. "All the big players are doing it now. Garbo, once only a processor, is now buying directly at the dock. So is East Coast Seafood. It will make it difficult for small operations like mine to compete."

"How so?" asks John Alden, a Maine native whose namesake was on the *Mayflower*.

"The middleman gets squeezed out. Before, I'd make, say, thirty cents a pound buying lobster and reselling it. Now Garbo or another big company buys direct from the boats and gives that thirty cents back to the lobstermen to reestablish loyalty. I cannot match that. They call it 'vertical integration.'"

"My cousin got integrated," says John. "It killed him and the other middlemen. It's killing families and our communities. The last three years, lobster prices have been too low. Now the big distributors are taking a bigger bite out of the pie."

"I've told my son, Josh, to give up lobstering," says Peter. "Told him to quit and get certified for heating and plumbing maintenance. He already helps out with a plumber in the wintertime. Now, there's a dependable job."

"Josh won't ever quit," says John Alden. "He's like you."

"I know. But I had to try. Reckoning is coming. The statewide land-ings wobbled last year for certain; we're just waiting on the bean counters. It may be a significant drop. I feel we've reached our peak. I just can't believe what we've been catching the past five years. Holy cow! It can't go on."

The next morning, I meet Peter and John at the wharf at 4:00 A.M. to go lobstering aboard *Sasha,* their thirty-five-foot boat. The fog is soupy, thick as clam chowder. Josh has already boarded his boat, *Dorcas Anne.* The younger generation has more ambition than the old men.

During the day, we work the following: the Humps, four hills at twenty fathoms (120 feet); Chapel Rock, a lobster haven at the same depth; and the footprint of Southern Island, where the painter Jamie Wyeth lives. The latter, Peter shares, is the setting he likes best: working the ledges off an island or the shore, in clear water, where he can actually see his gear on the bottom. Others must agree. The eastern end of Southern Island is surrounded by a cove of colored buoys.

Peter talks about how fishing has changed. "Thirty years ago, I'd lob-ster the channel in spring, then move up and tight, near shore, for the shedders in summer. Now, today, I'm just as likely to find a shedder in deep water. It must be the warmer water that's doing it. Lobstering has shifted offshore. It's a whole new game."

By noon today, Peter finishes tending 170 traps on rotation. He looks in the tank and says, "Oh Lordy, we're gonna be rich!" He's bluffing. We have only three hundred hard-shell lobsters or so, but Peter is an opti-mist, though not wide-eyed. He says, "Today is a good reason to have a wife that works."

On the voyage home, Peter seems pensive for a while, searching for something out across the water. We motor like that, in silence, for twenty minutes. Suddenly, he speaks. "Fisheries are fragile, they say. But I'll tell you, people seem even more vulnerable than lobsters these days. Com-munities are tested; our town has changed. Twenty years ago, Tenants Harbor was more of a fishing town. The General Store was a real mer-cantile; now we must go to Rockland for a lightbulb. Cod End was a thriving restaurant; my sister was in charge; now we must let it go. Lawn maintenance is the biggest job for young men today. Well, old men, too.

We have more people now—more outsiders with more money. What does that get you? We didn't need any of that in the old days."

Peter swings the boat toward his float to unload our meager catch. "And those are just local concerns," he continues. "The whole world is warming. No question about it, the Gulf is heating up. No question at all. And, speaking of temperatures, the Chinese may be the hottest thing on the block. That's the one thing that may cool off—the demand from Asia.

"But, look, I'm here for the long run, even if I sell the business. I'll never retire. If I won the lottery tomorrow, I'd still go out lobstering. If I had one day left, I'd go. I love it that much."

9

Tragedy of the Commons

Maine fishermen are not especially religious compared to, say, the Methodist watermen of Chesapeake Bay. Fisherfolk attend church suppers of any denomination, but the majority avoid Sunday sermons. Sunday is still sacred, however; it's the lobsterman's only day off. On Sunday mornings, the lobstermen and their spouses seek spiritual fulfillment in informal, creative ways. The Clamdigger Bar is one avenue; Suzy's Scissors is another; Frank's garden a third. By far the most original substitute is the Church of the Morning After on Main Street. Morning after, as in recovering from the wicked ways of Saturday night.

By 7:00 A.M., ten musicians have assembled in Steve Robbins's repair shop along the waterfront between Marlinspike Chandlery and Dockside Books. This is half the capacity of the place, not because it is small, but thanks to the lobster traps, buoys, and warps scattered about the room, as if a tornado had just rushed through. The first ten are the core of the orchestra—well, of the chorus, too. Admirers linger at the entrance and overflow into the street. There are no pews, but prime seats are reserved for the musicians—about five more to come, making fifteen. The first ten lift their instruments—guitars, banjos, ukuleles, dulcimers, violins (fiddles), and accordions—and begin to play. Steve's Church of the Morning After is a gathering of the best musical talent in town, an end in itself. It is a self-described halfway house. The theory is: All sins will be absolved with a little harmony. What they create beyond that is more than a family, nothing less than a community, an antidote to self-conceit.

Steve Robbins, seventy-three, sits in the middle of his shop, holding court. He is a longtime, full-time lobsterman but moonlights as a repairman of other captains' gear. He is a big man—over 240 pounds—and completely bald, an odd but commanding look for a guitar player with an angelic voice. Nobody is certain when Steve began his Sunday service, least of all Steve, but it's likely that a few friends came over to play one Sunday, then another, and before they knew it, they had a tradition. Today, the band assembles fifty-two weeks of the year. New musicians are welcome but must introduce at least one new song, to which the varsity joins in—seamlessly. They know all the classic tunes—rock, country, folk, blues, bluegrass, and beyond.

The lobster traps, in various states of disrepair, occupy three piles on the floor, one next to Steve, where he has set his thermos and cigars. Heaps of coiled rope, four feet high, take up more floor space. On a workbench sits a purple-and-gold felt bag of Crown Royal, the preferred poison of the band. But the most ubiquitous objects are the recently painted lobster buoys hanging from columns and ceiling struts. Most are adorned in black and hot pink, Steve's colors. A few dozen dangle like ornaments. On the floor beneath them, unpainted buoys lie waiting. Like some sinners, they haven't yet been resurrected.

Another musician, Renée Sewell, arrives and wiggles her way into a cubbyhole between two traps. Real estate is precious at church. Renée opens the case to her bass guitar and sets her car keys in a Maxwell House can, where Steve keeps nails and screws. She kicks a paint can out of her way and tunes up.

As the ensemble warms up, it is clear they can harmonize with one another, in any key, as easily as changing lanes on the highway. Steve leads with a riff from George Harrison's "Here Comes the Sun," and the rest of the pack climbs on board for the hayride. Steve taps his foot, or, rather, his shoe, covered with hot-pink paint. "That pink is coordinated with my pants," he shouts. Sure enough, his neatly creased khakis have swirls of pink and black, reminiscent of a Pollock painting.

One more straggler, Lori Connor, tiptoes past the buoys and paintbrushes to the back of the room. She holds a ukulele. Still playing, Steve says, "You're late, dear one."

"I know," says Lori.

"Drunk, as usual, I suppose?"

"Not on your life."

Steve smiles and chuckles and lets it go. "Sun, sun, sun," he sings.

"Yes, here she comes," Lori ad-libs.

Twelve voices now rise in chorus, "Here comes the sun." They're all in the same chord, regardless of the instrument. Steve encourages them to take risks with a wild strum of his guitar. He drops a chord by mistake and shrugs. He does not preach temperance, just forgiveness.

The warm-up complete, the musicians jockey for position, dragging chairs here and there. "Can someone hand me a saw," a guitarist calls out, "so I can cut the arms off this chair?" Then his Gibson will fit.

The older man with the banjo says, "I can smell the bait on these rubber gloves."

"Oh, good, I love a little atmosphere," says Renée.

Make no mistake, atmosphere is what they have got.

The guitarist with the Gibson finishes sawing the arms off his chair, then stands up, gently lays his classic guitar on its case, and pulls out a harmonica. That's the first hint he's going to play "Know You Rider," the traditional version. With the first three notes, the seven guitars in the room join in.

Well I know you rider, gonna miss me when I'm gone
Well I know you rider, gonna miss me when I'm gone
You gonna miss your mama from rolling in your arms
Just as sure as the bird fly in the sky above
Just as sure as the bird fly in the sky above
Life ain't worth living if you ain't with the man you love

Now the accordion and banjo figure out the tune. The ukuleles and dulcimers climb aboard. It sounds like they've been practicing for weeks, not just freelancing a five-minute jam session.

The sun's gonna shine in my back door someday
The sun's gonna shine in my back door someday
The wind's gonna rise and blow my blues away
To love you baby, it's easy as falling off a log
To love you baby, it's as easy as falling off a log
Wanna be your baby but I sure won't be your dog

At the end of the classic song, two spectators who were listening at the doorway step inside to find seats. One is a Greek who fixed my deck. The other is Julie Eaton. They join Dick Bridges, Andy Gove, and Bill Sargent, three lobstermen, in the bleachers. Next through the door are Frank and brother Bob Gotwals, who carry guitars and a trumpet. The brothers stand tall in a position of honor, opposite Steve Robbins. No need to saw any more chairs. Frank discreetly drops a jar of raspberry jam, produce from his garden, into Steve's guitar case. An offering to the gods.

Steve notices this but makes no acknowledgment. He lights up his first cigar of the morning. Smoke drifts across the room like a bank of fog, a sweet smell that cancels the residual odor of bait. Steve takes a long drag. He's serious now. When it comes to the music archive—the long parade of traditional American ballads—Frank is his only peer. Now Steve has his audience.

He strums a few chords, puts down his cigar, and sings:

Has anybody seen my Corrine?
No matter where Corrina might be
Tell my Corrina to come right back to me
I want some lovin' sweetie dear

Besides the chorus, "Corrine, Corrina" has two more stanzas. But Steve stumbles on these. "There are more words," he says, "but I was drunk when I learned that one." This is an act; Steve doesn't drink at all anymore.

Frank responds with a solo of the traditional song that led to Jerry Garcia's "Going Down the Road Feeling Bad." When Frank comes to the line "Going where the water tastes like wine," the whole room jumps in with "Yes, the water tastes like wine."

Frank and Steve switch bands to the Animals with a duet of "The House of the Rising Sun." They work their guitars in such a lovely way that there is no need for words. The mood of the instrumental places the crowd right in a house in New Orleans.

The congregation plays for two more hours—songs of longing, disappointment, and hope. They also hit some high notes of humor, singing "Dead Skunk in the Middle of the Road."

Julie makes a request. "How about something southern?"

Frank does the honors of introducing a southern zinger as the last song, or what everyone thinks is the last song, "Dixie Chicken."

If you'll be my Dixie chicken, I'll be your Tennessee lamb
And we can walk together down in Dixieland.

The throng picks up on this chorus instantly and repeats it enthusiastically with each musician taking a turn to feature his or her instrument or to ad-lib new lyrics.

At this point, a yellow Lab barges through the front door and inspects the room, licking all the seated musicians, knocking over coffee cups with his tail. The spilled coffee blends nicely with the paint on the floor. Satisfied with his havoc, the Lab exits with gusto, nuzzling Julie on his way out. Never missing a beat, the harmonica whistles out "Down in Dixieland," at the end. Suddenly, they are done, but there is a call for an encore.

This is inevitable, since Frank has not yet played one of his own songs, and many in the audience are loyal fans. One of them says, "What about tomorrow, Frank? You got a ballad about what's coming next?"

"An Unfamiliar Sea," he says, echoing the title of a recent album of his—all songs written by him. He lifts his guitar strap back over his head and strums a few chords. In his soft voice, he sings:

The captain tells me stories with a proud but thoughtful look
We ripped the fish out of the sea with just a compass and a hook.
Passed along the knowledge gained from father down to son
And learned through generations that the work was never done.

I should have seen this coming all too easily.
Too many seek these treasures and there's much less for me.
No one here's worked half so hard or quite so long as me.
And the fog keeps getting thicker on this unfamiliar sea.

The room is silent for a moment, the crowd thoughtful. Then the spectators launch into applause, and Julie Eaton whistles like a mynah bird. Patrons and performers hoof it to the Harbor Café for a late Sunday breakfast. To the Stonington crew, eating breakfast before church is sacrilege. So they keep hunger in check. Daily bread is later-day French toast. All patrons agree to that—or pancakes.

A community like this "Sunday church" group tries to find common ground. For Steve Robbins and friends, music is the great melting pot. So if you ask a Stonington resident if he or she has been to church recently, they know exactly what you mean—Steve's northern revival. Most have run the gauntlet of pots and paint for spiritual renewal at one time or another. This may come as a surprise. Fishing towns are better known for selfish behavior than for cooperation. That's why overfishing and seafood wars are commonplace in coastal towns throughout the world.

In Steve's case, however, the community is a shared and cherished commodity. Fearing the loss of it, fishermen are fighting hard for its survival. Yet for centuries around the world, fishing villages and common grounds have hosted a tragedy of greed. The depths of that calamity are most obvious elsewhere in the Gulf of Maine.

From Cape Cod to Nova Scotia's Cape Sable, the Gulf encompasses one-fifth of the Atlantic seaboard, a territory the size of Lake Superior. Commercial fishermen exploit the nearly thirty active fisheries found here, bringing in over $600 million each year. Lobster comprises 80 percent of the take. All other species trail in single digits. The lesser species are largely overfished. Most experts agree the American lobster is one of the few marine species that is not overexploited—at least for now.

Around the globe, fishing stocks are plunging. From New England flounder to Atlantic and Pacific bluefin tuna, from Grand Banks swordfish to Peruvian anchovy, from Gulf of Mexico mackerel to coastal sharks, marine species have been overfished. After exploiting pelagic and bottom-dwelling species like herring and halibut, respectively, industrial fishers are now moving on to deepwater and Antarctic species, such as orange roughy and krill, the food upon which baleen whales depend. The oceans resemble an enormous chessboard on which most of the pieces have toppled. Checkmate on us: The fish are nearly gone.

By net, trap, trawl, and hook and line, fishermen are taking far more produce out of the seas than can be replenished by the breeding stock that remains. As a consequence, 53 percent of global fisheries are "fully exploited," says the World Wildlife Fund, and nearly a third are "over-exploited, depleted, or recovering from depletion." Unless the trend reverses, all species harvested for food may collapse by 2048.

If asked to single out one factor that prompts such a gloomy forecast, scientists point to "overcapacity" of the world's fishing fleets. The roster of boats is two times larger than the level that oceans can accommodate sustainably. Experts argue that the industry could return to the profile of fewer, smaller boats of the 1970s and still produce the same yield. The same argument is made for lobster boats and traps.

How did this overcapacity develop around the world? Declining stocks prompt more competition for a limited resource—a "gilded trap," in Bob Steneck's words, if you will. This led to overcapitalization of larger and larger boats, of more nets, of a bigger fleet. When a fishery goes bust, the whole armada steams toward a new patch of blue, as if suffering from some unquenchable addiction.

The solution offered for this dilemma is usually aquaculture, which may take some pressure off overfished seas. But lobsters, it turns out, are not well suited to sea farming. Larvae can be raised in hatcheries, but they take five to seven years to mature. Meanwhile, they require a huge food input. If not, they become cannibalistic. So if aquaculture is to help Maine lobstermen, it will be to augment stocks of other species—clams, mussels, scallops—that lobstermen might harvest in their spare time. Right now, lobstermen have only one prize in mind: lobster.

Such single-mindedness is the Maine lobsterman's potential downfall. In Newfoundland, where single-minded fishermen watched their exclusive cod fishery collapse in 1992, some forty thousand people lost their jobs overnight; ten thousand of them were fishermen. More than twenty-five years later, the cod have shown only a slight rebound on the Grand Banks. Thanks to ocean warming, they may never recover completely. Canadians have few places and species left.

Just to the southwest, the Gulf of Maine has its own challenges. Maine has a long tradition of overfishing. Its track record is poor: Herring, hake, halibut, croaker, and cod have been overexploited. Same goes for flounder—winter flounder, witch flounder, and windowpane. Trawlers have also depressed pollock and redfish populations. In fact, all groundfish have been overharvested. Invertebrates like clams and sea urchins have succumbed. Pelagic species like mackerel are not exempt. Unless managed well, black sea bass will likely be next. Does anyone learn from their neighbor or from the past?

Overfishing may be generally defined as harvesting from a population at a rate greater than the population's reproduction capacity to replace the harvested animals. However, for each species, managers have developed a more specific measure of overfishing. The Atlantic States Marine Fisheries Commission (ASMFC), along with the National Marine Fisheries Service and the state of Maine, manages lobster stocks in the Gulf of Maine. The ASMFC's official definition of overfishing lobster reads: "The American lobster resource is overfished when it is harvested at a rate that results in egg production, on an egg-per-recruit basis, that is less than 10 percent of the level produced by an unfished population."

In other words, the average female lobster should be allowed to live long enough to produce at least 10 percent of the eggs that she would produce if she were allowed to live her natural life. If she is harvested ahead of that schedule, overfishing is in play.

Out of the many casualties in the long parade of Maine fisheries, let's look at the most recent: northern shrimp. In December 2013, the ASMFC banned all shrimp fishing in the Gulf of Maine, citing overfishing and ocean warming. The shrimp population had collapsed so swiftly in just two years that the ASMFC considered there was "very little hope for recovery in the near future."

"It's the lowest biomass in history," said Terry Stockwell of the Maine Department of Marine Resources at the time. The shrimp have suffered a one-two punch. First, overfishing depressed stocks. In 2010, for example, shrimpers caught 2.2 million pounds over their federal limit of 10.8 million pounds, a 20 percent overage. Subsequent years showed a similar excess. Second, the warmer waters have affected the shrimp by killing off the phytoplankton that shrimp consume. Since overfishing is a relative concept, it was hoped that the moratorium on fishing would allow the small crustaceans to replenish themselves.

But the initial ban had little effect. The numbers of shrimp from 2012 to 2016 were the "lowest on record." Like cod, once northern shrimp are knocked down, they don't seem able to get back up. Ocean warming has compounded the effects of overfishing.

Ironically, climate change may keep fishermen from having to face up to the responsibility of overfishing. In the long run, warming seas may overshadow the impact of exploitation. In the short term, their impacts may reinforce each other's impacts. This synergy has happened with both cod and northern shrimp, bringing on an intense search for the last remaining stocks.

Old-time lobstermen know the trap well; they can remember years of low catches, followed by frantic hauling and a further decline in stocks. The 1920–1940 lobster seasons fit the pattern. Young lobstermen have shorter memories, and the senior men warn them, to no avail. Today, even in the face of a historic boom, old-timers are cautious. They warn of the threat of overfishing from a new generation of lobstermen who captain bigger boats—some over fifty feet long—bearing traps they turn over more frequently. These mavericks go farther out in the ocean and lobster all year, instead of taking the traditional midwinter break. By adding three months to their season, the cowboys augment their catch by one-third or more. Today's winters tend to be milder, so it's no sacrifice. More and more lobstermen are trying their hand at winter. Meanwhile, a 120-million-pound season could turn into 150 million pounds, a new record. But would it be sustainable?

We do not know yet, since climate forces coupled with overfishing have not reached their zenith. In the shadow of ocean warming, prevention of illegal harvesting and other forms of overfishing will be even more important. Climate change intensifies overexploitation. Both are immediate threats to the livelihood of lobstermen.

Ecologists, the scientists who study organisms in relation to their environment, claim there is a common thread to shared resources like ocean fisheries, and a common tendency to overexploit them. In many ways, the bluefin tuna fishery, the cod fishery, and the herring fishery have the same history. Fishermen act in their own self-interest, catching the maximum amount of fish, sometimes contrary to the best communal interests of the fleet. They deplete the common resource even when they would be served better by conserving it.

This common paradox, or psychology, if you will, was characterized by ecologist Garrett Hardin in 1968. He pointed to short-term selfish behavior as the critical personality trait of the ranchers, farmers, and fishermen who landed in trouble, especially when they ignored what was best for the group. He identified Aristotle as the first observer to write about the phenomenon, so the dilemma had gone unchecked for centuries. Thanks to Garrett Hardin, the issue took center stage again. Hardin's revolutionary thesis has been at the center of debate in ecology and economics circles ever since.

Hardin presented a parable, called "The Tragedy of the Commons," which teaches a simple lesson—initially set in farming country—with powerful implications for managing fisheries and other common resources. The parable imagines a pasture "open to all," a sea of grass. Several herders graze their sheep there, motivated to expand their flocks—infinitely, if possible—even though it is not in the best interest of the community. Quickly, each animal added to the turf degrades the commons by a small amount, eating the grass, leaving the soil bare. The herder receives all the benefits of an additional ram or ewe, while the damage to the commons is suffered by all. If all the owners continue the pattern of overuse, the turf becomes overgrazed. The commons is destroyed. Therein lies the tragedy: Each owner is locked into short-term selfish behavior that causes long-term environmental harm to everyone.

A classic example of the tragedy is the imperiled cod fishery on the Grand Banks. Many of those fishermen had hailed from Maine. Refusing any sensible quotas, each fisherman loaded his boat, until the fishery crashed in the 1990s. Afterward, fishermen returned from the Grand Banks with nearly empty boats. Selfish interests interfered with the collective good. Reaching its own nadir, the predicament forced the collapse of a fishery. Freedom in the commons brought ruin to all.

Looking at this predicament, we can easily despair over the unsustainability of human behavior. Being selfish about a shared resource can clearly hurt others. But it does not always have to, as Hardin's critics have pointed out. When Hardin's paradigm was first published, he considered the only solutions to the tragedy he described to be the adoption of draconian government regulations or turning the commons (air, land, water) into a private enterprise. The reasoning went that owners of private property protect their resources, while those exploiting public property do not. One solution: A commons can be placed in private hands—enclosed.

But what about the freedom of the seas? The oceans are not and cannot be owned. Hardin's idea might work for land but apparently not for water. Moreover, fishermen resist government regulations and, in fact, lobby successfully against them. So, many argue, Hardin's two answers would not work in the Gulf of Maine. In the ensuing years, new solutions have emerged, for a few had been operating in other parts of the world for centuries. Examples include grazing and forest lands in Switzerland and Japan and irrigation systems in the Philippines and Spain. In all these cases, local citizens came up with solutions to the commons dilemma themselves. Elinor Ostrom, the 2009 Nobel laureate in economics, championed such alternatives to Hardin's scenario in the 1990s. She found that various communities have been able to manage their common resources equitably and sustainably over many years. In most cases, they banded together to limit access by adopting institutions that provided incentives for wise use. That cooperative behavior stands in contrast to Hardin's "selfish" behavior, which he claimed was always the rational course of humanity. In Ostrom's world, because of the long-term benefits, mutual cooperation is a more rational action than independence.

Hardin's forecast for the inevitable overuse of a commons relied on open access, where anyone could enter the mutual ground and exploit it. But when you consider commons with limited access, like some fisheries that have a set number of licenses allowed (e.g., Alaskan king crab), cooperative management is possible. An instinct for altruism within a small community—especially one that limits access—is an antidote for the events Hardin delineated. However, before the 1990s, the Maine lobster fishery was wide open to whoever had a boat.

Ostrom showed that societal controls can regulate the use of a commons without having to resort to private property. She says a commons does not have to be placed in private hands. Besides restricting access, remedies include creating community institutions that police the commons and designing incentives to follow the rules, such as shares in the resource, bonuses for limiting the catch, or fines for exceeding it. Paramount to the success of the group effort is the free flow of information on stock abundance, prices, weather, and the like. Accepting the latest scientific information is important, too. Are you listening, climate deniers? The more valid news a person has, the more secure he or she is in making rational decisions.

For example, access to the North Pacific halibut fishery was not restricted, and it thus suffered losses, until news and action brought individual quotas. Catch limits were also imposed. The twin measures of restricting access and offering incentives turned the fishery around.

When gathering her success stories around the world in 1990, Elinor Ostrom said, "Tragedies of the commons are real, but not inevitable." If she had waited five years, she would have come upon a nascent institution in Maine, struggling to assert itself, called "comanagement." This initiative has broken new ground in fisheries stewardship. It may have circumvented the "tragedies of the commons" right at home.

In 1995, at the urging of Marine Resources Commissioner Robin Alden, the state legislature established the seven "lobster zones" off the coast. These management areas are mostly rectangular, running perpendicular to the coast from Kittery in the southwest to Cutler in the northeast. They are contiguous, nestled from front to back like lanes in a swimming pool. Fishermen from a nearby township with a license for a given zone can lobster only in that particular lane. The zones are modeled upon local lobstering territories, those exclusive grounds guarded by fishermen's families. That framework was recognized by Robin Alden as having helped to conserve lobster populations for decades. Now, with the seven zones superimposed on the lobster grounds, local fishermen had two jurisdictions to defend: family territories and their broader zone.

To administer the zones, a council was elected to each with the responsibility of recommending conservation measures to the commissioner of Marine Resources—a whole new paradigm. This form of advice and consent constitutes comanagement, for in breaking with traditional top-down governmental management, it allows a partnership between resource stewards and fishermen. Comanagement could be of special utility as climate change gathers strength.

At first, the legislature empowered the zone councils to propose rules on three issues: limits on the number of traps per boat, control over the number of traps on a line or buoy, and setting the hours when lobstering is allowed. Then, in 1999, the legislature gave zones the power to recommend limitations on the number of licenses in a zone, the so-called limited-entry system. Unbeknownst to fishermen, closing access in this way was one of Elinor Ostrom's solutions to the commons dilemma.

The idea was to put a cap on the number of licenses (or an entry/exit ratio) for each zone. The calculations are complex. With over 4,900 lobster licenses issued in the state, many lobstermen retire each year, exiting the fishery and allowing the entry of student and apprentice lobstermen. In fact, some 22 percent of all licenses are inactive but not turned in. Lobstermen tie their identity to having a commercial license, even if they are too elderly to make use of one. This inactive group, consisting of perhaps 1,085 former lobstermen, has created a bottleneck for young lobstermen wanting to join the profession. Over three hundred fishermen sit on waiting lists for various zones.

Six of the zones have restricted entry—the exception being Zone C, the area off Stonington, which has remained open until recently. The council of lobstermen for Zone C have just considered a closure of their area. With it, all of the Maine coast will have limited entry, a protection of the commons. Because fewer new lobstermen have been approved than have retired or died, there has been a net reduction in issued licenses—by 12 percent since 1997.

The system is not perfect. The average wait for a license is six years; for some, it has taken twenty years. This is a frustration for some fishermen, but it's a rule that largely has worked so far. The lobster grounds—the zones and the territories within them—are not overrun with outsiders. By empowering the local fishermen to limit access, everyone helps protect the industry from overfishing. So does Maine's law, which states lobster licenses are restricted to owner-operators. The captain must be aboard while fishing. No corporate fishing is allowed.

Surprisingly, over the years, there has been a steady increase in deployed traps overall (now approaching three million), so it is doubtful that restricting entry alone can control effort effectively. Nonetheless, it puts one conservation mechanism in place. Should the lobster population decline, a combination of limiters may be needed, including catch quotas and stricter trap limits.

Limited entry, or closed access, plugs one hole in the leaky facade of the "tragedy of the commons." Still, if the resource collapsed, says Don Perkins and his team at GMRI, "the current system would not be able to respond fast enough to prevent overfishing, which could be catastrophic to Maine's lobster fishery and coastal communities." Four thousand lobstermen would simply overwhelm a lobster population at half the current size.

Stricter trap limits are one way to be better prepared. When the zone management law was written, the zone councils were given authority over setting trap limits, provided that the number did not exceed a maximum limit of twelve hundred. At first, each zone agreed to adopt a limit of twelve hundred traps, largely because most fishermen had grown weary of "hogs" who set and hauled more than that number. Subsequently, under a zone council referendum, all zones switched to a limit of eight hundred traps. The exception is Zone E, off Boothbay Harbor, which lowered its cap to six hundred traps. Since then, no other zone council has cut its limit. Although Zone E's move appears to be a selfless conservation gesture, the rumor was that the move was simply to discourage other fishermen from colonizing its waters. Further efforts to lower trap limits in various zones have come to naught.

Still, marine scientists and economists agree that reducing the trap limit would likely put more money in the pockets of fishermen. At five hundred or six hundred traps, a lobsterman would save on trap construction, bait, and fuel, while catching a similar volume of lobster. What's more, if the volume did decrease a bit, the price would likely climb and make up for the drop—in that remarkable balancing act of supply and demand. Simultaneously, the stricter lobstermen would conserved the resource more.

There is no rule etched in the water that says lobstermen must harvest close to 90 percent of the adult population each year—the overfishing threshold. They could leave more behind for the ecosystem and the species that depend on lobster.

Furthermore, as shown earlier, there is evidence that reducing the number of traps in an area actually increases trap efficiency. Lobstermen can recite the experiment. Meanwhile, in a coastal survey of lobstermen throughout the seven zones, 63 percent agreed with the statement "There are too many traps in the water." Only 14 percent disagreed. However, only 13 percent were in favor of voting to enforce stricter trap limits. Lobstermen seem to be of two minds: They see a problem with trap densities, but they do not want to fix it. Not yet. Ironically, they are set in their ways.

"When you're a fisherman, you're an optimist," says Robin Alden. "You wouldn't leave the harbor if you didn't think you could fill your boat."

That optimism keeps the trap numbers at the upper limit. Not only are lobstermen allowed eight hundred traps; they also carry that many. If the Gulf of Maine were drained for a day, it would appear as cluttered with traps as cars in rush-hour traffic on an L.A. freeway. As experiments show, three million traps is simply overwhelming and unnecessary for the fishery. Sooner or later, comanagement will be called on to respond.

Comanagement is inherently very fragile. It requires nurturing to keep it running right. It also requires a steady flow of reliable information—news on experiments with trap limits is one example. Science news on ocean warming and its impacts is another. Comanagement in Maine is not structured to act quickly on conservation needs. After twenty years, entry limits are just now being successfully negotiated for Zone C. In a crisis, the Department of Marine Resources and the legislature may have to step in to effect change. Nonetheless, this awkward twenty-year-old system is growing into the best remedy for the commons.

A new challenge for the lobster zone councils is fast approaching on the horizon: ocean warming. They now recognize high lobster population densities are shifting northeast in the Gulf of Maine. Bob Steneck was the first to track this movement by looking at landings and temperature by counties for the fifty-year period from 1965 to 2014. Once concentrated in

Casco Bay off Portland (in the 1970s), the center point of the Gulf of Maine lobster population is now in northeastern Maine.

This shift coincides with a warming of the eastern zones in each successive autumn, when lobster postlarvae are sounding. For example, the waters of Hancock County, which contain Stonington and most of Zone C, surpassed the 12° C threshold suitable for lobster settlement in 2011 and subsequent years. For that period, landings skyrocketed to 19,800 pounds per mile (15,000 kilograms per kilometer) of coast. Meanwhile, Cumberland County, to the southwest, the home of Casco Bay, leveled off to half that harvest.

During October 2016, a trap war erupted at the border of Zones B and C in Hancock County. Over $350,000 worth of gear was destroyed by the two factions in the territorial dispute. The movement of lobster from Zone C to Zone B and the reaction of lobstermen "pushing the edge" were to blame. The Marine Patrol posted a fifteen-thousand-dollar reward for any information on the culprits, a bounty that brought silence to the waters fast—the fisherman's code. The lesson is that more disputes over warming waters and displaced lobster are coming soon, but few will hear about the violence and vandalism that accompany any possible lobster war.

For the lobster zones in general, the northward trend means high lobster densities are shifting from zone to zone, west to east, up the coast. The councils will likely want to reexamine the rules for crossing zone boundaries and for hauling outside the three-mile line. Otherwise, within a given zone, fishermen may find lobsters less abundant from one year to the next. This scenario is ripe for contention. It may be difficult for lobstermen to settle for less than they had the previous year.

Disturbances like the northward movement of lobsters draw into question the future of lobstering in Maine. Lobsters are no longer evenly distributed along the coastline. And yet, Maine lobsters are considered a "sustainable" marine resource. The history behind this classification—and its benefits—is illuminating.

In 2013, the London-based Marine Stewardship Council (MSC) certified the Maine lobster as sustainable. This award from the premier international certification institute for wild-caught fisheries was welcomed by the state of Maine. The blue MSC label on seafood promises to boost demand and prices. It is also prestigious. The certification process is rigorous. The MSC investigates the health of the fish stocks, how environmental impacts of local fishing operations are minimized, and what management systems are in place that might respond to changing conditions. Maine lobster seems to qualify. So do over two hundred fisheries around the world—about 10 percent of all fisheries—ranging from North Atlantic swordfish and Greenland cod to Alaskan salmon and North Pacific halibut.

The irony is that lobsters are vulnerable to climate change and an increase in predators—and thus a downturn—regardless of what good management is in place. The most current stock assessment places the Gulf of Maine population at 248 million lobsters, approximately double the annual harvest. (Exploitation has been calculated to be 48 percent.) This assessment measures the height of the boom, not a twenty-year average. So the MSC evaluation of the health of the lobster fishery is skewed by whatever factors—for example, ocean warming and lack of predators—that caused the anomaly in the first place. Conservation measures put in place more than a hundred years ago did not prompt the *current* bonanza. No new conservation rules have been created in the past thirty years. Instead, they may have nearly doubled the strength of the boom. Something new is at work.

Climate change adds another dimension to considerations of sustainability. Just as fisheries management must now factor in ocean warming, so, too, must evaluations of the longevity and health of a fishery.

Comparing a 120-million-pound harvest to a standing stock of 248 million lobsters, one gets that 48 percent exploitation rate. This is far below the 90 percent threshold for overfishing. And, in fact, this level of fishing may be sustainable for now, but what happens when the landings climb or stocks decline? The ratio can quickly collapse.

Lobstermen, scientists, and resource managers will need to be vigilant as these parameters shift. Yet few have taken notice, easily distracted by the doubling dockside price, now even tripling since the first days of the glut. In coastal towns like Stonington, an observant few are worried about last autumn's weak harvest. They would hear soon about the verdict for the year. (The statistics on the year's lobster landings were due for release in spring 2016.)

In Stonington, the probable news of the harvest and other issues of comanagement and sustainability are hotly debated in summer along the waterfront. One gathering is under way on the east side of the harbor. The Maine Center for Coastal Fisheries, a marine policy institute created by Ted Ames and his wife, Robin Alden, is holding a meeting, which includes board members like Bob Steneck.

Bob tells me later the conversation went something like this:

Steneck says to Robin, "Your lobster zones have been such a success. As you say, we could model multispecies management areas after the lobster zones and territories. For finfish. The size and shape of the areas would vary with each fish. Species from scallops to alewives to cod could be regulated together under local comanagement. That's similar to what they do in Chile, where fisheries are spatiallly constrained. They operate small exclusive fishing zones and they work."

"Yes," says Ted, "we could have ecosystem-based management under local area councils."

"And possibly limited entry for all boats," adds Robin, "if that makes sense."

"We will need diversity in fishery stocks," says Steneck. "Just as they now have in Newfoundland, where variety buffers any storm. Up there, fishermen are making more money on scallops, shrimp, and hake than they were with a single fishery of cod."

"Scallops and haddock are coming back here, too," says Ted.

"The focus would be on sustainability of the fishermen, rather than on the species," says Steneck. "The trick is getting the feds aboard. We may need new production of species like alewives to fit under the law."

"We'll take it to Washington next month," says Robin.

The enthusism is contagious. This Stonington solution may tame the commons dilemma a bit more in the Gulf of Maine. Robin, Ted, Bob, and their community will lead the way.

Meanwhile, above town, Frank Gotwals's band, Archipelago, is serenading the Island Heritage Trust membership at a fund-raiser for preserving public lands. If successful, a beachfront will be set aside as a commons for all to enjoy.

I arrive late, after all the boiled lobster is gone. The spectators are a little giddy from the beer. At that hour, Frank is singing only requests. People choose from the American songbook, tunes from the Church of the Morning After, and ballads from Frank's albums.

"An Unfamiliar Sea" is coming around again on the old guitar.

The captain tells me stories with a proud but thoughtful look
We ripped the fish out of the sea with just a compass and a hook
I fear there is no good solution for a man who's been so free
And the fog keeps getting thicker on this unfamiliar sea.

Those in the crowd tap their feet, the cadence of a march, as if welcoming an old friend.

Frank responds with an instrumental riff that puts everyone on a cloud and takes them home for the night.

10

Spring, Southeast Harbor

Some say dawn brightens first in Stonington on the bay windows of the Harbor Café. The place is on a slight rise and faces southeast. The sun may not arrive here first at all times of the year, but in mid-May, a few weeks before the solstice, that reckoning is dead on. At 4:00 A.M. I am sitting at the watering hole, watching the faintest glow in the east, waiting for Frank. As tradition has it, he will have breakfast with his stepson, Jason, just as the new lobster season is getting started. Jason, ten minutes early, as always, sits across from me at a lacquered table adorned with local marine charts—not at all necessary, since Jason knows the Maine coast by heart.

Jason is pensive, distracted, but all smiles.

Looking through the bay window, he scans the eastern horizon. "Red sky in morning," he says. "Halibut take warning."

I tell him his rhyming couplet is a new one for me.

"Better get used to it," he says. "Memorize it. Halibut is what I mean to catch today."

An extra benefit of May lobstering is that northern halibut—pronounced "hullibut" in Maine—is in season. A lobsterman can take a break from hauling at midday and rig up for the huge flatfish. Regulations require a minimum size of forty-one inches—just shy of three and a half feet long. Jason offers to take me along today to take the measure of the twin spring fisheries—lobster and halibut both.

Frank slips through the door and joins us at a table for six. Julie Eaton's photographs of the eagle Majestic stare down at us from the walls. Katie, the waitress, pours coffee for the three of us and takes orders, our selections from memory.

Jason's face brightens when he places his order. Not just the prospect of blueberry pancakes or a halibut on the hook has him grinning. Jason has some familial news for his father.

"Your granddaughter has taken to the water," he says.

Frank raises his eyebrows.

"Jill is going lobstering with me." Jill, fourteen, is Jason's middle daughter of three, a fan of soccer, basketball, and drums.

"Really?" says Frank.

"Yes. We've painted twenty-eight buoys for her to work this summer. I'm setting half today. The other half will join them on Southeast Harbor next week, when Jill gets out of school."

"Does she know what to expect?"

"She's not so enamored with the water as yet; she just wants the money. Let's see if she has the grit to last the season."

"The physical work is the easy part," says Frank. "The rubber meets the water with the mental challenge of it. Even her first summer could be up and down: the catches, the money, the setbacks, the success."

"That's what you taught me when I was a teenager," says Jason. "I'll pass the lesson forward." The young father seems pleased the game is on. *Young* is a relative term. At forty-three, Jason has been working the water for twenty-five years.

"I suppose you'll teach her to respect another man's buoys," says Frank. "She should never mess with someone else's traps."

"You taught me that—to be one hundred percent honest."

"That's all there is out there—your reputation in the fleet. That's everything. If you lose that . . ."

"The trust."

"The trust, that's right. If you lose that—it's our currency—to get it back is hard. To have the trust of the fleet makes your life livable on the water. The rest of lobstering is just practice and experience."

"You learn by watching, then hold your head high and go," says Jason.

"You have to show up to be a good lobsterman. After a good day or a bad day, either one, you still have to wake up and go again tomorrow. You're always fishing for tomorrow, if you're any good. Jill will learn that."

If the baton has not already been passed, it is making its way around the track.

Katie steps into the room, balancing three plates hot and heaping full from the kitchen. She serves Jason and me our blueberry hotcakes; she delivers a spare bagel to Frank. Katie returns with the coffeepot to administer lifesaving refills. We are set for a feast.

Frank bites into his bagel, then sets it down to free up his hands to dig out from his shirt pocket the latest press release from the Maine Department of Marine Resources. The announcement tallies the state lobster landings for the previous year, first available the following spring.

"From my perspective of the last forty years," says Frank, "the tally for 2015 is as good as it gets in terms of volume and value. Maine nearly topped half a billon dollars in lobster. That's a lot of shellfish."

"We had a really good catch," says Jason, "and—"

"A really good price. No fisherman ever wants to say they've had a good season really. He hates to jinx it and always wants more. But we're doing very well."

The catch came in at just over 121 million pounds, a drop of 5 percent from the all-time record of 127.8 million pounds in 2013. The winter fishery was down 12 percent and the summer/fall fishery had declined 3.4 percent. However, this decline was more than compensated by a 10 percent increase in average price, registering $4.09 per pound. The yield: an all-time record value of $501 million, a boon to the Maine economy.

"The price climbed to over four dollars a pound," says Frank. "That's what did it. Last autumn the volume sank a little, but prices rose. We haven't seen a four-dollar price tag since 2007—since before the recession."

"If landings fall some more this year," says Jason, "the price may rally even more and make up the difference."

"Sure. The boat price will help," says Frank, "but it can't recover everything if volume really sinks in the future."

"That future may be tomorrow or five years from now," says Jason. "Those larvae aren't settling on the bottom like they used to."

"No telling, not knowing," says Frank. "Forty years ago, I never would have predicted this kind of boom. That's why I don't like to make predictions. There is no doubt landings will change again—go higher still or lower. But no one knows for sure. The five percent drop last year is not a big downturn. Let's see what happens next."

"Everyone's expecting a downturn," says Jason. "Downturn to what? Twenty years ago, we were only catching one-third of what we land now. We're way ahead. If the harvest cuts in half, I can still make it. I won't lose everything. But I'm unusual. Others are very vulnerable. A downturn by a third could ruin some of these guys."

"Ever since the glut, scientists have predicted a crash," says Frank. "Always doomsday. And the scientists have always been wrong." Frank glances at Jason. "How many predictions that you've made have come true?"

Jason laughs. He takes another bite of blueberry pancake. With a full mouth, he says, "I have to disagree. These big catches are definitely not sustainable. The boom-and-bust roller coaster is cyclical. Whatever goes up must come down. That's a rule of nature. We just don't know when the downturn is coming."

"From my point of view," says Frank, "I have no reason to think it's not going to be a good season coming up."

"Sure," says Jason. "One more good season. We don't know beyond that. For whatever reason—I don't know if it's the climate, the weather, food, or lack of predators—this coast has been perfect for growing lobsters. But it cannot last forever."

Frank smiles like a politician but will not cast a ballot. "We make assumptions, because that's what human beings do," he says. "We make assumptions based on our personalities. Some people are naturally optimistic; they think it's going to get better. Others are naturally pessimistic; they keep predicting bad things are going to come true. Eventually they'll be proved right. Okay, Jason?"

Jason smiles. "I guess that makes me a wide-eyed pessimist."

Katie brings the check, and all of us wave off a fourth refill on coffee.

Frank says to Jason, "The most important advice I'll give Jill is what I passed on to you: Follow the code, the lessons learned."

Jason nods and cranes his neck to look out the front window. "It must be close to five A.M.," he says. The sun burns on the horizon. "Well, I better go catch that halibut. I know it's waiting for me. Yep, spring is just like you're a kid again."

Thirty minutes later, Jason is driving the thirty-six-foot *Seahawk* into Southeast Harbor, heavily laden with sixty-four traps on deck. (The dock crew at the Co-op stacked them four-high while we were at breakfast.) The white boat splits the blue waters, casting a green tint in her wake. We dodge and weave through the Jericho islands as if we were on a slalom course, reaching our destination in half an hour, not as a crow flies, but as a fish swims. Famous for its early shed, Southeast Harbor is a shallow cove beyond Lazy Gut Island to the east, generally ranging in depth from five to thirty feet, with a few deeper holes. Lobstermen can see the rocky bottom while working. It is a crucial staging area for Stonington lobsters each summer.

The deepest hole, at 102 feet, has a singular story. To seed the Southeast Harbor nursery, several old-time lobstermen over the years have released berried females into the hole. Those captains believe baby lobsters have emerged from the hole and populated the shallows of Southeast Harbor. It's hard to argue with success. That hole has made the lobstermen rich.

Jason catches 10 percent of his summer harvest here, even though the bonanza here lasts a mere month. The July shed runs big, runs brief.

Yet it is not the holes that grant these nursery grounds their greatest significance, but the general shallowness of Southeast Harbor. Because they are shallow, these waters warm up quickest in spring and summer. The first shed occurs here typically one week to ten days earlier than in the rest of Stonington waters. When the molt does come, fishermen expect a run of large male shedders first, followed by females a week later. Southeast Harbor is known throughout town as the site of the first shed. The secret is out. Yet it is not a mob scene. Jason and a few cousins have carved the territory out for themselves. And, knives ready, they defend it by cutting traplines if need be.

Jason's goal for May, the start of the 2016 season, is a time-honored one—to get ahead of the shed. He tries to time the setting of his traps to a week or so in advance of the first molt. This requires a crystal ball and his fair share of good luck.

While his stepfather, Frank, relies on ripening raspberries as his first clue that the shed is near, Jason is more scientific. He listens to reports of the sea surface temperature from the National Oceanic and Atmospheric Administration. When the temperature hits 50° degrees F, as it did last week, he tunes in to signs in the lobsters themselves. This past Thursday, Jason noted that males in his traps off Fog Island were splitting their shells—a crack appeared in each carapace. In addition, their abdomens, normally white, were black—a sure sign that shedding is imminent. According to his calculus, Jason knew it would be only two weeks before the big shed at Southeast Harbor.

Jason, Frank, and Julie pride themselves on beating lobsters to the punch.

Still, waiting for and forecasting the local shed can often be an inexact art. So, Jason hedges his bets. Since April, he and his sternman, Chris "Kit" Bruce, have carried 240 traps—in four boatfuls of sixty—to another favorite area: the waters outside Spoon Island, the last outpost in Jericho Bay. Here, the depth is two hundred feet or more. At this time of year, they can catch stragglers from the winter, all hard-shell lobsters. In May, the market for hard-shells is strong, while the whole state awaits the shedders.

Jason says, "We can make enough money from hard-shells to pay for our bait and diesel while we set our traps on Southeast."

As we swing past Lazy Gut Ledge and close in on Southeast Harbor, Jason speaks of his secret weapon. "We've got two kinds of bait aboard—salted herring for the lobsters and fresh alewives for the halibut. The alewives were caught in a spawning run past Ellsworth last night. They're still full of blood, which I'm hoping the halibut will love. I just need one big halibut. To catch him, I've got three hundred alewives ready for the hook."

Chris Bruce is busy stuffing herring into bait bags to set on Southeast.

The captain warns him not to touch a single alewife. The alewives are set aside, as if they were a bouquet to win a bride.

Upon arrival, the first thing we do is set Jill's fourteen traps in very shallow water—about ten feet—at the head of the harbor. It is high tide, and the team must set her traps before the water ebbs. After school last week, Jill painted her buoys with her chosen colors: a white nose, teal middle, and yellow bottom. These differ from her father's in just one stripe: Jill's teal replaces Jason's blue. On the west side of the harbor, there is just room for Jill's fourteen buoys; her next fourteen will go on the east side next week.

Setting the traps requires care when fifty cages are still stacked on deck. There's not much room for the crew to maneuver. The trick is to get each trap on the rail and overboard with just a single motion—one line (warp) and buoy going over with it. Separating each warp is half the challenge. The tangle of blackened lines on deck resembles spaghetti— spaghetti with squid ink.

Jason's own fifty traps are distributed at different depths—six, nine, ten, twelve, fifteen feet—as if he were picking numbers on a roulette wheel. The bet is blind. In any given year, one depth does better than another, but past performance offers no hint of future outcomes. However, one thing is certain: Southeast Harbor will produce the first shedders, if you cover every depth. To do this, Jason will bring out another fifty traps next week, for a total of a hundred. If he catches six shedders in each trap, he will clear over $2,500 from Southeast each day.

With the light building in the east, the clouds burnished orange and black like tiger stripes, Jason casts his eyes into the blue water to see where his traps settle on the bottom. Southeast Harbor is so shallow and the water so clear that he can see the gravel and rocks on the bottom. The traps stand out like little lanterns. Just to double his bets, Jason tracks each trap on the GPS plotter. Yet he has never forgotten a trap, especially one in plain sight.

"I dream about my traps," says Jason. "It's a bad habit. It started when I was sterning for Frank. I banded so many lobster claws that I dreamt about those yellow bands at night. One, two, three, four. I could count up to a thousand in my sleep. Now I rehearse where my traps are placed. Luckily, the cages are always chock-full. Lobsters busting at the seams."

Mostly, Jason dreams about how and where to get ahead of that next shed. After Southeast Harbor hits, he will place traps on Mud Flats, just south of Whaleback Ledge. Typically, shedders appear on Mud Flats, deeper water, about ten days after Southeast Harbor. From here, over the next two weeks, Jason moves down the bay, staking out Fog Island and the other isles of Jericho Bay. Soon, the whole area—shallows and deep—will be crawling with shedders.

While the dawn sky has been orange for the last twenty minutes, the sun now rises a bloodred over Mount Desert Island. Just think: Jason enjoys this kind of light show every morning. The light illuminates the faces of captain and crew. Jason McDonald is tall and dark, like a Scottish Highlander. Chris Bruce, thirty-eight, is blond, perhaps from a rival clan. Jason sports a Garbo Lobster sweatshirt and cap. Chris is stripped to shirtsleeves, which show off his tattoos. Both arms bear dragons, and a devil adorns the back of his neck.

I shake Chris's hand, turning to the captain to say, "Your sternman's name is a little too like mine."

"Don't worry," says Jason. "I rarely call him by his Christian name. I usually hail him with something with a little more color." The sternman doesn't laugh, so it must be true.

An hour past sunrise, all traps are set. Just in time—the tide is ebbing. The buoys float at the edges of Southeast Harbor like a toy armada. Jason reaches into his red-and-white cooler for a power bar. Other than a few snacks, his cooler is empty. "There will be no lunch today," he says. "I hate to stop once I'm in the rhythm of hauling. Nearly drove me crazy growing up with Frank. Come ten o'clock, he halts everything for a picnic."

Jason turns the boat south, parallel to the length of Jericho Bay. He is heading for open water. In the far distance, we can see the eponymous Spoon Island at the mouth of the bay. In fact, Spoon comprises a pair of spatula-shaped islands, indistinguishable ten miles away.

The first obstacle on the run south is North Popplestone Ledge, a broad rock outcrop that has sunk a few boats in years past. Like most underwater ledges, it has a gaping jaw at low tide. With the tide ebbing, its two sharp teeth are becoming exposed. Jason gives them a wide berth. Next is South Popplestone Ledge, with its four teeth surfacing on the ebb tide. The tide rips and roils between them. Just to the west, Fog Island sits calmly and solidly. Jason catches 70 percent of his lobsters here and around neighboring islands during the course of a typical summer.

The next two hazards—Green Ledge and White Ledge (called "Way Ledge" by the fishermen)—are larger embankments. Chris Bruce points out a harbor seal and her pup on Way Ledge. "A sign of spring," he says. Chris is our onboard naturalist, flagging terns, puffins, and guillemots for us to see. "I picked up the knack for identifying seabirds one summer at Audubon Camp," he says.

The next danger is so treacherous, precariously situated in the main channel, that a state green can buoy marks it—Drunkard Ledge. The Drunkard looks like an oversize mammoth tooth. Random waves crash on the molar with abandon, crushing anything that gets in the way—except lobsters. Large males congregate in the Drunkard's teeth. To take advantage of the congregation, Jason has placed a string of traps—ten pair—around the rock. On the first haul, we reel in a big lobster—over two pounds—and four other selects. The trap itself is banged up a bit. "Storms can beat up your gear here," says Jason. "Between waves and granite, something's got to give. It's usually one of my traps."

In the surf at the edge of the Drunkard, Jason misses the next buoy with his boat hook. He is a little off balance in the racing tide. "How embarrassing," he says, rocking on his feet. "If I miss three, we go home."

Farther south, between Great Spoon and Little Spoon, Jason stops for another string, testing the waters at each turn of the tide. He tells me the shed typically manifests here in August or early September. "But," he says, "lobstering is changing every year with the warming, so I don't know what to expect next. One thing's already clear: Lobsters are shedding farther out."

For now, his test string produces only hard-shells—about thirty. This is satisfactory for a May harvest. After the last buoy, the morning work is done. Captain and sternman look past Little Spoon to the Gulf. A searching look. Then they turn to each other and both shout, "Halibut!" Their faces are like mirror images; they break into wide grins.

We motor three miles past the Spoons to the federal limit, where the depth is 250 feet, the bottom sandy. "Halibut habitat," says Jason. "Try saying that fast three times in a row."

Jason shifts the boat to idle so they can rig their fishing lines for halibut. The quiet is fitting for this spiritual experience.

Jason and Chris lay out one thousand feet of white fishing line on deck and attach eighty hooks—one every ten feet or so. The sternman is responsible for baiting the hooks with alewives—one fish threaded through the eyes for every hook. An iron anchor and a buoy are attached to each end of the fishing line. Jason drags the line behind the boat until the entire length is positioned on the bottom.

The rigging process is repeated twice so that, upon deployment, three one-thousand-foot fishing lines form a U shape on the sandy bottom. Jason says, "I bet we're gonna catch one. I can feel it." We will return in three hours to see if he hooked one. Of course, three hours is just an estimate. No self-respecting lobsterman wears a watch. He knows the tide turns in six hours and twelve minutes, and that's enough of a measure for him. So when the tide begins to slack, halfway through the cycle, we'll head for the halibut. In the meantime, the captain returns to hauling lobsters.

Just inside the federal line, Jason's 240 deepwater traps await his inspection. At this distance and depth, he has rigged triples—one buoy for every three traps. Since these are faster than pairs, chances are we'll be able to find and haul eighty buoys and their 240 traps in two or three hours. To navigate between them, Jason has the GPS turned on high resolution.

The first few hauls produce one legal lobster per trap. All hard-shells, which today's market will price at $4.50 per pound (plus an eventual $1 bonus). We catch a lot of "junk." Pistols and barely legal lobsters—what was perhaps caught but not kept last fall. Garbo says, "Seventy percent of spring lobsters go to the processors, while only thirty percent are pretty enough for shipping overseas." The ratio reverses in July.

I'm impressed by how patient a lobsterman must be at certain times of the year. Jason says to me now, "If we can catch an average of one pound per trap, we're doing good for this month." In August, he expects three or four times that amount. Lobstering is a game of perseverance.

Chris shows the captain and me two small females with eggs adhered to their abdomens. The eggs are not the black color I witnessed last autumn, but green and opalescent. This means the eggs are close to hatching. Summer is around the corner. Chris notches their tails with a hunting knife and releases them to the nurturing waters.

"These females are too young to be pregnant," says Chris. "But there you are. With the warming, lobsters are maturing faster. The rules of the game have changed." Just about every day on the water, lobstermen confirm the suspicions of scientists.

"The older I get, the less I know," says Jason. "The world is changing fast. Of course, Frank says the same thing, so I guess when I get to be his age, I really will ask questions all the time."

Ever the naturalist, Chris now holds up two males. He asks if we see a difference. "No?" he says. "Notice one is right-handed—the big crusher claw on the right—and the other male has its crusher on the left, which is rarer. Human left-handedness occurs in about twelve percent of people. I'd like to apply for one of those million-dollar research grants to pin down the percent for lobsters. Yes sir."

About halfway through the gear, Jason lifts a big female out of one of the traps. She has green eggs on her abdomen, but our eyes are drawn to another piece of anatomy. She has three white barnacles growing on her head, an indication that she hasn't molted in over a year; she would not molt while carrying eggs anyway. Her carapace is pockmarked and eroded—nearly shredded in places. She has lobster "shell disease," a debilitating condition that manifests when naturally occurring bacteria destroy the shells of living lobsters. The bacteria render the lobsters ugly, unmarketable, and often weak. Eventually, the ruination of the shell makes it difficult to molt and sometimes the lobster dies. Perhaps more often, the damaged shell is discarded. Diseased lobsters are edible, not harmful to humankind. However, lobsters with shell disease can be sold only to a processor; they are too unsightly for the more lucrative live trade.

Scientists are uncertain whether high water temperature, relative acidity, low oxygen levels, population density, or another stress is the dominant trigger for the disease. It is not contagious, but, rather, appears spontaneously in individual lobsters. Large males and egg-bearing females are most often infected, since they molt less than once a year, during which time the disease can get a hold. Lobsters appear to discard the disease when they do molt. The new shells grow back without any trace of scars or lesions. Unfortunately, however, the same lobsters can contract it again.

The ultimate cause of shell disease may prove to be climate change. While the warming atmosphere and oceans are the most obvious effect of excessive burning of fossil fuels, ocean acidity is another major impact. As atmospheric carbon dioxide levels have climbed—now in excess of four hundred parts per million, a 40 percent rise—the oceans have become 30 percent more acidic because seas absorb the gas, forming carbonic acid. Putting a lobster shell in that mixture is like placing chalk in a glass of vinegar. It will eventually dissolve.

In addition to the prospect of lobster shell disease brought on, in part, by this acidity, every marine organism with a shell could be vulnerable to the increasing acidity itself. Shellfish, from clams and oysters to shrimp and crabs, as well as the tiny plankton at the base of the marine food chain, may find it more challenging to accumulate calcium carbonate to build their shells in more acidic seawater. Acid dissolves limestone. Meanwhile, lobsters may succumb to double jeopardy—retardation of shell formation as well as shell disease. At risk is an ecosystem built on the backs of plankton and shellfish. Also at risk are thousands of jobs and billions of dollars to Maine's economy. The gulf widens when we look at the marine food web and ocean ecosystems around the world. All are vulnerable to acidity.

"When I was a teenager, sterning for Frank," says Jason, "we never saw shell disease. It's all happened in the last twenty years. We mainly see it in big males out here past Spoon Island."

According to David Cousens, president of the Maine Lobstermen's Association, who fishes out of Thomaston, near Tenants Harbor, the incidence of shell disease in his home waters has doubled over the past couple of years, from two or three in a thousand to six in a thousand. He's seeing half a dozen rotting shells in a good boatload.

That rate may not seem high, but it's enough to get the attention of Maine lobstermen. Looking south for a milepost, Maine fishermen find that in 1996 in Rhode Island, the prevalence was about ten in a thousand lobsters, or 1 percent. Now it ranges between 18 and 34 percent. The disease may be creeping northward to the Gulf of Maine.

Chris picks another big lobster with shell disease—this one an oversize male—out of a trap and hands it to his captain. Jason holds the two elderly selects aloft. They catch the light but don't shimmer like young ones. Their dark shells are leathery and pitted, reflecting little light.

"I'll begin to worry," says Jason, "when it shows up in the younger ones. That would give me pause. Lobster is all we got." He drops the senior lobsters back in the drink. "They say it's the climate again. Everywhere we turn, it's the climate these days."

"You cannot get away from it," says the sternman. "Good or bad. No telling, not knowing."

While talking, Chris marks each buoy or trawl (three traps) with a fish. He places one herring in an empty box, until he reaches five fish, a string of fifteen traps. Then he writes down on a pad the number of lobsters for a given string. "Otherwise, I lose my place," he says as he sets another herring in the box. "Now, you wouldn't want to do this at home," he continues. "If you're cooking dinner with your wife, marking the number of eggs you crack into a bowl with a dead herring may not go over so well. I mean, these fish are ripe!"

The last trawl of the day, comprising three traps, is like all the others. If hooking the buoy begins the hauling sequence, then stuffing the bait bag is the middle, the odor primed for a deep breath. I count twelve steps of the hauling process, which flash by like frames of vintage photographs. I watch each stage—hooking, pot hauling, reeling, railing, picking, measuring, baiting, banding, setting—memorizing the precise movements of the team, until the lobsters with their yellow bands are placed, crawling, in the tank. They appear as ancient rituals of fishermen, ancient yet ephemeral, typical of fishing the world over.

We now have ten traps in the stern, ready to move inshore—to Fog Island. Over the next few weeks, most of the Spoon Island traps will be moved inside, to the main islands, searching for a shed.

But before he motors into Jericho Bay, Jason must check his three halibut rigs. Those fishing grounds are only a mile from the lobster traps. While we cross the water, *Diamond Girl*, a Stonington boat, pushes past us, laden with traps, headed inshore.

"That's Donny Jones," says Jason, "shifting traps from ocean to bay. Good to see him heading inside. Summer's coming."

We arrive at the fishing grounds, the location of the third rig. "Thar's the fishing buoy," says Chris, pointing at the white sphere. "Better be a big 'un."

"I don't see that halibut pulling it under," says Jason. "That big shark in *Jaws* pulled under three."

Jason puts the buoy line on the pot hauler and reels it in, removing the empty hooks as they surface. He is smiling, full of anticipation.

After ten minutes, the end of the line comes up, the bait eaten by crabs. "It was just a practice run," says Jason. "Let's try number two."

The second line comes up empty. Jason says, "That was just fooling around. Lucky I don't do this for a living."

The last trawl is the one we set first. It has had the longest set, an extra twenty minutes.

The pot hauler whines. The diesel chugs. Chris lights a Camel, and the acrid smoke mixes with the scent of bait and diesel exhaust.

Halfway through the line, the hooks empty, Jason turns to Chris and me and winks.

Then it happens. Jason shouts, "Fish on!"

With the help of a gaff, Jason and Chris pull the huge brown-and-white halibut aboard. He flaps on deck. They measure him with a tape. He is forty-four inches long, just four inches shy of four feet, and three inches over the legal limit. Jason grins like a ten-year-old.

"Makes my day," he says.

"Steaks or fillets?" asks Chris.

"Fillets," says the captain.

"Mighty tasty, I'd say, either way."

"Wicked awesome."

The butchering style is always the captain's prerogative, and there are many choices, but the pearly white flesh is invariably grilled one way—over charcoal, Stonington-style—to perfection.

As for the lobster, Jason and Chris caught 242 handsome hard-shells, one per trap, or $1,090 total—not world-shaking but there's the promise of summer. Jason is still praying for one more good season.

Indeed, on this glorious day in May, captain and sternman seem unaware the downturn may be just around the corner. On the voyage back to town, they speak of fishing—the possibility of hooking a four-foot striped bass. "Thanks to the warming, you see more stripers swimming into the Gulf of Maine," says Chris. "No better time to catch one."

Yet not every consequence of the high temperatures is a good thing, they admit. The conversation switches to the global scene. "I heard on the radio," says Jason, "that last month was the twelfth month in a row of record high temperatures around the world." At this, Chris joins Jason in staring over the bay, perhaps a little numb to all the bad news at hand. *Climate change,* once unspoken of, has become a dirty term.

Jason speaks next, without taking his eyes off the horizon. "The warming may be coming," he says, "but the Gulf of Maine doesn't mix with the warmer Gulf Stream, so I don't think we're gonna be affected like Rhode Island and Connecticut, which are heating up something wicked. If it does happen here—any more than it has already—it's gonna be scary."

Jason rounds Fog Island and sets his course west into Merchant Row, the broad channel where thousands of lobstermen, dozens of generations, have made their way into Stonington at the end of a beautiful day. He's still talking. "The greatest concentration of lobsters in Maine is right off Stonington," he says. "But if and when they move farther northeast, we cannot follow the lobsters. We can't fish outside our zone. We're stuck right here." Jason takes off his baseball cap and wipes his brow, smooths his hair back on his head. He replaces the cap, tilted now slightly, as if he favors his right eye.

"We need to change the regulations," he says, "so that we can cross the boundaries, but they won't do it. The state government doesn't get it. A guy from New Hampshire can come up here and fish outside the three-mile line anywhere he wants, but we can't do it."

Living on the water, on warming waters, has become more complicated.

We pass by familiar islands—Isle au Haut, McGlathery Island, Round Island, Wreck—on our way to port. "The footprints, the underwater ledges, of all these islands produce the best lobsters in the world," says Jason. "You just have to read the signs and know where to go first. I'm still picking up clues after twenty-five years."

Other signals become apparent. Already, within Zone C, lobsters are densest to the east. Also, within the zone, lobsters are accumulating at the eastern side of family territories. Consequently, lobstermen are focusing on the eastern edges of their territories. This crowds the next man. "Pushing the edge," says Jason, "is something that will likely happen more and more as populations decline. We'll see some tensions flare up."

"Not on Southeast Harbor," says Chris. "I think we're safe there."

"The only thing we're pushing there," says Jason, "is the shallows— the threat of running aground. I hope Jill's traps do well, even better than mine."

"Spoken just like a proud daddy," says Chris.

"If she or a child of hers someday decides to be a full-time lobsterman, I hope we have enough crustaceans. I hope she will be able to make a good living. Ten years ago, I was certain of it. Now I'm not so sure. It's going to keep getting harder to go."

"That's why you gotta love what you do," says Chris, "or what's the point?"

Jason spins the wheel to starboard and we turn north between George Head and Crotch Island, the once and future granite quarry that brought Stonington its first grandeur. Jason starts to whistle a sea chantey. He's happy to be headed home to his girls. Meanwhile, Chris mops the deck, erasing all traces of bait and bottom mud. He sees his wife up ahead at the Co-op dock, and waves. All five deckhands wave back with her. They've forgotten his tumble on the dock the other day. The community is small and tight—accepting of one another and forgiving.

"The taxidermist is gonna have a heart attack when he sees this halibut," says Jason.

"Forget the souvenir," says Chris. "Let's have a barbecue."

"Sounds great to me," says the captain, pushing the throttle and leaving a wide arc in his wake.

Epilogue

By now, everyone is expecting the next big shed—a second wave for the summer. Counting on it, here in August 2016. Yet the town is subdued. Stonington's streets are unusually quiet. Semis gather seafood sporadically, their diesel engines intermittent. The harbor is nearly silent. Boats go out a mere three or four times a week. Lobster cars at the Co-op are floating fifty-deep, waiting to count a hundred before the Garbo trucks come to claim them. Old-timers are characteristically stoic; younger men lament. For the Stonington lobstermen, the first shed was only a week early after all. And middling. It tiptoed in on June 30 but never gathered steam. No drumroll, no whistle.

"I'm only hauling lobster four days a week," says Julie Eaton, remembering her old six-day schedule in West Penobscot Bay. "We're catching three to four hundred pounds a day on average. July, August. That's a third of what I was landing last summer. On top of that, we've got another bait shortage. The herring quota's been cut, so the price of bait has nearly doubled. And some days I can't find any herring. I've resorted to cat food and tuna fish. That's expensive, too.

"It's a bump in the road, I bet. I'm sure everything will be fine. This is my livelihood, so I have to keep the faith. I'm not afraid I'm going to starve, after all. The lobsters always come."

East of Stonington is no better. "Jericho Bay is slow," says Frank

Gotwals at the end of August. "The last couple of weeks have not been so good." Most boats at the Co-op are pulling in less than five hundred pounds, although they range between one hundred and eighteen hundred pounds, the latter for the bigger boats. Those big boats are performing best in deep water. The volume for the Co-op overall, serving eighty boats, has dropped to four hundred crates per day, ninety pounds each. That's down from 750 crates per day in 2012. "We had a good winter," says Frank, "so the Co-op annual tally still looks good, but fishing is definitely off, now that it's summer—typically our best time of year."

Even Southeast Harbor has not matched its legendary performance. "Each shed has dried up quickly this summer," says Jason McDonald in September. "I did catch a thousand pounds for the first three weeks— and Jill did well—but it's dropped to six to seven hundred pounds, or less, a decrease of a third. One to two lobsters per trap is not what I'm used to looking at. And September's worse than August. Like Frank, we're only going out five days a week. Even then, bait—at four hundred dollars a day—is killing us." Jason takes his cap off and wipes his brow.

"Everyone's kind of nervous," he continues. "I haven't seen it look like this since I began in 1990."

Up and down the Maine coast, the news is much the same. Dealers bitch; lobstermen worry. The Maine Lobstermen's Association publishes a "Lobster Price Report" weekly that is annotated with comments from lobstermen and dealers. For June 27, 2016, to the northeast, Beals Island reports, "Catch is poor inside, worse outside." By August 29, Cutler reports from Down East, "Fishing is extremely poor." Meanwhile, to the southwest, Boothbay Harbor at Mid-Coast reports, "Catch is terrible." By November 7, Cutler flags the catch as "poor and dropping." From Swans Island to Tenants Harbor, the breadth of Penobscot Bay, the harvest is slow.

By February 2017, the harvest statistics for 2016 are released by the state. Lobster landings come in at just over 130.8 million pounds, an increase of 2.3 percent over the previous record of 127.8 million pounds in 2013. It would appear that by the end of the year the fishery's slide has been arrested. Yet where is the impact of the summer/fall slump?

At face value, the new annual record is clearly deceptive. It gives a false signal of the lobster harvest. If one groups the monthly landings into the first half of the year and the last half of the year, a very different picture arises. The winter/spring fishery had a huge increase of 45 percent, accounting for all of the annual rise. Meanwhile, the summer/fall fishery had a decrease of 2 percent over 2013. In other words, the winter lobstermen, dominated by bigger boats operating in warmer seas, caught enough lobsters to drive the annual catch into positive territory, while the traditional summer lobstermen lost ground again. Fewer summer shedders caught for the third year in a row.

Contributing to the heavy winter harvest may be elevated ocean temperatures. Bob Steneck suggests that a warmer-than-average autumn may have prompted a second molt. These second shedders would have added to the legal stock available to the winter fleet.

The average dockside price for 2016 was $4.07 per pound, down just a couple of pennies. The yield: $533 million, a $32 million increase over the previous year. Landings are best utilized as a barometer of dollar value; they do not closely reflect the abundance of lobster in the ocean. Despite a weaker summer harvest, lobstermen were holding their own in terms of value.

Poor years tend to be cumulative. With a dip of 3 percent in 2014, 5 percent in 2015, and now the summer catch off 2 percent in 2016, Maine has a three-year slip in summer landings. At the Co-op, Jason overhears lobstermen wary of the future. If the same loss is repeated over the next several years, they fear a 30 percent drop. If this is sustained over a few years, it would be considered the mark of an entrenched downturn. From there, it is not far to the 50 percent decrease that marks the beginning of a true crash. Even Stonington lobstermen predict they cannot absorb a loss of that magnitude. Banks and other lenders will come knocking on their doors. Houses, trucks, and boats may be repossessed. Call it a lobster bubble—ready to burst.

Nonetheless, recent catch statistics as well as lower postlarvae settlement data show predictions of a crash in the next three years as inconclusive. Trends are difficult to discern. The precariousness of lobstermen is not always obvious from the previous year's harvest. "If the lobster population is about to fall off a cliff, you won't see it coming," says Diane Cowan at the Lobster Conservancy in Friendship, Maine.

By summer 2017, a headlong fall over the precipice may be under way. It began with a cold winter and spring. Those frigid months were compounded by a poor showing of lobsters; there was little to catch. This year would have no boost from heavy winter landings. The chilly waters forced a late shed, which was unusually brief. It ran for only a week in early July and was "unimpressive," says Jason. By August, he is only snagging five hundred pounds a day, half his take from two years ago. Last year's harvest of between six hundred and seven hundred pounds no longer looks so bad.

"The Co-op is landing two hundred crates a day [18,000 pounds], down from three hundred crates in August 2016," says Ron Trundy, Co-op manager. "So far this year, volume has dropped twenty-five to thirty percent." The stimuli for the downturn could be a cold spring on top of poor settlement from several warmer summers.

For captains like Jason, the current catch is the worst in ten years. Anxiety has given way to dread. And he has a theory: Since the past two seasons—one a warm early shed and the other cool and late—have produced similar slumps in August, he thinks the problem is a lack of volume, not temperature or timing—too few lobsters to shed. This thesis points to poor settlement approximately seven years before.

Autumn brings no relief. "We're having as bad a September," says Julie, "as we had last year. I can't seem to do better than four hundred pounds. I'm already hoping for next season. It's kind of like gambling: You just don't know what will happen next."

By the end of 2017, landings for the entire State of Maine total 110.8 million pounds, an overall decline of 16.4 percent.

The price did not rebound quickly enough to keep lobstermen out of hock. It averaged $3.91 for a catch value of $433.8 million, a decline of $106.6 million to the lobstermen. It's not a bust but air may already be hissing out of the lobster bubble.

In the wake of this news, three leading marine biologists in Maine have a similar take on the future:

"We've been expecting a downturn for some time," says Rick Wahle at the University of Maine. "The young-of-year have not settled in any big numbers since 2007. And 2016 is no better."

Bob Steneck agrees but is cautious about future scenarios. "I think lobster will decline," he says, "but they won't go extinct."

Brian Beals, a colleague of Steneck's and Wahle's, sums it up this way: "We know there's a crash coming. I hope it doesn't happen, because a lot of lobstermen communities are going to get hurt."

While scientists are united that a collapse is coming, many fishermen have a different reading. "Barring a disease outbreak or a further change in the Gulf of Maine," says Frank Gotwals, "I don't see the fishery crashing over the next five to ten years. Of course, in fifteen years we could see the harvest cut by more than half or, if conditions are more favorable to the lobsters, even doubling. Up or down, it's anyone's guess. Who really knows for sure?"

Yet Frank recognizes the gravity of crossing the 50 percent threshold. "If we only caught fifty percent of our current annual take," he says, "we'd have a crisis. Not so much because of the lobsters being in trouble, but because of the economics of it."

Frank is pointing to financial realities. Lobstermen would not be able to cover daily expenses—bait, fuel, traps, line, loan interest—not to mention the cost of living and lifestyle expectations, which are higher now. Some fishermen have put all their savings into their boats. Eventually, they'll have to hang up their sou'westers.

Julie Eaton talks about survival of the fittest, the most prepared. "It's all about planning for what's coming," she says. "We've all been expecting changes. Those that have planned for them will survive. But some— those who are overextended—won't endure. Nature needs to cull the herd."

The boom-and-bust cycle of each sector of Maine seafood follows a familiar track. A fishery is stable for a number of years until some factor or pressure changes. Fishing pressure can increase, as it did for groundfish, shrimp, scallops, tuna, and clams, bringing a temporary bonanza to the market. Or, in the case of lobsters, an environmental factor changes. After a few short years of stratospheric landings, the fishery declines. It tends to stay depressed for decades. Perhaps the low predator pressure or the supplemental feeding with bait will give lobsters a safety net and they will not fall through the floor right away. But, sooner or later, the conditions that have suppressed the lobsters in Long Island Sound since 1999 will head north. At best, the Maine lobster has a limited window for success. Have no doubt, the seas are warming and the warm ocean masses are aimed at Maine.

Those warm waters are getting close. In Massachusetts, halfway between Long Island Sound and the Gulf of Maine, rising ocean temperatures have encouraged the destruction of lobster stocks. In 2016, the Massachusetts harvest was only 17.6 million pounds, which is 60 percent below the 1998 peak. Conservation measures, such as seasonal closures and trap reductions, have been applied, but to no avail. Lobstermen fight against further measures, claiming they've already faced enough hardship. Besides, those conservation efforts may be in vain. If temperature is the prime factor in the collapse, managers and fishermen believe it may be impossible to save the lobsters south of Cape Cod.

So it's time to ask how much climate change is responsible for the lobster's predicament. Is it the single factor or one of many? Humans tend to want to reduce every issue—political, psychological, or scientific—down to a single cause. This reductionism marks our history and politics today. Yet, it seems pretty clear that the lobster is caught at a crossroads, an intersection of factors in its boom off Maine and its bust off Long Island. Everyone has a favorite angel or villain: size limits, V-notching, predators, kelp, bait ranching, larval settlement, fecundity, currents, temperature. And the devil incarnate in Long Island Sound: shell disease. The best answer right now for the source of the boom is that it's a combination of all the usual suspects. However, some carry more weight than others. Brian Beals, a marine biologist at the University of Maine, ranks the likely influence on the lobster boom as follows: one, climate change; two, predators; three, sea urchins and kelp. Lists vary, but every scientist I encountered placed ocean warming as number one. They point to younger females breeding, rapid molts, and expansion of warm, deeper waters. Lobstermen either accept climate change as a factor or not. They are split right down the middle.

In September 2016, carbon dioxide passed the threshold of four hundred parts per million (ppm) concentration in the atmosphere. With the current rate of global pollution, the value climbs two ppm per year. At that rate, in 2040, when the concentration of carbon dioxide approaches 450 ppm, the global temperature will have risen 3.2° F (1.8° C). This will place Gulf of Maine surface temperatures in the mid- to high-fifties in summer.

Ocean surface temperatures will shadow atmospheric readings. However, there are likely to be hot spots around the globe. The Gulf of Maine is one of these. A new climate model out of Princeton, New Jersey, projects warming of three to four degrees Celsius in the northwest Atlantic sixty to one hundred years from now—2080 to 2120. This brings the water temperature off Stonington to nearly 60° F, close to the threshold for metabolic distress in lobsters. As in Long Island Sound, where this line was crossed in 1999, millions of lobsters would likely die.

That year, shell disease and thermal distress claimed 90 percent of the lobster stock off the coasts of Connecticut and Rhode Island. The fishery has never recovered. Average water temperatures in Long Island Sound are now routinely at the record-breaking 1999 level—over 68° F. Local lobstermen are looking at closures of their season.

Meanwhile, Canadian lobsters are robust, once again breaking all records. Between Long Island Sound and the Bay of Fundy, Maine straddles the middle temperatures and living conditions for now.

Even if water temperatures do not match worst-case projections, ocean acidification will likely wreak havoc with shellfish. Any creature with a shell—lobsters, crab, shrimp, clams, mussels, oysters—will be vulnerable to erosion of its exoskeleton and susceptibility to disease. This intermediate threat was addressed by Andrew Pershing of the Gulf of Maine Research Institute: "The extreme weather of climate change could lead to one really hot year that stimulates an outbreak of shell disease. That would destroy the fishery. Lobsters could be long gone before the ocean is consistently much warmer."

In the short term, how far could the lobster fishery retreat? Many experts consider the late-1990s levels (one-third of today's catch) to be possible. Twenty years ago, in 1998, the Maine statewide landings were 47 million pounds, 36 percent of the 2013 peak. The fishery was valued at $137 million, close to three dollars per pound. Such a gross sale would be offset more today by higher operating costs. A lobsterman would take home less money and have less purchasing power with it. Frank and Jason discuss those economic realities all the time. They are watchful of their finances, even more so with the prospect of a downtrend.

The dockside price has not been kind to lobstermen of late. In September 2017, the Canadians were released from an 8 percent tariff on lobster shipped to Europe. This made Canadian lobster cheaper relative to Maine lobster, forcing the Americans to drop their price at a time when it normally would have rebounded, thanks to low supplies. Maine lobstermen were blindsided, but promise to be more wary in the future.

It will also be important, in the wake of climate change, to be vigilant against overfishing—to avoid repeating the mistakes of the cod fishery. When the cod was down, climate warming kept the population from rebuilding. Despite this fact, managers did not adjust their quotas accordingly.

Yet, the prospect of the lobster supply drying up is only one of two climate threats to the Maine coast. Besides a shift downward in volume, the new fear is a geographic shift in the location of the lobsters that remain. The anxiety forces eyes to turn toward Canada.

In 2017, as lobster supplies falter and prices flatline, an armed conflict between lobstermen from Canada and the United States is possible. We pick up the story in midstride from a couple of years ago at the Canadian border—where it crosses the Gulf of Maine. The fog does not simply drift in from one direction one Friday in May. Instead, the mist materializes directly and ubiquitously from the sea, as if on the exhalation of right whales. But the lobster boats are too thick to allow a breaching whale. They are after a more cunning beast. Located in the Bay of Fundy, the narrow arm of the Gulf of Maine between Nova Scotia and Maine's northeastern tip, the fishermen vie for the hottest new spot for lobsters.

In the confusion of the whiteout, at least two boats—one from Maine, the other from Grand Manan, New Brunswick—haul opposite ends of the same trapline. On another day, an American loses his thumb while doing the same thing—disengaging his traps from tangled Canadian lines. Tempers flare on both days. Yet this is not the first time those on both sides of the border have threatened to take matters into their own hands. Several denizens of this no-man's-land carry guns on the water.

The Bay of Fundy is known for its tides, fog, and whales—and now for its lobster. The center point of the species' range is approaching. Almost as famous is Machias Seal Island, a disputed twenty-acre outcrop halfway between Maine and Canada. The two countries are fighting over the sovereignty of the island and its surrounding waters, known as the "Gray Zone" in diplomatic circles. Both sides lobster here, including the two flotillas today. Both sides are on guard. Both fear bloodshed.

"This is a ticking suitcase out here," says Brit Carver, sixty-four, of nearby Cutler, Maine. "It's just a matter of months before someone gets killed."

Each side has heard death threats as fishermen react to the stealing of gear, sabotaging of lines, and setting of traps atop those already on the bottom.

"Tensions have intensified," says Specialist Mark Murry of the Maine Marine Patrol. He worries about the likelihood of violence. "It's all about the lobsters. The lobstermen are seeing red."

The Gray Zone is a 277-square-mile oblong patch of sea. Machias Seal Island is right in the middle of it. The island is barren and treeless. The seals have departed, but the rock hosts colonies of seabirds, mostly puffins, razorbills, murres, storm petrels, and terns. Its commercial value is found in the fisheries of its encompassing waters. Its political value is its real currency.

The dispute over the island and its waters is in its 235th year. In 1783, the Treaty of Paris, which ended the Revolutionary War, gave the United States all islands within seventy miles of the new country, with certain exceptions. Its ambiguities have prompted several border disputes between the United States and Canada. All have been resolved except for one. The Treaty of Paris excluded from U.S. ownership all islands considered part of Nova Scotia. Canada has insisted that Machias Seal Island falls within the definition of "Nova Scotia" in a 1621 land grant by King James of England. In other words, Canada argues that the island is grandfathered into its domain.

The United States begs to differ. The U.S. State Department claims subsequent treaties negated the land grant. "Our historic position is that Machias Seal Island belongs to the United States," says one Foggy Bottom spokesman.

Nobody is budging. In fact, more and more Canadians have been entering the Gray Zone to lobster. The word is out that there's a wealth of lobster around Machias Seal Island. Canada has recently allowed non–Nova Scotians to acquire lobster licenses to the area. Cutler lobstermen are incensed about the northern hordes, yet they are stumped on a peaceful course of action. With lobster stocks booming, even more Canadian lobster boats are likely to come soon. The rising price of lobster has emboldened Canada to assert its sovereignty and keep the Gray Zone in play.

Since 1832, a lighthouse has continuously been occupied on the island—first by the British, now the Canadians. Today, all lighthouses in eastern Canada, except Machias Seal Island Light, are unmanned; the lights are automatic. The two keepers for Machias Seal Island are helicoptered to the station in twenty-eight-day shifts. Surprisingly, Machias Seal Island Light is also automatic, though manned. The keepers have nothing to do but mow the lawn. They stay on post simply to maintain Canada's sovereignty claim.

The Canadian flag flies over the lighthouse station. In an act of frustration and defiance, the Cutler men have threatened to replace the Canadian maple leaf with the Stars and Stripes. In the meantime, negotiations in Washington and Ottawa have gone nowhere.

The great irony is that lobsters do not observe international boundaries. They are on the move toward the Gray Zone and beyond. No treaty or trap cutting or gunfire can stop them. Just a ban on fossil fuels.

Since I first visited Stonington four years ago, the center point of the lobster population has migrated twelve to seventeen miles northeast. It has followed the warming seas. At this rate (from 3 to 4.3 miles per year), the center point will reach Machias Seal Island, one hundred miles away, somewhere between 2036 and 2046. By 2037 at the earliest, the majority of "American" lobsters might reside in Canada.

Predictions of what this scenario will look like are difficult to make. Yet some observations are useful. The temptation for Cutler fishermen (and other anxious Maine lobstermen) to cross the line could be immediate. The value of lobsters might be more lucrative than today, drawing trappers from distant counties and provinces. Just as Canadian lobstermen slip into contested seas now, Maine fishermen might become the lead trespassers, testing Canadian waters.

The chance of a hostile border dispute increases with each passing year. As if anticipating it, in 2017 the marine patrols from New Brunswick and Maine elevated their vigilance over the Gray Zone. They were on the lookout for violators. More waters could be grayer very soon.

A standoff in 2037 is not far-fetched. Border fights over the control of fisheries are popping up around the globe. Bordering countries often claim the same island, shoal, or bank, or even fish. Not surprisingly, most disagreements have been fueled by climate change, resulting in warming seas.

Schools of mackerel moved recently, in part, from the North Sea to Icelandic waters. This movement was likely prompted by ocean warming, bringing a new commercial species within legal range of Icelandic fishing boats. Although catching virtually no mackerel before 2006, Iceland quickly allocated herself a 130,000-tonne quota. In the last two years, somewhat under that theoretical quota, Icelandic catches have added up to 18 percent of the total northeastern Atlantic haul. This has stirred up a mackerel war between the European Union (predominantly Scotland), the Faroe Islands, Norway, and Iceland—reminiscent of the cod war of the 1970s, when Icelandic gunboats clashed with a Royal Navy frigate. In 2014, an interim agreement was signed by all parties except Iceland, reallocating country quotas out of the 210,000 tonnes of mackerel agreed upon for the North Sea. Instead of staying within the established total to make the country allocations work, the quota has been extended by 100,000 tonnes, nearly doubling the take—a "tragedy of the commons" on an international scale. This still means Iceland may catch 38 percent of the whole Atlantic pie, a larger share than before. Sooner or later, Scotland will come looking for its fish.

Scarborough Shoal in the South China Sea is another fisheries battleground. Claimed by both China and the Philippines, the shallow bank accounts for 12 percent of the total global fish catch. Because of fishing pressure, virtually all South China Sea fisheries are collapsed, overexploited, or fully exploited. China alone consumes 34 percent of the global fish supply, or $280 billion (3 percent of GDP)—a revenue worth fighting for. Fishing by the Philippines amounts to 2 percent of its own GDP and, like Chinese fishing, is part of its national culture. Tensions between the two countries commenced on April 8, 2012, when the Philippine navy apprehended eight Chinese fishing vessels on Scarborough Shoal. In retaliation, China imposed a fishing ban for other countries in the South China Sea for the summer months. The Philippines did not recognize the ban and imposed its own ban. In April 2015, the China Coast Guard employed water cannons on Philippine fishing vessels and seized their catch. Patrol boats edged arriving Philippine boats out of the contested area. The battle seemed ready to escalate.

Suddenly, in October 2016, the Chinese patrol boats departed Scarborough Shoal, signaling a warming of relations between China and the Philippines. The previous week, President Duterte of the Philippines had visited Beijing, where he announced he wanted a "separation" from the United States. Next, in Tokyo, Duterte announced he would revoke an agreement that gives the United States access to five military bases, including airstrips, in the Philippines. Limiting or removing American access to the bases would delight China. Fish for F-16s.

The border disputes between China and the Philippines and between Iceland and Scotland are illustrative of the level of intensity that fighting over food can bring. However, there is at least one constraint over the prospect of Maine lobstermen rushing the Canadian border. By Maine law, the only lobstermen with access to the Bay of Fundy are fishermen from Zone A, the northeasternmost of the lobster zones. That means lobstermen from Cutler, Machias, and Lubec. Everyone else to the southwest must stay in their respective zones, unless they get a transfer. In Zone C, Stonington lobstermen cannot reach the Canadian border—it's two zones too far—unless new legislation alters their access.

Yet, right now, the people of Stonington are busy with their own challenges. More than ever, the lobster fleet is pushing the eastern edge of Zone C itself. Captains are working close to the line and, within their own family territories, are "working the east'erd." That's where the lobsters are densest as the population moves to the northeast. Where it will end up, no one knows for sure. Yet already, Zones A and B are gaining on Zone C, the leader in the state since 2009. Perhaps it will not be for long. In proximity to the Canadian border, Zone A could be poised for a bonanza, and residing there will prove to be a cherished and profitable advantage for a few.

Another battle erupted in Zone C recently, one that could only be fought in the state capitol, rather than on the water. For twenty years, all zones except Zone C have enforced a limited-entry policy, whereas in eastern Maine, the number of new licenses available each year depends on the number surrendered—mostly due to retirement or the death of a lobsterman. Otherwise, the number of licenses is secure. A fear of visiting or incoming lobstermen moving to a place like Stonington to acquire lobster licenses has finally prompted locals to close the last zone. A benefit of limited entry here could be a better-regulated commons, a closed fishery. An additional benefit will be fewer lobster boats in Stonington Harbor, and fewer traps in the water.

The port itself is strong for now, once again ranked number one in the state, with sixty million dollars in overall fisheries landings (2016). That amounts to 25 million pounds, most of it lobster. Stonington is still beautiful, still authentic. You can come home again, but for how long?

Success brings an air of complacency. Some assume the boom will continue. As several lobstermen say, perhaps a downturn like that in summer 2017 will be temporary. "We'll bounce back," they say. Some are betting on a bright future. Greenhead Lobster, the largest buying station on the harbor, has just built a twenty-thousand-square-foot processing and shipping facility in Seabrook, New Hampshire, within range of Logan International Airport. Hugh Reynolds, the owner, has a well-oiled machine. Yet spinning those gears requires an enormous supply chain of lobsters and a steady (or growing) demand from Asia. Reynolds has nerves of steel.

The situation is the same in Tenants Harbor, where Peter Yee at Wildcat Lobster has bought out his partner, Steven Yip. Wildcat will now acquire more buying stations, perhaps that one in Stonington, with Pete Yee as the solo pilot. He still has an eye on one million pounds in annual exports to China, but he is having trouble locating the lobster.

Peter Miller has sold his lobster-buying station to the new Tenants Harbor Fisherman's Co-op. In a checkmate move, he sold his parents' restaurant, Cod End, at the same time to Luke's Lobster, a successful and popular chain that specializes in lobster rolls. Luke Holden, the owner, is expanding at a feverish pace, with several restaurants in New York City, Chicago, Boston, and Tokyo. He will look for shedders from the new co-op next door. His customers will come from the town's gentry.

A third business in flux in Tenants Harbor is Linda Bean's Perfect Maine. Linda has parlayed part of her L. L. Bean inheritance into lobster operations. She owns buying stations in Port Clyde, Tenants Harbor, and Vinalhaven. She also owned a lobster-processing plant in Rockland, which she subsequently sold to her employees. For a while, she was vertically integrated. So was the Sea Hag lobstering plant, right up the street. However, Sea Hag has closed its door—bankrupt and on the auction block. Two dozen workers were laid off. Sea Hag is the first Maine lobstering plant to go bust. The reason may have been poor financing, more than any issue of supply and demand. Yet the other lobstermen and entrepreneurs in the area—Luke Holden, Peter Miller, Linda Bean, and Peter Yee—will take notice, on the heels of a shaky year in landings.

What will happen to Stonington and the remaining expanse of the lobster coast? Lobsters and lobstering may not disappear altogether, but the quality of life may change. Stonington and neighboring villages are vulnerable to any prolonged downturn, which most experts agree would lead to an irreversible gentrification of the Maine coast. Some say that when the world changes, residents will adapt or move. Yet, for Maine, few fishermen can change their stripes. Their skills are not transferable, their originality not to be tamed. Only a few will choose the big city— Bangor or Augusta. During any exodus on the road, lobstermen will likely pass people from away, steering for Stonington—moving in and buying up the captains' homes. The first thing the interlopers will do is build fences between houses. Next: NO TRESPASSING signs. The fishermen had little need for either. Or for the cruise ships that gentility brings—up 6 percent in traffic statewide this year. Culture will begin to collapse: the end of lobster bakes and races and the Church of the Morning After. Also on the horizon: The price of seafood could double, putting lobsters out of reach of all but the wealthiest tourists.

It's hard to imagine the local lobster culture disappearing—all that untamed beauty vanishing overnight.

The locals speak of such a future in hushed tones. They talk about the worst, then disavow it. Talk of the town losing its authenticity is just rumor, they will say. There is little talk of a plan B, a life with fewer lobsters, or lobsters retreating up the coast.

Without planning for it, however, locals will likely react to a fragile future with all the resiliency and character they can muster. The glut may be coming to an end and, with it, the easy life. Yet, in all likelihood, they will do their best to meet the new challenges of ocean warming, prices, Canadian competition, bubbles, diversification, unions, and comanagement. Another action of resiliency will be to continue with conservation practices.

"Just how precarious these communities are is quite sobering," says Robin Alden, now executive director of the Maine Center for Coastal Fisheries in Stonington. "I don't want to think what Maine would be like without lobsters. Families would have to move away. There just isn't much to do besides lobster."

A concern about the future of the Maine coast in the wake of climate change has led to a major investigation by the GMRI. It is pursuing a $1.8 million grant from the National Science Foundation to study the impact of ocean warming on fishing communities in Maine. The project takes an integrated look at ecology, economics, and social concerns. It examines how temperature affects the distribution of lobster and fish and how that impacts local seafood operations.

The first news-breaking product of GMRI's study is a population model that predicts lobster abundance will shrink 40 to 62 percent over the next thirty-two years, due to rising ocean temperatures. "We are coming off the peak right now," says Andrew Pershing. "We're returning to a more traditional fishery." In 2002, a traditional year, Maine lobstermen landed 63 million pounds of lobster, half the recent catch. Pershing says conservation measures nearly doubled the population explosion that would have been expected from warming alone. Without those measures, by 2050 the lobster stocks would diminish another 20 percent. From lobstermen to resource managers, the population forecast has been met with wide skepticism. No one knows what will happen in thirty years.

By June 2017, the halibut are once again running low. Jason's annual fishing fever has come and gone, but not Stonington's community spirit.

The Gotwals-McDonald clan joins Donna and me for dinner at Fisherman's Friend to land some fresh fish. A table for nine: Frank and Donna, Jason and Haley, Donna and me, and the three McDonald girls. Jill, now fourteen, has Jason's striking blue eyes. Addy, sixteen, and Kennedy, six, have brown eyes, like their mother's. The tenth tribesman, missing for the evening, is Frank's mother, eighty-nine, who is home tending her garden. That adds up to four generations. The girls are huddled around Haley's arms and legs like a brood of summer ducklings.

Haley catches my eye and says, "Yep, it's all girls. Jason is a sport to put up with a houseful of women. Even our male cat died. Sad. The captain's all alone now."

Jason hears this refrain. "At least the toilet seat is never up," he says. "I'm not complaining. Besides, I get to take my daughters out in the boat from time to time. Jill now every week. Those are awesome days."

Jill has been lobstering with her father once a week ever since her first traps were set—since her eighth-grade class let out for the summer. Now she has twenty-eight traps soaking in the water. June is always the month for getting straight, for preparation before the big push. Nobody, except Jill, is laying odds for the coming season.

Her grandfather Frank is the first to broach the subject of lobstering. Breaking the claws, so to speak. Frank says he picked a dozen lobsters out of a trap this morning.

Jill's ears perk up. "Yesterday, I caught fourteen lobsters in one trap," she says, beaming.

"A family record," says Frank, grinning. "What about the rest of your gear?"

"I'm betting on a hundred and fifty pounds one day soon—five pounds per trap—if the big shed shows up. That's five hundred and twenty-five dollars, right, Dad?"

Jason smiles. "I imagine you'll catch every lobster in the ocean the way yer going," he says. Frank and Jason exchange winks. But Jill catches them and responds with a wink of her own. There's no sidelining Jillian McDonald.

Meanwhile, Frank and the two Donnas order halibut from the menu. Jill and her sisters insist on hamburgers, while Jason and I vote for fried clams. Haley has lobster Alfredo. She's slim; she can afford the butter.

When the fish arrives, Frank tackles the halibut with abandon. The

Donnas and he exchange knowing looks. But Jason falls into a cold silence. He had his fill of halibut fillets from our day on *Seahawk* a year ago. Then again, last month he hooked two with sweat and swagger. He cannot eat another bite. Not until next May.

But it's late June now and eleven months till baiting another hook with alewives. In the interim, Jason and Jill have plenty of lobsters to win, herring and pogies to bait, and buoys to color and claim.

Photographs are passed around of Addy's modern dance class. She's light on her feet and has perfect posture. Then the conversation returns to Jill's summer endeavor, requiring balance on the rail, not balance on the floor.

"How do you juggle setting and hauling?" asks her grandmother from across the table. It is the role of grandparents to ask too many questions.

"I like the hauling, but setting—with all the warps and buoys—is harder than I thought. My sports training helps. It's tough work lifting those traps, especially when they're full of creatures. But I like inspecting all the sea life that comes aboard. It's like hide-and-seek, the starfish and whelks appearing, then disappearing under the waves."

"So you like the ocean's bounty?" says Donna Gotwals.

"It's not just the marine animals that attract me. I like the look of the water at dawn, when the red sky washes over the blue. I've painted that sky when we return home in the evening. I love being on the water, but I like the money, too."

"Frank, it's been a long time since *you* felt that way about it," says Donna, teasing him.

"Yeah, like *since* this morning."

"Exactly." The words of a lobsterman's widow.

Frank and Donna nod their heads, pleased with Jill's progress. "You may want to stern with Alyssa and me someday on *Seasong*," Frank says.

"Not on your life," quips Jason. "She's crewing on *Seahawk* till school starts. She's booked tight. We're going after shedders tomorrow on Southeast Harbor."

On a chilly, crisp morning, I think of the captains of Stonington going through the paces of their lives. Jason wakes at 3:00 A.M., Frank at 3:30, and Julie at 4:00. You can set your watch by them. They wear none. They navigate by the moon. By dawn, they are hauling the first trawl, hoping for a good catch. Frank and the others always take a moment to appreciate the sunrise—it's the first gift of their day. Then the parlay begins, moving traps to a better bottom, to wherever they gamble might be the winning play. The whole day is like a game of blackjack: betting the right cards, figuring the right configuration will turn up. With the downturn, lobstermen may conserve the resource—and their bets—by limiting their traps. But no time soon. Nobody is holding his breath.

For now, lobstermen are still busy playing the commons. There are just enough lobsters for three million traps. There is no overfishing yet, per se. That may change. In the future, fewer lobsters and fewer traps—perhaps a necessity in the next decade—may meet resistance until they translate into a higher price.

Climate change is now a fact of life along the Maine coast. Playing the commons now means mastering supply and demand—and politics—in the face of ocean warming.

Fishermen are flexible, adaptive, at sea; now they must be versatile at the state capitol to modify regulations. They must adapt to unpredictability. They will also need a different price structure to balance the lower catch if the roller coaster of the boom-bust cycle proceeds.

The parable of "The Tragedy of the Commons" works just as well for the climate as it does for a farm field or a stretch of water. The atmosphere is a pool, a reservoir of clean air. Into the sky, we dump carbon dioxide. But the atmosphere has a carrying capacity of carbon and other gases. We happen to have surpassed the threshold for what the climate (and Earth) can tolerate. Carbon dioxide is a major greenhouse gas, and loading it is causing the temperatures of the planet to climb. Heat drives the climate; the oceans are warming. Fish and shellfish are reacting, moving hundreds of miles.

Can Mainers arrest climate change? They can try. Vinalhaven has those three towering windmills, beacons of sustainability; the Maine coast needs more. And, besides fighting the heat, they can keep the local impacts at bay. Living with climate change requires adapting, finding ways to optimize the future. Senior lobstermen have the advantage here: They have survived lulls in the harvest before. The difference: how declines in the catch today are brought on by warming waters.

Remarkably, communities are already adapting. In just three years, boosting demand helped double the price of lobster paid to fishermen. The next widespread adaptation will likely be diversification. Southern species, such as black sea bass and summer flounder, that have invaded the Gulf of Maine due to warming could turn into valuable fisheries. And aquaculture is catching on. Already, "cowboy fishermen" are turning into "sea farmers," learning how to use aquaculture to harvest mussels, clams, and oysters. So far, lobsters have been too difficult and expensive to raise. The survival of fisheries, the diversity of seafood, the price of the product—all these can be manipulated to a degree if the lobstermen are wise.

The people of Stonington will not give up easily. They do not play the victim, as if some perfect storm had barreled through town. Rather, they are ready to fight. Stonington is a community uncertain of its future, but it will do combat, engaging on every front. As Julie Eaton says, "Sure, let's start a Skippers Program, let's tie up, let's train an apprentice, let's form a union, let's open up a new export market. No time to waste. Let's go."

And the forecast for the fishery? At the start of the next season, seemingly out of nowhere, Julie whispers in her Mainer lilt, "The lobstah will come." She bluffs her way through any uncertainty. But she may be right. She has had to be optimistic in her life to survive. And she's mastered her world.

I think back to Julie's big fear, the nightmare of finding her traps completely empty one morning. Or just one specimen there: the last lobster. If that happened, how would she face the next day?

Despite the best of intentions, lobstermen may not be able to master climate change. It keeps coming, worse than before, wave after wave. The year 2017 is another one for the record books. Julie and I talk of the spike in sea-level rise—five inches—off Portland last year. "My house is safe," she says. She lives mid-island, but at the harbor, water is nipping at our heels. "I'll fish for the rest of my life—that I'm sure of," Julie shouts from her skiff, halfway across the harbor.

School is already out for summer, and the kids huddle along the wharf, waving at Julie. She yells back to us, "The lobstah will come!"

That optimism sums up the uncompromising character of Maine fishermen. But a lobsterman's voice may not be the last one heard. One way or another, Mother Nature is likely to have the final word.

Jill McDonald rises at 4:00 A.M. to greet the first big shed of the season. Her internal clock is now set to that hour, but her father tickles her under her chin. Across America, the only other teenagers waking so early are Olympic hopefuls and a few of Jill's friends who are sterning for their fathers.

She gazes out her bedroom window at the obsidian night sky. A million stars wink back at her. It's a go.

It's been a go all June. The true test of her commitment is heading out every week—sun or storm, slick calm or tempest. Her father does not even check the weather radio. In summer, he's always prepared to go. It's part of the code, to which his daughter has signed allegiance.

A stiff breeze stirs the trees outside. She knows now this means choppy seas, not her favorite; however, she takes the good with the bad.

In the truck, Jill asks her father if the shedders will show up in this wind. "Don't they run for cover?" she asks.

"There's no fear under the ocean," he says. "All the turmoil is in the waves." On the drive to the harbor, her father reassures her. She sighs.

He whispers, "The lobstahs will come."

He tells her the lobsters have been shedding off Deer Isle for thousands of years. But, he adds, the ecosystem is changing and nobody knows how far it will shift. Or where the lobsters will go.

"So we don't know anything," says Jill.

"We know this day will be stunning."

At the Co-op, Jill casts off the lines of *Seahawk*. As she swings off the piling into the boat, the first flickers of dawn are enflamed with red. Rising from the water, the sun is oblong, vertical, ascending like a nascent candle flame from its molten wax. It drips cinnabar into the sea. If she endures, Jill will have sixty years of sunrises to look forward to, each one a blessing, each one remembered well. She memorizes the colors, planning to paint the sunrise over the blue water when she retires this evening.

If the oceans hold a memory, the lobstermen are etched into the water as if it were stone. We are in awe of their beauty, their originality, their defiance in an age of conformity. They are the last shepherds of the sea.

The captain swings *Seahawk* in a wide arc and points the bow at the lobster grounds. The boat is bathed in the warm summer light. The sunrise voyage is twenty minutes long. Southeast Harbor might as will be in their backyard. Jill stands on the bridge, casting her eyes eastward, absorbing the dawn colors and thinking of dozens of lobsters.

Over her shoulder, the white windmills loom across the cold cobalt sea. Like three sentinels, their solitary eyes pierce the distance, as if watching Jill. She returns their gaze. With such vigilance, perhaps her generation will pay better attention to ocean warming.

However, right now, for father and daughter, all navigation is across this immediate stretch of water. They catch the morning tide, carrying them over any perceived obstacle or obstruction.

She takes off her cap and lets the summer breeze freshen her long ginger-blond hair. The peak of the season has begun. It has all the promise and peril of every boom-and-bust decade of her grandfather's day. She's heard the stories, was weaned on them. She knows the only antidote to fretting is to show up for your buoys—every day. It's the only way she can remember where they are located the next day or week.

Her sterning girlfriends are just as punctual—as if they're carrying a torch for all female fishermen and for all their families, as well. Jill has pride in the lineage and in the sisterhood. Yesterday, she dreamed of captaining her own boat. She's beginning to love the life.

Yet, just now, she's looking for her own wicked good catch as a sternman. Under her breath, she repeats her father's words, "The lobstah will come."

She smiles now with all the anticipation of a fourteen-year-old girl. Who can blame her? Penobscot Bay has always delivered. After all, it's the lobster capital of the world.

Acknowledgments

Dozens of people, often in bewilderment, have asked why write a book about Maine lobstermen. The long answer can be found in the pages of this book. The short answer is: what a perfect way to spend time with some of the most genuine and fascinating people in the world. I traveled to Maine with an open mind, eyes, ears. As serendipity would have it, on my first visit to Stonington, I met Frank Gotwals and Julie Eaton, around whom the story revolves. Patriarch of the east side of the harbor; matriarch of the west. Shortly afterward, Frank introduced me to his stepson, Jason McDonald, wise beyond his years. I am indebted to these three captains, who welcomed me onto their boats, into their homes, into their lives. I expanded my understanding of community from them. Their spouses—Donna Gotwals, Haley McDonald, and Sid Eaton—were generous as well, despite the odd hours I would appear at their doors.

I am also thankful for other captains of the Maine lobster fleet who took me out on the water: Genevieve and Cory McDonald, also of Stonington, and Peter Miller of Tenants Harbor. They gave me updates as the lobster harvest peaked and faltered.

Six marine biologists regularly gave me background on lobster biology and the state of the fishery. I appreciate the help of Brian Beals, Diane Cowan, Kathy Mills, Andrew Pershing, Bob Steneck, and Rick Wahle. Malin Pinsky shared the background data for his research on lobster migrations with me. Resource managers at the Maine Department of Marine Resources were also helpful, in particular Kathleen Reardon and Carl Wilson.

My partner, Donna Grosvenor, accompanied me on three sabbaticals in Maine and, with her great passion for people, opened doors with lobstermen and their spouses. Her exquisite photographs grace these pages. Additionally, Donna was the first reader of the manuscript and offered many helpful comments. She has that rare gift for editing a turn of phrase without losing its resonance. The second reader was Richard Adams Carey, who has written of these waters before. His suggestions brought the many drafts to a happy conclusion. He helped make the dialogue more real. I appreciate their critical eyes and encouragement.

I would also like to thank some of the many people in Stonington who assisted in research for the book: Ted Ames and Robin Alden, John Boyce, Tony Bray, Chris Bruce, Virginia Burnett, Peter Buxton, Ami Carver, Bill and Amelia Damon, Tom Duym, Megan Flenniken, Andy Gove, Barrett Gray, Derrick Gray, Carla Gunther, Caleb Hardie, Vicky Hardie, Alyssa LaPointe, Jillian and Adeline McDonald, Elliott Nevels, Liz Perez, Hugh Reynolds, Debbie Robbins, Steven Robbins, Jr., Steven Robbins III, Bill Sargent, Suzy Shepard, Ron Trundy, Al Webber, Todd West, John Williams, and Bob and Lynn Winters.

Elsewhere in Maine, my efforts were assisted by John Alden, Frank Alley, Jeff Bennett, Ami Carver, Philip Conkling, David Cousens, Allyson Dailey, Mark Farquhar, Matt Jacobson, Emily Lane, Patrice McCarron, and Peter Ralston.

In Santa Fe and across the country, I'd like to thank many friends who were supportive of the project, including the following: Jan Adesso, Diane and Walter Burke, Kay Carlson, Jefferson Davis, Monica DeRario, Paul DeStefano, Wren Green, George Johnson, Dorothy Massey, Melinda Morrison, Kate Naylor, Steve Reed, Katerina Rollins, Claire Romero and David Bomse, Eric Rounds, Becca Schwarzlose, Bill Sidman, Don and Linda Terpstra, and Rob Wilder. And, of course, great appreciation to Stonington and Matinicus, our Maine coon cats, who were spiritual advisers on the project.

Thanks also to Michael Flamini, my editor at St. Martin's Press. He was enthusiastic about the book from the beginning. The story seeks to match his enthusiasm for lobster and Maine. Gwen Hawkes and Vicki Lame, associate editors, were always gracious and helpful.

My gratitude also extends to my agents at the Strothman Literary Agency, Lauren MacLeod and Wendy Strothman, who handled this book with care. They offered helpful suggestions along the way with characteristic passion for narrative nonfiction.

With all these helpful hands, I had a smooth race, zigzagging among the lobster buoys for three seasons to the finish.

Selected Bibliography

Abel, David. "Gulf of Maine Fishermen Face 6-Month Cod Ban." *Boston Globe,* November 10, 2014, 1–3.

———. "In Maine, Scientists See Signs of Climate Change." *Boston Globe,* September 21, 2014, 1–3.

———. "Losing Hope for Lobster South of Cape Cod." *Boston Globe,* December 3, 2017, 1–2.

———. "US, Canadian Fishermen at War over Lobster Waters." *Boston Globe,* May 28, 2015, 2–10.

Acheson, James M. *Capturing the Commons: Devising Institutions to Manage the Maine Lobster Industry.* Lebanon, NH: University Press of New England, 2003.

———. "Co-Management in the Maine Lobster Industry: A Study in Fictional Politics." *Conservation and Society,* November 2011, 1–15.

———. *The Lobster Gangs of Maine.* Lebanon, NH: University Press of New England, 1988.

Acheson, James M., and Robert S. Steneck. "Bust and Then Boom in the Maine Lobster Industry: Perspectives of Fishers and Biologists." *North American Journal of Fisheries Management* 17 (1977): 826–47.

Ames, Edward P. "Atlantic Cod Stock Structure in the Gulf of Maine." *Fisheries* 29 (2004): 10–28.

Arnold, Chris. "She's No Man; She's a Lobsterman." NPR, August 19, 2012.

Associated Press. "American Lobster: The New Chinese New Year Delicacy." *Washington Post,* February 17, 2015, 2–4.

———. "Black Sea Bass Influx Threatens Lobster Population." WMUR-TV, September 27, 2015.

———. "Lobstermen Keeping Eyes on Spread of Shell Disease." *Portland Press Herald,* August 11, 2013, 3–6.

———. "Lobster Wars Still Simmering." *Bangor Daily News,* July 20, 2010, 2–3.

———. "Mainer Sentenced to Prison for Selling Lobsters Under the Table." *Portland Press Herald,* April 17, 2015, 4–5.

———. "Shrimp Fishing Banned in Gulf of Maine for 2014 Due to Overfishing, Warming Oceans." *Huffington Post,* December 5, 2013, 2–3.

Baumer, Jim. "Chinese Appetite for New England Lobster Boosts Industry." *Boston Globe,* March 13, 2015, 2–3.

Bell, Tom. "Gulf of Maine Lobster Forecast to Give Industry Early Warning." *Portland Press Herald,* December 19, 2014, 2–3.

———. "Maine Fishermen Cash In as Lobster Cracks $4 a Pound." *Portland Press Herald,* October 9, 2015, 1–5.

Benson, Judy. "Lobster Fishermen Taking Enforced Break (Long Island Sound)." *The Day,* September 8, 2014, 1–3.

Bidgood, Jess. "A Fisherman Tries Farming." *New York Times,* October 10, 2017, 1–3.

Bigler, Taylor. "Stonington Lobster Boat Captain Photographs Her Life on the Water." *Ellsworth American,* August 6, 2015, 1–3.

Billings, Cathy. *The Maine Lobster Industry: A History of Culture, Conservation and Commerce.* Charleston, SC: History Press, 2014.

Brophy, Jessica. "Hundreds Gather to Celebrate 25th Annual Fishermen's Day." *Island Ad-Vantages,* July 24, 2014, 1.

Brown, Mike. *The Maine Lobster Book.* Camden, ME: International Marine Publishing Company, 1986.

Colombo, Jesse. "China's Bubble Economy." *The Bubble Bubble,* October 2, 2012, 1–9.

Conathan, Michael. "Ocean Warming Means a New Paradigm for the World's Fisheries." *Climate Progress,* May 20, 2013, 1–3.

Conkling, Philip. *Along the Archipelago: Essays and Observations from Maine's Islands and Working Waterfronts.* Rockland, ME: Island Institute, 2012.

Conkling, Philip, and Peter Ralston (photographer). *Islands in Time: A Natural and Cultural History of the Islands of Maine.* Rockland, ME: Island Institute, 2011.

Corson, Trevor. *The Secret Life of Lobsters: How Fishermen and Scientists Are Unraveling the Mysteries of Our Favorite Crustacean.* New York: Harper-Collins, 2004.

Curtis, Abigail. "As the Ocean Gets Warmer, Are the Lobsters Heading to Cooler Northeast Waters?" *Bangor Daily News,* March 2, 2014, 1–2.

Daley, Beth. "For Maine Lobstermen, Less Could Mean More: Officials Want to Cut Number of Traps." *Boston Globe,* April 21, 2009, 2.

Deer Isle Granite Museum. *Stone Slabs and Iron Men: The Deer Island Granite Industry.* Stonington, ME: Deer Isle Granite Museum, 1997.

Dismore, Sandra. "Every Fisherman Has a Story to Tell and Every Story Is Different." *Fishermen's Voice,* September 2013, 1–12. (First of a four-part series.)

Dukes, Jesse. "Consider the Lobstermen: Boom and Bust in Maine's Last Great Fishery." *VQ Online,* Summer 2011.

Editorial Staff. "Maine's Lobster Industry Might Not Last Forever. Then What?" *Bangor Daily News,* March 14, 2014, 1–2.

Editorial Staff. "Record Catch of Lobsters Raises Fears of Overfishing." *New York Times,* April 23, 1996, 2.

Fahey, Anna. "Lobster Prices Hit Rock Bottom Thanks to Climate Change." *Alternet,* August 9, 2012, 3–4.

Felice, Flavio. "Elinor Ostrom and the Solution to the Tragedy of the Commons." Translated by Maria Bond. *American Enterprise Institute,* June 27, 2012, 1–5.

Formisano, Ron. *The Great Lobster War.* Amherst: University of Massachusetts Press, 1997.

Foster, Joanna M. "The Lobster Bubble: Maine's Lobster Boom, and Why Experts Predict a Dramatic Bust." *Climate Progress,* August 4, 2013, 2–8.

Goode, Erica. "Cod's Continuing Decline Linked to Warming Gulf of Maine Waters." *New York Times,* October 29, 2015, 2.

———. "Fish Seek Cooler Waters, Leaving Some Fishermen's Nets Empty." *New York Times,* December 30, 2016, 1–6.

Gotwals, Frank. "Let's Celebrate the Maine Lobster." *Bangor Daily News,* June 17, 2014, 1–2.

Graves, Liz. "Marketing Powerhouse Chosen for Lobster Effort." *Ellsworth American,* December 24, 2014, 1–3.

Greer, Adam. "The South China Sea Is Really a Fishery Dispute." *The Diplomat,* July 20, 2016, 2–3.

Guilford, Gwynn. "The Enigma Behind America's Freak, 20-Year Lobster Boom." *Quartz,* October 6, 2015, 1–34.

Hall, Jessica. "Lobster Forecast Causes Concern, Not Panic, for Maine's Industry: Lobstermen See a Need to Plan for a Smaller Catch in Several Years, but Say the Change May Raise Their Prices." *Portland Press Herald,* April 24, 2014, 1–5.

Hardin, Garrett. "The Tragedy of the Commons." *Science,* December 13, 1968, 1–17.

Idlebrook, Craig. "Lobster Processing Plant Purchase Holds Promise for Gouldsboro." *The Working Waterfront,* December 5, 2012, 1–2.

Jackson, Derrick Z. "New England's Threatened Lobster." *Boston Globe,* October 12, 2013, 1–3.

Kessler, Rebecca. "Fast-Warming Gulf of Maine Offers Hint of Future for Oceans." *Yale Environment 360,* November 17, 2014, 1–2.

Koenig, Seth. "Will Chinese Market Prove Lucky or Lethal for Maine Lobstermen." *Bangor Daily News,* September 9, 2011, 2–3.

Koopman, Heather N., Andrew J. Westgate, and Zachary A. Siders. "Declining Fecundity and Factors Affecting Embryo Quality in the American Lobster (*Homarus americanus*) from the Bay of Fundy." *Canadian Journal of Fisheries and Aquatic Sciences* 72, no. 3 (2015): 352–63.

La Flamme, Mark. "'We Feel Like We Have a Voice': Maine Lobstermen Union Recognized." *Bangor Daily News,* March 23, 2015, 2–4.

Maine, Anna. "Lobstermen Stop Fishing Due to Low Prices." *The Working Waterfront,* July 10, 2012, 1–3.

Martinez, Andrew J. *Marine Life of the North Atlantic: Canada to Cape May.* Locust Valley, NY: Aqua Quest Publications, 2003.

Matthiessen, Peter. *Men's Lives.* New York: Random House, 1986.

McCarthy, James. "Exports Boost Lobster: Demand from Asia Boosting Sales at York Shellfish Dealer." *MaineBiz,* May 4, 2015, 1–3.

McFarlane, Andrew. "Why Is Britain Braced for a Mackerel War?" *BBC News Magazine,* August 24, 2014, 3–9.

Munshi, Neil. "Lobster Industry Squeezed by Oversupply." CNBC, August 7, 2013.

Murphy, Edward D. "Maine Lobster Industry Wary as Warm Waters Suggest Repeat of Disastrous 2012 Season." *Portland Press Herald,* February 4, 2016, 2–7.

National Science Foundation. "Warmer Future Oceans Could Cause Phytoplankton to Thrive Near Poles, Shrink in Tropics." *Science Daily,* October 25, 2012, 1.

Oragano, Christina Lemieux. *How to Catch a Lobster in Down East Maine.* Charleston, SC: History Press, 2012.

Ostrom, Elinor, et al. "Revising the Commons: Local Lessons, Global Challenges." *Science,* April 9, 1999, 1–14.

Pew Charitable Trusts. "The Story of Atlantic Bluefin Tuna." *Global Tuna Conservation,* October 8, 2013, 1–9.

Pinsky, Malin, et al. "Marine Taxa Track Local Climate Velocities." *Science,* September 13, 2013, 1239–42.

Proctor, Noble S., and Patrick J. Lynch. *A Field Guide to North Atlantic Wildlife: Marine Mammals, Seabirds, Fish, and Other Sea Life.* New Haven: Yale University Press, 2005.

Rappaport, Stephen. "Lobster Landings Skyrocket in Value." *Ellsworth American,* February 26, 2015, 1–2.

———. "Lobster Prices: Going Up, but How Far." *Ellsworth American,* January 12, 2017, 1–2.

Robbins, Brian. *Bearin's: The Book.* Belfast, ME: North Wind Publishing, 2011.

Russell, Eric. "Are Lobstermen Keeping Their Traps Shut?" *Portland Press Herald,* July 14, 2012, 1.

———. "Ocean Scientists Report 'Unprecedented' Spike in Sea Level off Portland." *Portland Press Herald,* February 26, 2015, 2–3.

Seelye, Katherine Q. "In Maine, More Lobsters Than They Know What to Do With." *New York Times,* July 28, 2012, 2–3.

Steneck, Robert S., and Richard A. Wahle. "American Lobster Dynamics in a Brave New Ocean." *Canada Journal of Fisheries and Aquatic Sciences* 70 (2013): 1612–24.

Steneck, R. S., et al. "Creation of a Gilded Trap by the High Economic Value of the Maine Lobster Fishery." *Conservation Biology* (2011): 1–9.

Stewart, Jeanine. "Dungeness Crab Prices Flying Up and Away." *Under Current News,* January 28, 2014, 2.

Trotter, Bill. "Lobster Price Plummet Prompts Talk of Industry Shutdown." *Bangor Daily News,* July 11, 2012, 3–4.

———. "Lobster Shell Disease Inching into Gulf of Maine." *Bangor Daily News,* August 15, 2013, 6–7.

———. "Maine Lobster Catch on Track to Hit Lowest Value This Decade." *Bangor Daily News,* October 12, 2017, 2–4.

United Nations Intergovernmental Panel on Climate Change (IPCC). "IPCC Fourth Assessment Report, 2007." Retrieved from http://www.ipcc.ch /publications_and_data/publications_and_data_reports.shtml (accessed June 22, 2012).

Van Allen, Jennifer. "Maine Women Welcome a Sea of Opportunities." *Portland Press Herald,* October 5, 2014, 2–4.

Wahle, R., and N. Oppenheim. "American Lobster Settlement Index: Update 2016." Retrieved from http://umaine.edu/wahlelab/current-projects/american -lobster-settlement-index/ (accessed May 15, 2017).

Whittle, Patrick. "The Big Story: Maine Baby Lobster Decline Could End High Catches." Associated Press, April 22, 2014, 1–2.

———. "Lobster Population Shifting North as Ocean Temps Warm." *Portland Press Herald,* August 18, 2015, 1–4.

————. "Maine Lobster Is Booming in China." *Business Insider,* February 17, 2015, 3–5.

Wilkinson, Alec. "The Lobsterman." *The New Yorker,* July 31, 2006, 56–65.

Wines, Michael, and Jess Bidgood. "Waters Warm, and Cod Catch Ebbs in Maine." *New York Times,* December 14, 2014, 1–4.

Woodard, Colin. "Mayday: Gulf of Maine in Distress." *Portland Press Herald,* October 25, 2015, 1–10. (First of a six-part series.)